Philosophy through
Science Fiction Stories

Also available from Bloomsbury

An Ethical Guidebook to the Zombie Apocalypse, by Bryan Hall
Cosmopolitan Aesthetics, Daniel Herwitz
Everyday Examples, David Cunning
Fiction and Philosophy in the Zhuangzi, Romain Graziani
Problems in Value Theory, edited by Steven B. Cowan
The Philosophy of Science Fiction, James Burton

Philosophy through Science Fiction Stories

Exploring the Boundaries of the Possible

Edited by
Helen De Cruz, Johan De Smedt,
and Eric Schwitzgebel

BLOOMSBURY ACADEMIC
LONDON • NEW YORK • OXFORD • NEW DELHI • SYDNEY

BLOOMSBURY ACADEMIC
Bloomsbury Publishing Plc
50 Bedford Square, London, WC1B 3DP, UK
1385 Broadway, New York, NY 10018, USA
29 Earlsfort Terrace, Dublin 2, Ireland

BLOOMSBURY, BLOOMSBURY ACADEMIC and the Diana logo are
trademarks of Bloomsbury Publishing Plc

First published in Great Britain 2021
Reprinted 2021 (twice), 2022

Cover design by Louise Dugdale
Cover illustration © "Lyla's Island" by Helen De Cruz

A catalogue record for this book is available from the British Library.

A catalog record for this book is available from the Library of Congress.

ISBN: HB: 978-1-3500-8122-2
       PB: 978-1-3500-8121-5
       ePDF: 978-1-3500-8123-9
       eBook: 978-1-3500-8124-6

Typeset by RefineCatch Limited, Bungay, Suffolk
Printed and bound in Great Britain

To find out more about our authors and books visit www.bloomsbury.com
and sign up for our newsletters.

Contents

Acknowledgments   vi

Introductory Dispute Concerning Science Fiction, Philosophy,
and the Nutritional Content of Maraschino Cherries
Helen De Cruz, Johan De Smedt, and Eric Schwitzgebel   1

Part 1   Expanding the Human

Introduction to Part I   *Eric Schwitzgebel*   11

1 Excerpt from *Theuth, an Oral History of Work in the Age of
Machine-Assisted Cognition*   *Ken Liu*   17

2 Adjoiners   *Lisa Schoenberg*   35

3 The Intended   *David John Baker*   53

4 The New Book of the Dead   *Sofia Samatar*   75

Part 2   What We Owe to Ourselves and Others

Introduction to Part II   *Johan De Smedt*   95

5 Out of the Dragon's Womb   *Aliette de Bodard*   101

6 Whale Fall   *Wendy Nikel*   123

7 Monsters and Soldiers   *Mark Silcox*   133

Part 3   Gods and Families

Introduction to Part III   *Helen De Cruz*   153

8 I, Player in a Demon Tale   *Hud Hudson*   159

9 The Eye of the Needle   *Frances Howard-Snyder*   175

10 God on a Bad Night   *Christopher Mark Rose*   193

11 Hell Is the Absence of God   *Ted Chiang*   209

Concluding Ventilation   *Helen De Cruz, Johan De Smedt,
and Eric Schwitzgebel*   235

List of Contributors   243

Index   247

Acknowledgments

The editors wish to thank the following people and organizations for helping this project come to fruition. We would like to thank the British Society of Aesthetics for their small grant which allowed Helen to organize a workshop on philosophical fiction writing (Oxford Brookes University, 2017). This workshop led to the conception of this volume, and brought some of the editors and authors together. We also wish to thank the Berry Fund for Public Philosophy at the American Philosophical Association for a small grant that allowed us to organize a competition for philosophical science fiction stories. The winning entry of this competition, Lisa Schoenberg's *Adjoiners,* is reprinted with minor revisions in this volume. Many thanks to Yiling Zhou for proofreading and formatting the manuscript. We are also grateful to our editors at Bloomsbury, in particular Colleen Coalter, Becky Holland, and Helen Saunders for suggestions and support throughout the process, and to an anonymous referee for their helpful comments. A final word of gratitude is due to all those science fiction authors, both classic and contemporary, who have informed our thinking about the relationship between philosophy and fiction.

"Adjoiners" first appeared in *Sci Phi Journal* in 2017 as "The Adjoiners", URL: https://www.sciphijournal.org/index.php/2017/06/30/the-adjoiners-by-lisa-schoenberg/, and is reprinted here with some revisions.

"Hell is the Absence of God" first appeared in *Starlight 3,* ed. Patrick Nielsen Hayden (pp. 15–47). New York: Tor, 2001

Introductory Dispute Concerning Science Fiction, Philosophy, and the Nutritional Content of Maraschino Cherries

Helen De Cruz, Johan De Smedt, and Eric Schwitzgebel

"—this dialogue, for example," said Johan, folding his arms, gazing across the table in the hotel bar at the meeting of the American Philosophical Association. "It didn't even happen. Fictional philosophical dialogue is out of fashion for excellent reason."

"But that's the beauty of it!" replied Eric, looking slightly hurt. His imaginary cocktail was bright pink, with three cherries and an umbrella.

"No one will believe it. What's the point? It's a waste of time. If you're doing philosophy, just lay it out straight. Say what you want to say. Don't decorate it with fiction." Johan pointed accusingly at Eric's cocktail. "I mean, why an umbrella? It's silly froufrou."

"It's cute!" said Helen, who you didn't picture until just now, but who had been sitting at the imaginary table all along. "It enhances the mood. It adds color. Even if strictly speaking it has no nutritional content, its vivid turquoise complements the pink and red of drink and cherry. Fiction dresses an idea, invites you to engage with that idea, makes it attractive in a certain sort of way."

"The wrong sort of way!" said Johan.

"Fiction is the very flesh on the bones, not decoration," said Eric.

"Imagine a man who is explicitly sexist," said Helen. "He is committed to patriarchy, thinks that women should only have certain roles. They should only be mothers and homemakers. Now give him a story to read. Tell it from a woman's point of view. Make it some future dystopia where women are oppressed in a way that even he would say is bad. Get him to sympathize with those fictional women, really feeling their plight. Tell the story vividly, emotionally, with depth and detail over three hundred pages.[1] When he pokes his head back up out of the story, maybe he'll see the world a little differently. Maybe he'll have a little more sympathy for women in oppressive systems. Maybe he'll see similarities between the exaggerated situation in the fiction and the experiences of women in his own society, and maybe he'll be a tiny bit more open to change. He'll have shifted a little, philosophically, in his view of the world. That's the kind of work philosophical fiction can do."

Johan looked around the bar. For a long time, academic philosophy in Europe and North America had been almost exclusively the province of white men, and—since what is not made explicit in fiction conforms to the reader's beliefs about the actual world[2]—it still showed in the demographics of the discipline[3] in this imaginary hotel. Aristotle, Kant, and Locke could probably have benefited from imaginative exercises like the one Helen was describing.[4] And yet . . . "that's not really philosophy, exactly, I'd say." Johan paused, gauging Helen. "Philosophy is about rational argumentation. Of course, things other than rational argumentation can change your worldview. Even listening to a great piece of music, such as Beethoven's Eighth Symphony[5], can be emotionally profound. It can fill you with awe just by its very sound, with no rational content at all. And maybe, in the right circumstances, it could color your future perspective. But that wouldn't make Beethoven a philosopher or his symphonies philosophical works."

"If the work explores or promotes a worldview," said Eric, "I don't see why we shouldn't call it philosophical." He pierced a maraschino cherry with the stem of the umbrella, then lifted it to eye level. "Now suppose that the intent of this cocktail, in its pink and turquoise flamboyance, is to celebrate life's capacity to delight us with sweet, luxurious, unapologetic indulgence. The manager highlights this drink on the cocktail list with that very intent, and knowing that intention, the bartender mixes and presents it. This cocktail[6], then, is itself an act of philosophy, even if certain dowdy no-funners are unable to appreciate it." With one finger, Eric flicked the cherry off the umbrella, high into the air, aiming to catch it in his mouth on its downward arc. The cherry struck him on the chin, then bounced to the floor. The bartender, who in mixing the cocktail had no such intentions as Eric described, glanced critically in their direction.

Helen stooped to retrieve the cherry, then set it on a napkin in front of her. "So, we can drink philosophy as well as read it, Eric? Should we invite the bartender to give a colloquium talk?"

Eric lifted his cocktail. "That would be awesome! But of course she will need to perform in her accustomed liquid medium."[7]

"Argument by cocktail? I wouldn't go as far as that," Helen said, gazing absently at the hotel's logo on the crumpled napkin. "But maybe a great painting can express a philosophical idea more vividly and effectively than an expository essay. Take Picasso's *Guernica*—such an austere, quasi-monochrome study in the horrors of war.[8] A few days ago, I was in a museum and saw a painting by, I think, a French painter, of glossy horses standing in the shade and bedraggled donkeys standing in the glaring sun.[9] It showed how they kept those animals for hire, but clearly it was also a social commentary. Its basic content was kind of obvious and simple—but it was political philosophy. And maybe it would reach people better than an essay. I imagine some aristocrat contemplating the painting, pitying the donkeys. Maybe later, as he's rolling along in a lovely carriage, he sees someone selling apples in the bleaching sun and thinks "What are we doing? We're treating people as badly as those donkeys!" It's not like he couldn't get similar ideas from prose and think the same thing non-metaphorically, but the vividness of the metaphor hooks him in, leads him along, makes the idea salient and emotional and memorable in a way it wouldn't otherwise be."

"But, Helen," groaned Johan, "now everything will become philosophy. You can't sustain the compromise position you want. Every work of fiction, implicitly or explicitly, critiques or celebrates a worldview. The main characters have ideals and values, they make life choices, and by portraying these sympathetically or unsympathetically, and by showing us how those values and choices play out in the story, the fiction nudges us toward a worldview. But surely, we don't want to say that all fiction is philosophy. And it isn't just fiction. All movies and TV shows, all lyrical songs, and maybe all songs of any sort—maybe even architecture and fashion and product design. If you say that painting is philosophy, lots of things risk becoming philosophy, until you end in the inanity of turquoise-umbrella cocktail philosophy. Eric's ability to appreciate the cocktail in phenomenological terms does not turn the bartender into a phenomenologist. Where do you stop?"

"Why stop?" said Eric. "I rather like the idea that everything you do is implicit philosophy. Every choice you make manifests your worldview. Every public act is a kind of advertisement for a way of being. We are all always philosophers. Why does philosophy need to be some rarified, privileged activity?"

"Are we doing okay here?" The server appeared in severe gray and black hotel uniform—a uniform that expressed, if Eric was right, the hotel management's particular philosophy of hospitality. Smoothly, she cleared the cherry and napkin. "More drinks? How about some food?"

"We're discussing the philosophy of cocktails," said Helen. "If you don't mind my asking, in your opinion, is there a philosophy of cocktails? Would you describe yourself as a philosopher?"

The server looked annoyed. "I don't know about any of that. Are you guys okay on drinks, then?"

"We're fine," said Johan, sympathetically. "Thanks."

"Okay, maybe she wouldn't be a good choice for a colloquium slot," conceded Eric.

"There have to be boundaries," pressed Johan. "If everything is philosophy, then nothing is. To be a coherent discipline, you need to rule some things in and other things out. A work of fiction, or maybe even a cocktail, might be in some broad sense 'philosophical'—but unless you have an expository argument for a philosophical thesis, you don't really have a work of philosophy."

"How about Wittgenstein, Confucius, Thales?" suggested Helen. "They didn't always present arguments for their claims, but we recognize them as philosophers, right?"

"Wittgenstein did provide arguments, even if they were sometimes sketchy and fragmented. Confucius and Thales make an intriguing case. I think it's fair to say that many don't consider them to be philosophers by today's analytical standards," said Johan.

"How about the famous 'trolley problem'?" said Helen, arranging peanuts on the glossy, dark brown tabletop, five nuts[10] in one row and an outlying nut about eight inches away, near Johan. She grabbed Eric's maraschinoed cocktail and started sliding it along the tabletop toward the group of five nuts. "An out of control trolley is headed toward five people who will certainly be killed if nothing is done. But wait. You see that you're standing next to a switch that can shunt the trolley onto a side-track. If you flip the switch, the trolley will be diverted away, saving the five people. Yay!" Helen diverted the glass from its path toward the five nuts, aiming instead toward the lone nut. "Sadly, there is one person on the side track who will now be killed by the trolley. The question is, if you're standing there with that choice, should you flip the switch? Should you kill one person in order to save five? Or is killing such a forbidden and horrible act that you shouldn't do it, even if it means five people will die as a result of your inaction?"[11]

"Yes, we all know the trolley problem," said Johan, rolling his eyes just the tiniest bit. "It's a colorful way of posing the ethical question of whether you should do what maximizes good consequences or whether you should instead abide by rules such as 'do not kill' even in the face of bad consequences. My point is that you don't need that fluff. You don't need to make a story of it. In fact, the story is distracting. It contains irrelevant detail that could illegitimately influence your judgment. And then again, it doesn't contain enough detail for your purposes. No blood splatters, no anguished screams, no frantic arm-waving by those people who apparently can't leave the tracks. I mean, what are these people doing on trolley tracks anyway? Why can't they get out of the way? Are they tied down, or what? And it's even sillier the way you've done it just now, with this pink cocktail and peanuts, as though somehow having these legumes here helps us think about it better. The whole thing is absurd, not conveying the gravity of real life and death choices. And because it's so comical, maybe it's easier than it should be to just count up the peanuts, and say 'flip the switch'. You might actually reach a different and worse judgment than you would in real life. Better to stick with the core arguments and considerations, rather than add irrelevant details."

"Johan, you have too high an opinion of the rationality of philosophers," Helen replied. "Maybe some god or ideal cognizer could just think about abstract principles like 'maximize good consequences' or 'don't kill innocent people' and then figure out all the implications, weigh them against each other, and reach a well-grounded ethical conclusion undistracted by irrelevant details, as you call them. But that's not how the human mind works—not even the minds of great philosophers. We need a story to think through the implications. We need something specific to consider, something that ignites the imagination and the emotions. That's what fiction, especially, is so great at, and why it can have such philosophical oomph. A superhuman genius could maybe think abstractly about a government with the power to rewrite history and the news and see all the horrible things that would flow from that. For the rest of us, to really grasp its awfulness, it helps to read George Orwell's *1984*.[12] Or consider . . ." Helen thoughtfully munched a peanut saved from the trolley, "what if we could upload our consciousness onto computers and live in artificial computational worlds? So much of philosophical interest could follow from that! We could duplicate ourselves, back ourselves up, totally rewrite our own values and priorities if we wanted, give ourselves any sensory experiences we desire. The nature of risk, selfhood, scarcity, and death would all change radically. Thoughtful science fiction stories, like Greg Egan's *Permutation City* and *Diaspora*, can help us imagine what it might really be like, help us see aspects that might not be immediately obvious.[13] If you try to just sit and think about it abstractly, you'll fail. To make progress you need to think narratively—what someone would do if such-and-such, and then how others might react, and what would happen next. That's how human brains work.[14] Even just 'abstractly', once you really start to think about it, you begin to write a mini-fiction. That's why philosophers so often use thought experiments, to help their audience think along with them. So why not just acknowledge that fiction is part of how we do philosophy?"

"Okay, maybe most of us need fiction as a crutch," acknowledged Johan, looking down critically at Helen's diminishing peanuts. "But we should try not to rely on fiction. We should avoid it as much as we can. Think of your trolley problem. There's this interesting study that suggests that if the one person you have to kill to save the five is named "Chip Ellsworth III" and you're a political liberal, you're more likely to divert the trolley to kill him than if the one person is named "Tyrone Payton," and vice versa if you're a political conservative.[15] The irrelevant details confuse you. You imagine the annoying rich white guy, and suddenly you're a consequentialist! You're fine sacrificing him to save others. But if it had been someone different, you'd have embraced a different moral principle. In a fiction, if you tell the story one way, maybe you sympathize with the protagonist and then you think, okay, what he's doing is fine. If you tell the story some other way, maybe you don't sympathize with the protagonist, and you come to a different conclusion. What drives those sympathies might be how the person talks, their race, whether they're funny, whether they had a sad childhood—irrelevancies. Fiction, maybe, can be a partner or an aid to philosophy, but we should be wary of it, and the best philosophy ultimately pushes such details away to focus on fundamental principles without all the peanuts and umbrellas."

"That's exactly wrong!" intervened Eric, who had been making steady progress on his cocktail while Helen and Johan were arguing. "Take everything you just said, Johan, and reverse it. Standing just by themselves, abstract statements like 'maximize good consequences' or 'act on that maxim that you can at the same time will to be a universal law' are empty slogans.[16] To give them flesh, they need to be applied to real and hypothetical cases. What does it mean to say, with Thomas Jefferson, that 'all men are created equal'? It's vacuous until we figure out how it applies. Does it mean that all men should get the vote? That all *people* should get the vote, and not just men? That no one should be enslaved? That there should be no hereditary titles?[17] Jefferson and his friends could all agree on the slogan, while they disagreed on these other issues. There's no substance until you include the details that you, Johan, want to strip away as irrelevancies. Helen says that fiction is useful for thinking through philosophy, given that we aren't superhuman geniuses, but I'd go farther. Fiction isn't merely an aid. The examples are the heart of the matter, where the best philosophical cognition happens. It's the abstract slogans that are the crutch. Abstract slogans can serve as aids to memory or give hints about a general direction of thought. To treat 'everyone as equal' can mean a great many different things, depending on who says it in what context with what applications in mind. You're right, Johan, that the trolley problem is silly. But you react by running in the wrong direction. It's silly because it has too little detail rather than too much. As you said, we want to know why these people are on the tracks, how did you come to be standing near the switch, what kind of trolley it is, and why it is out of control. Working out the full story in plausible detail will take much more than a paragraph. It will take a fiction. Really thinking through the ethics of a fully-developed imaginative scenario—that's every bit as much philosophy as is some abstract theorizing by Plato or Kant."

"But Eric!" spluttered Johan.

Helen interrupted him with a finger in front of his lips. "Johan, don't forget. *You're* a fiction."

Johan tossed both of his hands into the air. "So what? I'm still right. Pay attention to my abstract content!"

"As you said at the beginning, this whole conversation didn't even happen. We've only met Eric in person once, and at that time we didn't even discuss these issues. Plus, I happen to know that the real flesh-and-blood Johan doesn't agree with you at all."

Johan narrowed his eyes. "That has nothing to do with the merits of my argument."

"Well, we could have you win by wishing Eric away, for example, or having him say something obviously foolish." And indeed, suddenly, Eric and his now-empty cocktail glass were nowhere to be seen. All that remained was a wobbling cherry on the table near his seat.

"Yet another way to cheat in fiction," said Johan. "Give the other side a bad argument, an unappealing representative, or just write them out of the story altogether, maybe in a pink puff of smoke."

"Ah," said Helen, "but another great thing about fiction, much harder to achieve in ordinary expository writing, is that you can present the complexity of things without fully committing to a single authorial perspective. You can leave things unsettled. A fiction can speak to us with the same multivocality in which the world speaks to us. It can include details that surprise the author and that speak to the readers in ways the author couldn't foresee or understand."

"Such as this dialogue here, you're going to say next."

"If we've written it well enough," replied Helen.

"But that's—"

Johan disappeared in a pink puff of smoke.

Now please imagine Helen alone at the table, eating the cherry with a mischievous smile.

Notes

1   Atwood, M. (1985). *The handmaid's tale.* Toronto: McClelland and Stewart.
2   Lewis, D. (1978). Truth in fiction. *American Philosophical Quarterly*, 15(1), 37–46.
3   See e.g., Wilhelm, I., Conklin, S. L., & Hassoun, N. (2018). New data on the representation of women in philosophy journals: 2004–2015. *Philosophical Studies*, 175(6), 1441–1464. Schwitzgebel, E., & Jennings, C. D. (2017). Women in philosophy: Quantitative analyses of specialization, prevalence, visibility, and generational change. *Public Affairs Quarterly*, 31(2), 83–106. Botts, T. F.,

Bright, L. K., Cherry, M., Mallarangeng, G., & Spencer, Q. (2014). What is the state of blacks in philosophy? *Critical Philosophy of Race*, 2(2), 224–242.

4 Van Norden, B.W. (2017). *Taking back philosophy. A multicultural manifesto.* New York: Columbia University Press.

5 van Beethoven, L. (1812). *Symphony No. 8 in F major, Op. 93.* The work can be heard here: https://www.youtube.com/watch?v=9-f3iKeUJm4

6 On the philosophy of cocktails, see e.g., Bakewell, S. (2016). *At the existentialist café. Freedom, being, and apricot cocktails.* London: Vintage.

7 Schwitzgebel, E. (2020). *A theory of jerks and other philosophical misadventures.* Cambridge, MA: MIT Press, chapter 50, The philosopher of hair.

8 *Wikipedia, The Free Encyclopedia.* s.v. "*Guernica* (Picasso)" (accessed August 10, 2019). https://en.wikipedia.org/wiki/Guernica_(Picasso)

9 Actually, Joseph Stevens is a Belgian painter. We apologize for embarrassing fictional Helen in this way. The work is linked here: https://commons. wikimedia.org/wiki/File:Joseph_Stevens_-_Horses_and_Donkeys_for_ Hire.jpg

10 Real-world Johan wishes to point out that peanuts are technically legumes rather than nuts. Real-world Eric objects to Johan's privileging of scientific over culinary taxonomy, with its implication that you could make a fruit salad from zucchinis and tomatoes. Dupré, J. (1981). Natural kinds and biological taxa. *Philosophical Review*, 90(1), 66–90.

11 The original papers describing the trolley problem are Foot, P. (1967). The problem of abortion and the doctrine of double effect. *Oxford Review*, 5, 5–15. Thomson, J. J. (1985). The trolley problem. *Yale Law Journal*, 94(6), 1395–1415. Since then a whole cottage industry has sprung up analyzing the problem.

12 Orwell, G. (1949). *Nineteen eighty-four. A novel.* London: Secker and Warburg.

13 Egan, G. (1994) *Permutation city.* London: Orion/Millennium. Egan, G. (1997). *Diaspora.* London: Millennium.

14 Gottschall, J. (2012). *The storytelling animal. How stories make us human.* New York: Houghton Mifflin.

15 Uhlmann, E. L., Pizarro, D. A., Tannenbaum, D., & Ditto, P. H. (2009). The motivated use of moral principles. *Judgment and Decision Making*, 4(6), 476–491.

16 On maximizing good consequences, see Sinnott-Armstrong, W. (2003/2019). Consequentialism. *Stanford Encyclopedia of Philosophy* (Summer 2019 edition). URL: https://plato.stanford.edu/archives/sum2019/entries/ consequentialism. On universalizing maxims, see Kant, I. (1785/2006). *Groundwork for the metaphysics of morals* (A.W. Wood, trans). New Haven, CT: Yale University Press.

17 Finkelman, P. (1996). *Slavery and the founders. Race and liberty in the age of Jefferson.* Armonk, NY: M.E. Sharpe.

Part One

Expanding the Human

Introduction to Part One:
Expanding the Human

Eric Schwitzgebel

Oh, this primate body—so limited! Future generations could maybe shed it, or at least improve it. How attached are you to your primate form? Do you want to stay forever here on the ground, hooting to your conspecifics in slow language, with two legs, a weak mind, and a body that fails after eighty years if not sooner?

There is something beautiful about natural, unaltered *Homo sapiens*, with all their joy and misery, ability and disability, evil and good. A *conservative* about human enhancement might say: Whatever future technology arises to potentially improve us, let's have no part of it. We are good enough as is. Let's keep technology *outside* of our bodies and minds, an external tool, while we ourselves remain the same. Let's not treat humanity like some genetically modifiable crop to be enhanced for pickability, shelf-life, and resistance to herbicides. *Homo sapiens* ought to stand pat as the wonderful, if flawed, things we already are.

If you're a *moderate* about human enhancement, this reasoning might seem absurd—as absurd as rejecting the invention of penicillin so as to retain our beautiful susceptibility to fatal diseases. If we can improve, without fundamentally changing ourselves, why not do so? If we could extend our longevity to, say, two hundred years instead of eighty, wouldn't that be better? If we could enhance our cognitive capacities, holding more in memory, working better with complex ideas, being less susceptible to fallacies, wouldn't we make better decisions? If we could communicate more directly through brain-to-brain interfaces (with provisions for privacy of course) instead of being limited by slow, imperfect speech, why not go for it? If we can improve without leaving our core humanity behind, we should do it—or at least we should allow people to make such changes if they want.

If you're a *liberal* about enhancement, you might ask, what is this supposed core humanity? And why not leave it behind? Why not, if the chance arises, allow something new and radically different to grow alongside, or even replace, traditional humans? Maybe we could become gods—something fundamentally different and better, something that defies our meager human understanding in the same way that we defy the meager understanding of rhesus monkeys. Imagine some primate 15 million years ago hoping for the end of evolutionary change!

Some of the reasons for conservatism about human enhancement are essentially the same reasons that moved Edmund Burke in his classic defense of political conservatism: Well-intended changes almost always have unforeseen consequences, and those unforeseen consequences can be disastrous.[1] (Burke's example was the French Revolution.) Even if existing institutions, traditions, and policies have some obvious bad consequences, they have stood the test of time and so are, Burke argued, at least minimally adequate. Slow and moderate change is best, if change is to be pursued at all. An extreme technological Burkean could argue that we might even someday regret the invention of penicillin, if an antibiotic resistant superbug eventually destroys us all. Negative consequences might be non-obvious and slow in coming. The first story in this section, "Excerpt from *Theuth,*" explores the possible unforeseen consequences of initially innocuous-seeming cognitive enhancements for lawyers. The second story, "Adjoiners," likewise starts with something seemingly innocent, even joyful—transporting oneself into the mind and body of a bird—and ends by illustrating how the traditional concepts of selfhood and responsibility can break when your body is no longer experienced as your own.

All our values, all our laws, and our whole sense of the human condition are grounded in our particular evolutionary and cultural history: a history of embodiment in primate form, one body at a time, one location at a time, one mind at a time, within a limited range of variation. The Burkean conservative about enhancement holds that we have little idea what disasters might follow from changing this. What might be the consequences for our minds, societies, and personal identities? What unforeseen risks or losses might await us if we create, or become, conscious computer programs? Or if we learn to upload and duplicate ourselves, or merge our minds, or create the illusion of anything we want at our fingertips? Are we ready for the destabilization that would result?

Liberalism about human enhancement vividly raises one of the most fundamental questions in philosophy: What, if anything, is ultimately good? If we can imagine improving ourselves in various different directions, or even radically departing from our human form and past, what direction or directions should we go?

Consider an extreme example. According to *hedonists*, the ultimate good is pleasure (and the avoidance of pain). If pleasure is the ultimate good, here's something we could aspire to: Convert all of the matter of the Solar System into "hedonium"—whatever biological or computational substrate most efficiently generates pleasure.[2] The whole Solar System could become an unfathomably large, intense, constant orgasm. Wouldn't that be amazing? Such a system might know nothing about its human past, nothing about great art or literature or music. It might have no social relationships and no ethics. It might have no "higher" cognition whatsoever. The advocate of simple hedonism is unperturbed: None of that other stuff matters, as long as the pleasure is intense, secure, and durable. (We, the editors, guess that a small but non-trivial minority of our readers will embrace the Solar System orgasmatron as a worthy ideal to aspire to.[3])

According to *eudaimonists*, in contrast, the ultimate good consists of flourishing in one's distinctively human capacities, such as creativity, intellect, appreciation of beauty, and loving relationships.[4] In improving humanity, we should aspire primarily to enhance these aspects of ourselves. A eudaimonist might welcome enhancements, maybe even radical enhancements, that enable our descendants to be wiser, more creative, more loving, and more appreciative of the world's beauty. The third story in this section, "The Intended," articulates one eudaimonist vision. On the surface, the eudaimonists in this story embrace traditional values: monogamous love relationships, gardening, appreciation of nature. But furthering these goals requires, behind the scenes, a radical technology that is arguably oppressive.

In reading "The Intended" you might wonder why societies in the distant future, with great technological capacity, would look so much like our own, populated with people who live in one body at a time and who communicate in oral language through their mouths—and even more specifically, people who love gardening and who act like jerks in love triangles. A possible Burkean explanation is this: We have evolved so stubbornly into the primates we are that the societies that work best for us and for the descendants we grow or build will always take that familiar shape.

All conservatism is tossed aside in the final and most radical story in this section, "The New Book of the Dead," in which we transcend death to become godmachines. If in reading "The New Book of the Dead" you find that you only gain a glimpse of what it would be like to be a godmachine, and if you find the story to be full of metaphors that are hard to translate into literal language . . . well, of course that's because you are still only a weak-minded primate, and everything must be explained to you with pant-hoots and bananas. The godmachines will someday reminisce about us with tenderness and pity.

Recommended Reading/Viewing

Fiction:

- *Sirius* (novel, 1944, Olaf Stapledon). A dog enhanced to have humanlike intelligence struggles to make sense of love, value, and beauty in a world he doesn't fit into.
- *Flowers for Algernon* (short story, 1959, novel, 1966, Daniel Keyes). A low IQ laborer is cognitively enhanced to have superhuman intelligence, but his life does not improve in the ways he expected.
- *Gattaca* (film, 1997, written and directed by Andrew Niccol). A dystopia in which people designed to be genetically superior are privileged over the rest.
- *Diaspora* (novel, 1997, Greg Egan). A future populated with cognitively enhanced artificial intelligences living in simulated worlds, biologically engineered humans of various types, and robots, exploring a wide variety of ways to create a meaningful existence.
- *Feed* (novel, 2002, M.T. Anderson). A teenage character's perspective on a world where most of humanity has the internet piped directly into their minds.

Non-fiction:

- Haraway, Donna J. (1991). A cyborg manifesto. Science, Technology, and socialist-feminism in the late 20th century. In: D. Haraway, *Simians, cyborgs, and women. The reinvention of nature* (pp. 149–181). New York, NY: Routledge. A feminist, anti-essentialist critique of scientific and technological approaches to the body and the blurry boundaries between animal, human, and machine.
- Humanity+ Board, *Transhumanist Declaration* (1998/2009), https:// humanityplus.org/philosophy/transhumanist-declaration/ A brief but influential online statement of fundamental principles of transhumanism, affirming the value of "allowing individuals wide personal choice over how they enable their lives" through future technologies.
- Clarke, Steve, Julian Savulescu, Tony Coady, Alberto Giubilini, and Sagar Sanyal, eds. (2016). *The Ethics of Human Enhancement: Understanding the Debate.* Oxford: Oxford University Press. A multifaceted exploration of the ethics of enhancement from authors with competing views, including several treatments of the case for conservatism.
- Flanagan, Jessica, and Terry L. Price (2018). *The Ethics of Ability and Enhancement.* New York: Palgrave Macmillan. Essays that explore human enhancement from a perspective that does not assume that the lives of people with disabilities are worth less or that disabilities should always be "fixed".

- Schneider, Susan (2019). *Artificial You: AI and the Future of Your Mind.* Princeton: Princeton University Press. Could you upload your consciousness onto a computer? Would it still be you?

Notes

1   Burke, E. (1979/1993). *Reflections on the Revolution in France.* Oxford: Oxford World Classics.
2   Bostrom, N. (2014). *Superintelligence.* Oxford: Oxford University Press.
3   Bramble, B. (2016). A new defense of hedonism about well-being. *Ergo*, 3. URL: http://dx.doi.org/10.3998/ergo.12405314.0003.004.
4   Nussbaum, Martha (2011). *Creating capabilities.* Cambridge, MA: Harvard University Press.

1

Excerpt from *Theuth, an Oral History of Work in the Age of Machine-Assisted Cognition*

Ken Liu

Warren S., *Attorney*, 41:

Beforetellingyouabouttheproblemswithourmodernwayofdeliveringlegalser
vicesIwanttomakesurewegettoholdthatthoughtitsbettertostartevenearlier—

Let me turn off my booster. I assume you want as many people to
understand this as possible.

I've been at my firm—oh, let's make up a name for it: Drummond &
Coslett—for sixteen years. Most of my work consists of negotiating and drafting
commercial agreements—UCC 2.0, data aggregation and monetization, IP
licensing, blockchain fallbacks, that sort of thing. For compiled implementation,
I'm most experienced with the Res Iudicata platform, but I can work with other
blockchains or legacy off-chain contracts as well. However, I haven't seen the
inside of a courtroom in more than a decade.

I'll be honest: I didn't pick the law because I thought it a noble calling. My
grandfather was a judge, and I was proud to cite one of his opinions when I
clerked at the state business court after law school. My father, on the other
hand, was a litigator who hopped from firm to firm for twenty years, each
time earning more money. He put my sisters and me through private school
and college, retired early, and bought a boat to travel the world with my
mother. I wanted that.

The law has been good for my family, I suppose you'd say.

Back in college, I had an interest in the arts. I drifted around for a few
years after graduation, interning in New York publishing and the peripheries
of Hollywood until I realized that I was never going to make it in industries
where success seemed so tied to unpredictable trends and fashion. I needed
stability, a sense that I was objectively progressing up a ladder of expertise,
learning skills and getting better. The family profession grew more appealing.
But when I told my father I was applying to law school, he wasn't pleased at
all. "You'll regret it," he told me. "The business is changing."

I ignored him, the ways sons are supposed to ignore their fathers.

In law school, every Friday there was a presentation in the library from one of the legal tech companies: smart contract toolchain developers, discovery outsourcing vendors that relied on Mechanical Turk-style "crowd intelligence" to do mass document review, AI companies with digital research assistants that helped you track down obscure statutes and decisions. I went to as many of these as I could because I wanted to know what the cutting edge of the modern practice of law was like. The presentations that I found most interesting were on early versions of boosters—except back then everyone still said the whole name: "brain booster" or "cognitive enhancement device."

Back then, there was still a lot of controversy over neural enhancement, and only about a quarter of my 1L class had the brain-computer interface implants to make it work—most of us had been avid gamers or VR enthusiasts. If you had a compatible implant and signed the waiver, these companies would give you an unlimited subscription to their apps and services, free of charge. They weren't doing it out of the goodness of their hearts, of course. The point was to get you into the ecosystem while you were still a law student so that later, after you started practicing, you'd advocate for your firm to pay for a lucrative commercial license.

Compared to even the cheapest devices today, the interface hardware we had was primitive and the software crude. Due to concerns for safety and the limitations of the early technology, you had to initiate every interaction consciously, almost like learning to type using "phantom fingers." But if you put in the time to learn the interface effectively, you could put all your study materials into it and get instant search and recall on cases, case briefs, course outlines, classroom notes, and even lecture recordings. Similar software was just gaining acceptance at top-tier law firms, and people made wild claims about how cognitive enhancement was the real key to the next major productivity leap in the symbol-manipulation economy.

I loved tech and was always an early adopter, so I jumped at the chance to try the boosters. But others were more hesitant. My study group debated the issue endlessly. In the end, the argument that I found most convincing was that if boosters helped you be a better lawyer or doctor, then the interest of the client or the patient not only weighed in favor of enhancement, but actually compelled it. To *choose* to remain unenhanced while representing a criminal defendant with their life or liberty on the line would have to be considered a form of ineffective assistance of counsel, wouldn't it?

Some of my classmates mocked those of us who used boosters, saying that you didn't really learn the material if you relied on a machine. But I thought that was like arguing that you didn't really know math if you used a calculator. I used the booster only about half the time anyway—we were still worried about the implants "frying the brain," and even with the booster off, I still remembered the rule against perpetuities and could explain the importance of footnote four of *Carolene Products* (though with the booster on I'd be able to give you the exact quotes right away). The booster wasn't a substitute for learning; it just allowed you to read faster and think at a higher level, freeing you from the wasted effort of rote memorization. By taking care of the mechanical details, it unlocked your true intellectual potential. It was a bicycle for the mind, like a supercharged laptop or phone.

Despite the skeptics, the trend was moving my way. As the year-end law review competition approached, many of the holdouts signed up for boosters: nobody wanted to lose out because they couldn't spot an unitalicized semicolon or an improperly abbreviated old administrative agency name as well as someone with a booster that instantly brought up the right rule from the *Bluebook*.

They kept on improving the software. With machine learning and iterative personalization, the booster could pick up your thinking patterns and bring up the relevant information without your having to consciously invoke it. If I noticed an interesting line of reasoning in Supreme Court cases that no one else had commented on while running on the treadmill, I didn't have to scramble to write it down; the booster would track the idea (as long as I had remembered to turn it on) and suggest my own insight back to me when I sat down in my bedroom to write my law review note. When professors called on me in class, the booster observed my answer and anticipated my needs, bringing up relevant cases and canons so that I could rattle off cites and exact quotes, impressing even myself.

Not only did I study more effectively; I *felt* smarter, more confident. The booster didn't cheat me of an education; it made me a *better* me.

By the time I started at Drummond & Coslett, boosters were practically required for new associates. We all got firm-issued hardware that was a generation ahead of the consumer units. The personal data on our old implants could be transferred over so we didn't lose anything. But to keep client and firm data safe, we had to sign a waiver and agree to some additional surgical modifications to set up isolation protocols and encrypted enclaves.

You know how people always say that law is a conservative profession, and lawyers are the last to adopt a technology? That's only true up to a point. As soon as insurers—advised by AI analysis of malpractice trends—started to raise premiums for attorneys who refused to use boosters in their work, every white-shoe firm seemed to jump aboard overnight. Clients were also demanding more accountability in billing records to justify the ever-rising legal fees, and firms found the audit trail generated by boosters, which literally tracked every moment you spent thinking about a case, to be the best way to keep clients happy. Senior associates told us how lucky we were to not have to track our day manually in six-minute increments, and we thought it a sign of law firm culture progress that we got credited automatically for every minute we spent editing a memo on the subway or answering an email in bed.

I loved my time as a first-year associate. Everything was new, and I felt I was learning and growing every day. The hours were long and the work was demanding, but the pressure also brought the junior associates closer. We'd gather at a bar in the evenings to have drinks and share office gossip before heading back to bill a few more hours, and on weekends, sometimes we assembled in the office to binge-watch one of the new shows that were designed for booster-wearers, with twisty plots involving hundreds of major characters and flashy edits and dialogue delivered so fast that you couldn't follow the story without your booster on. Good times.

Not all of us were close. There were three un-enhanced associates in my class, and two of them didn't even last through the first year, leaving for less competitive places. The last one, Mina, mostly kept to herself. She had a physiological condition that made it impossible for her to be fitted with a neural implant. The firm went to a great deal of trouble to get her the assistive devices to compensate so she could do her work, but still she struggled, and the rest of us pitied her. She had to work twice as hard as the rest of us just to keep up: replaying recordings of meetings over and over at half-speed instead of trusting the booster to pick up the key points, poring over printouts and highlighting and summarizing instead of relying on instant recall, checking and double-checking her paper notes for a closing instead of having the auto-reminder cue her on what to do. And even with all her extra effort, she took so much longer to do everything. It was rumored that senior associates and partners didn't like working with her, since they had to write off so much of her time as overhead because clients refused to pay for the extra hours.

One night, I stayed especially late at the office to prepare for a closing. As I walked to the copy room, I passed by her office and heard crying inside.

Her door was open and I couldn't just pretend nothing was wrong. I knocked on the door and asked if there was anything I could do to help.

She looked up from her desk, tears glistening on her face. "I can't do this," she was sobbing. "I can't."

Almost by instinct, I waited for my booster to offer a suggestion, the way it cued me on etiquette during client meetings and firm parties. But the booster remained dormant.

So I did the first thing I could think of. I went down to the kitchen and made her a cup of instant noodles. Food was how my grandfather and father always cheered me up as a kid. I got a cup for myself, too, even though I wasn't hungry. Didn't want to make her feel weird to have me sit there watching while she ate.

We sat across her desk, chewing noodles, not talking at all. She had left the shade over her glass wall open, and through it, we could see the bright lights of fleets of cars streaking through the night streets far below us. The coordination software bunched them into tight clusters like freight trains hurtling along tracks, or pulses of information racing through fiber optic cables.

The warm food seemed to calm her. "Can you read this?" She pushed across a stack of paper.

I couldn't remember the last time I read a draft of anything on paper. The only time I worked with printers was when we did closings, which were ceremonial. The pages were meant to be bound and locked up in some vault, talismans to be invoked in the event of litigation. No one read from paper when it was so much faster to digest the electronic versions directly through the booster.

She had highlighted most of the text on five pages. NoIcantreadittoyou oughmyboosterjusthelpfullybroughtittomymindIhaventthoughtaboutthisin howlong—*oh.*

Givemeasecond.

Sorry about that. Since it's the middle of a work day, the booster is set to come back on every hour even if I manually shut it off. It's off again now.

I can't read Mina's five pages to you because the actual content is privileged, but, based on what the booster helpfully showed me a minute ago, I *can* tell you that the passage was in essence a single, meandering sentence spanning the five pages, a fairly unremarkable and inelegant provision, which, when greatly simplified and pruned of its ramified, knotty, dangling clauses, would read something like this artificial example . . .

"For the avoidance of doubt and notwithstanding anything to the contrary in this Amended and Restated Agreement, the aforementioned Optional Coverage that a Supplemental Insured that a Primary Insured that an Authorizer (defined subsequently in §§IV.B.1(a)-(c)) that a Committee (constituted pursuant to Appendix F (but only if said Appendix is in force as of the First Option Date)) that a Triggering Event that a Vendor Representative that the Company (but excluding any Subsidiaries and non-US Affiliates) designates pursuant to ¶VI.J.2(a)(ii) is present at causes to be formed or revives under ¶¶VI.J.3(b)(i)(D)-(G) appoints adds nominates chooses shall *not* be included in such Damage Calculation."

The margins of the printed pages were filled with doodles, which brought a smile to my face—Mina had always appeared so diligent, scribbling furiously at meetings and whenever we saw her at lunch. Who would have guessed that she was drawing crooked trees and winding mazes?

As I flipped awkwardly through the stack to feed the text through the booster, I noticed, almost as an afterthought, that the doodles and editing comments were growing sparse, more of them ending in question marks, until the comment on the last page was simply one large swerve of confusion, jagged from the force of the broken pencil lead.

"Did Howitt ask you to use his form?" I asked. "It's sloppy. Moran-Day has a better one, but Howitt hates her. What I would do—"

"I just asked if you can read it," she said.

I was taken aback by the heat in her voice. "Yes," I said, hesitant.

"No, I want to know if *you* can read it," she said. She took a deep breath. "Turn off your booster and try again." Her tone and expression had both turned frighteningly flat.

I didn't like turning off the booster while at work—actually, I had fallen into the habit of always keeping it on even outside of work. When the booster was off, it felt a bit like a part of myself was missing. People talked too fast; screens scrolled into blurs, and I hated the feeling of not *knowing*, everything like a word just at the tip of the tongue but refusing to solidify. The only time we associates shut off the booster was when we wanted to complain and commiserate about some firm policy and didn't want to leave a digital trail.

Still, I did as she asked.

The words wobbled on the page like gibberish. The beginning of the sentence escaped as I struggled to grasp the middle. Even having a vague sense of the overall import of the paragraph, I couldn't hold the entirety of the structure in my mind; there simply wasn't enough space. I could feel the clauses stacking on top of one another, toppling under their own weight and sinking into oblivion.

You have to understand that back then, the effects of booster implants weren't well understood. In the same way it took decades for people to come to terms with how the Internet fundamentally altered the way people communicated, injecting an element of orality back into literacy, we didn't fully appreciate how boosters would change the way we composed music, crafted art, devised mathematical proofs, programmed computers, or drafted legal documents.

One of the immediate, though perhaps least impactful, effects of booster implants was an expansion in the amount of working short-term memory available to the brain, which allowed wearers to naturally work with much more complex and larger parse trees, full of center embeddings and garden paths that required re-analysis, in both oral and written communication.

The drawings in the margins, I realized, weren't random doodles at all. They were parse diagrams, Mina's attempts at imposing a structure on the wall of text, at weaving a semantic web to capture the meaning before it slipped into the sea of incomprehension. But without a booster, she could not succeed.

"I thought I could make it work," she whispered, her fingers mechanically caressing the mouse of her old-fashioned PC. "I thought I just had to work harder."

There was nothing to say to that. Lawyers have never turned down a chance to use technology to build more elaborate structures out of the written word. A one-sentence handshake deal turned into a one-page handwritten contract, which turned into a ten-page agreement in the age of typewriters, which turned into a one-hundred-page bound volume with the advent of word processors, which turned into a ten-thousand-screen neural text module, which would be translated into Jura-SIC and then compiled into a one-hundred-thousand-kiloblock smart contract. The elaboration was driven by the impulse to specify a resolution for every eventuality as well as by the desire to build in strategic points of ambiguity that could be advantageous to the client, a quintessentially human contradiction at the heart of the law. The deliberate linguistic games were intended to clarify as well as to obscure, and that made them impossible to unravel by either pure AI or the unenhanced human mind.

The rest of us, blessed with genes that allowed our brains to adapt to this new upgrade path, were speaking and writing in a way that was literally incomprehensible to her.

I made some excuse and left. A sense of shame that I didn't even understand gripped me. I could do a job that she could not, even though she very much wanted to. My very presence was surely painful to her.

Mina left a month later, not for another firm, but dropping out of the law altogether. The rest of us never mentioned her, as though her very name held the power to bring bad luck.

By the end of our second year, another associate, Karl, collapsed in the middle of a client meeting and had to be rushed to the hospital. His body, it turned out, had developed an allergy-like reaction to the implant, and he had been taking a regimen of experimental suppressors despite warnings from his doctor. The only solution was to take his implant out. Karl messaged the rest of us to not come and visit him, and he never returned to work.

Insecurity hovered in the air like an oppressive thunderstorm. What if we were not, in fact, smart people who used technology to amplify our natural talents, but merely the lucky few who could use the boosters to hide our weaknesses, albeit only temporarily?

So we worked harder, and tried not to ask uncomfortable questions.

One day, the firm called a meeting of all the associates in the largest conference room on the first floor. The topic was simple: we would all be asked to upgrade our boosters to allow "passive billables."

Since you're probably not a lawyer, allow me to explain. At that time, the idea of using boosters to enhance professionals' mental processes had become routine and widely accepted, but not the idea of going the other way: where the machine would actively call on the brain to help *it* accomplish some task.

We'd always known that brains were better than computers at some skills: pattern detection, embodied spatial sense, adaptability and malleability, working with emotions ... But the brain was also remarkably inefficient. It didn't escape the notice of people who obsessed over new ways to "extract value" and "increase productivity" that much of the time, most of our neurons sat around, firing randomly and doing little else. Surely the brain-machine interface could be "leveraged" to put all that idle capacity to work. After all, artificial intelligence didn't have to be limited to the realm of intelligence crafted out of silicon; it could also encompass the mining of useful work from naturally-evolved but unproductive pools of latent intelligence.

You probably remember some of those early projects: tapping into the brains of networks of volunteers to fold proteins, evaluate product prototypes, train artificial creativity composers and designers to generate more appealing results ... But the technology didn't gain commercial traction until proper isolation protocols had been developed to protect the intellectual property rights of the companies that wanted to tap into this unused brain capacity.

Drummond & Coslett, like most of biglaw, was caught up in powerful economic trends. Older partners, who refused to adopt boosters or couldn't undergo the surgery for health reasons, were being forced out of the business. The younger, hungrier partners wanted more growth, which meant new capital structures, IPOs, data-driven management. The new managing partners, viewing themselves as pioneering CEOs, were under constant pressure to increase revenue, and the best way to do so was to escalate the number of billable hours from the existing pool of associates.

But even with boosters, it was impossible for people to work productively for much more than sixteen hours a day, day-in, day-out. And the audit records enabled by the boosters also made it harder to pad the timesheets, as in the old days. Passive billables, therefore, represented the most promising revenue-maximizing solution.

The idea was simple: instead of having associates go home at 10:00 PM and stop billing clients, the boosters would continue to stimulate parts of their brains and drive the idle neurons to perform billable tasks while the associate was driving home, taking a shower, catching up with their family, unwinding in front of the TV, or best of all, sleeping. Such "unconscious legal services" would be billed out to clients at a reduced hourly rate, similar to charges for smart contract compilation, litigation neural network training, access to research databases, vault services, and the like.

The kinds of jobs suited for passive billable processing varied, but most involved cognitive tasks for which pure AI was still unsuitable: role-playing negotiation strategies to identify the most effective approach, crafting recitations of facts and exhibits to optimize narrative and emotional impact on potential jurors or judges, identifying patterns of inconsistencies or contradictions in voluminous natural-language regulations, pre-compilation of contractual terms negotiated in human languages into pseudo-Jura-SIC, and so on.

They had the gall to pitch the proposal to us as a way to improve work-life balance. Advanced isolation protocols were supposed to keep the background processing from interfering with our consciousness. "You'd never know you were working!" the reps from the technology vendor gushed to a conference room full of associates with stony faces. "You could be billing while doing yoga, reading to your kids, going on a date!"—as if we had time for any of those things. There would be no negative side effects, they assured us. "Except maybe you'd be eating more to fuel those brilliant brains. But don't worry, your brain will burn off all those calories in your sleep!"

The head of associate development added that the firm would provide a hearty and healthy breakfast for the passive billers.

"Passive billables would be credited at 50% to your annual billing target for bonus purposes," said the lead managing partner. What he didn't say, but we all understood, was that the schedule of billable hours targets would also be revised up.

A group of associates got together for dinner after the meeting. Was this the life we wanted, we wondered. Toiling for long hours was one thing, but to be billing even when we were shopping, making love, eating, going to the bathroom, sleeping—was becoming a partner worth all this?

Without anyone suggesting it, we had all turned off our boosters.

"The partners are getting them too," someone said. "I read a profile in *Cutting Edge* that said they've been doing this in Silicon Valley for years. Some VCs now require founders as well as early-stage employees to have passive processing enabled and devoted to the company to maximize the chances of success. EverySort and Distparti made it mandatory for new hires this year."

"We can't stop it anyway," someone else said in a gloomy voice. "Not unless we all say no."

She was right. Whoever said yes was going to outbill the rest of us, and that competitive spirit, which had gotten all of us this far, was going to compel the rest of us to sign up if we wanted to stay in the game.

I called around to friends at other firms that had already implemented passive billable hours.

"Why not? Work's on the back of my mind all the time anyway," said one. "My wife already thinks I never pay attention to her."

I had questions. "Is it true that you don't notice anything different? Like, you can still veg out and watch TV while billing passively?"

"Well, since your booster will be churning hard on work-related tasks, you can't watch anything that requires booster co-processing," she said. "And don't try reading anything too complicated either. Stick to the bestsellers."

"But I really won't notice that parts of my brain are doing client work? They said that the isolation protocols are very tight."

"Sort of," she said. "I mean, my kids tell me I seem distracted—but they said that when I just used a phone, too . . . And I have weird dreams."

My ears perked up. "What kind of dreams?"

She was evasive, but I got the sense that they were unpleasant. "Who knows if they are from the passive billables or because the partner I'm working with is an ass?" she insisted. I wasn't sure if she was trying to convince me or herself.

That was the last straw. Over time, I had grown increasingly disillusioned with the law, at least as it was practiced at a firm like Drummond & Coslett. The high salaries and bonuses didn't give me a sense of security, not when I had no time for myself. I was also questioning the purpose of it all. For years, I had devoted my intelligence to devising elaborate legal structures that would escape the scrutiny of AI and human regulators in various jurisdictions, to constructing complex garden-path sentences designed to trip up computer parsers, to clever arguments on behalf of billion-dollar companies whose grievances were as abstract as the number of angels dancing in the cells of a flash memory card.

My one refuge had been the new art: new books, new shows, new music, new games designed to be enjoyed only with the best co-processing enhancers. It probably sounds like the sort of complaint for which you want to bring out the world's tiniest violin, but to have my dreams invaded by *work* was a step too far.

I began to call around to old law school acquaintances I hadn't heard from in years. Eventually, one of the unenhanced associates who had been in my first-year class, now working at a "lifestyle" firm, agreed to pass my resume to their head of recruiting. She agreed to meet me for an informational interview.

On the day of the interview, which had to be done discreetly, I turned off my booster and entered the time on my firm schedule as "personal meeting: unavailable." Leaving the booster off for so long felt unsettling. My mind was groggy, slow, as though I had been pulling multiple all-nighters. On the way over, I tried to fortify myself by reading the printout of my resume over and over. *"Lead counsel for restructuring a Fortune 100 company's international . . ."—I am smart; I am capable; I can adjust to change—". . . tax-optimized structure was subsequently re-deployed for other clients and marketed as the 'Gibraltar Quintuple-Decker' . . ."—I have accomplished great things; I know what I'm doing . . .*

"*You're a bit senior to be jumping firms,*" the recruiter said after we got the pleasantries out of the way.

I didn't think her question was rude. It was rare for a big firm senior associate, who had lasted long enough to be considered for partnership, to jump ship. I told her the truth. Her firm had low billable hours requirements (with commensurate low pay) and no passive billing at all.

"That's all true," she said. "Now, tell me, how much of your practice has been booster-free?"

That did surprise me. I knew lower-tier firms didn't have the latest technology, but I wasn't sure how that mattered. I was smart and experienced. I could adapt to slower and less capable hardware. "Probably none of it. But I don't depend on the latest technology. I started practicing back when—"

She held up a hand. "It's not about that . . . We also use boosters here, and I'm sure you can readjust to the pace of the less-advanced models . . . It's just that we find that associates who've always practiced with the booster don't transition to new places successfully."

"Why not?" I was confused.

"To put it bluntly, you don't know what you think you know."

She could see my disbelief.

"Your booster is off?" she asked.

I nodded.

She pointed at the resume and asked me to explain the "Gibraltar Quintuple-Decker."

I tried.

Those were the longest fifteen minutes of my life. I could see the words on the page, words that I had crafted myself. But I could recall nothing beyond them. I had a vague memory that I had worked for weeks to devise a wondrous, novel chain of corporate entities that appeared as a flow-through in one jurisdiction but a blocker in the other, that had the right to receive profits but not the obligation to suffer losses, that had saved my client tens of millions in half a dozen cryptocurrencies. I had delivered seminars on it to several practice groups and clients.

But I couldn't recall anything specific, draw any diagram, cite to any statute or case, make any analogy.

I sat there in defeated silence. The recruiter got up, left the office, and returned sometime later with a mug of tea. She set the steaming vessel down on the desk before me and left again, gently shutting the door behind her. There was nothing to say.

It wasn't about the hardware; it was about the data.

Lawyers, like just about any kind of skilled professional, don't store all their skills in their brains. The modern world makes it impossible to "know" everything you think you know. The bits of knowledge in our minds are really more like dangling pointers to actual stores of knowledge. Like beavers and dams and bees and hives, we externalize our knowledge in papers, forms, notes, electronic databases, blockchain entries. We know not *how*, only *how to find the how*.

The practice of law, similar to other symbol-manipulation industries such as management consulting and software programming, involves much less "drafting" than "copying, pasting, and tweaking." A plagiarism detection program would grind to a halt if fed contracts, since they were all copies of copies of copies, with no attribution. Lawyers almost never drafted anything from scratch, but began with existing forms, acquired from friends and rivals alike, and then cobbled existing sections of language together and tweaked them to suit. Like engineers who took apart old machines and recycled components to build new machines fitted to a new purpose, lawyers learned the craft of reusing forms over their apprenticeship, along with how far to push an opponent in a negotiation and how much time training a junior associate could be billed to a client.

The presence of such vast, unattributed copying in the law was a grey area when lawyers moved between firms. On the one hand, contracts, no different from novels or plays, *were* subject to copyright protection. But unlike novels or plays, legal documents were functional instruments, less about expression than service, and all contracts were, to some extent, plagiarized, being derived from a common pool of clauses and paragraphs that had been honed through centuries of litigation, reproducing and evolving along with generations of lawyers shuttling between firms, who served as their carriers. The practice of commercial law would grind to a halt if firms attempted to strictly enforce their copyrights via lawsuits: no lawyer wanted to cut off their own future ability to jump ship, and every firm lived in a glass house.

In my father's time, lawyers who switched firms would quietly take with them form agreements, notes, copies of motions and pleadings, favored partnership allocation provisions, preferred indemnification clauses. These were much more than mere shortcuts or libraries of ready-made magical incantations. A lawyer learned to practice by tweaking and customizing these tools, in which were embedded the wisdom of their mentors and colleagues, as well as the scars of their own failures and the proofs of their growing insight.

The practice was tolerated by the unspoken code that bound all lawyers together: the externalized repository of experience in an attorney's personal files was no less theirs than their memories and habits, and a lawyer could take them to a rival firm, so long as they did so circumspectly and discreetly.

But in the age of law firms being run as investor-driven businesses, quaint notions of professional courtesy and mutual respect had no place. The gradual corporatization of the work product doctrine emboldened firms to assert ownership over all forms of intellectual property, including intangibles like skill, experience, judgment, incorporated knowledge.

Best of all, the neural boosters gave them a way to enforce the claim absolutely by code, without the expenses and uncertainties associated with law and custom.

Remember that waiver I signed when I started at Drummond & Coslett to undergo extra surgery and receive the firm-issued implant? Beyond the ostensible need to keep client and firm data secure, there was another, unspoken reason for the procedure that I hadn't really grasped: preventing the employee from ever really *possessing* information.

Every contract I had drafted and modified, every term sheet I had negotiated and finalized, every deal I had shepherded through—they had all come through the filter of the firm-owned implant and were maintained in encrypted memory. With boosters in every employee, it was no longer necessary, or indeed possible, to download files onto personal devices. As soon as the implant was shut off, or, upon my departure, removed, I would no longer be able to recall a single line from those documents. I could take nothing with me.

But it was worse than that.

I told you earlier that a lawyer learned by shaping their tools, but the tools through which a lawyer learned also shaped the lawyer. When the booster implant is active, my thinking is no longer just in my brain, but spread out across silicon and cerebrum, in the machine as well as in the flesh. To enable this kind of close integration, the booster needed to carve out a region of my brain and reserve it for its own use—a secure enclave etched in neurons. Indeed, this isolation protocol was what made passive billing possible: the machine could cordon off a part of my mind from the rest.

All my skills, my experiences, the knowledge that I thought I had gained over the years through trying and failing, failing and trying again, were etched in that enclave. They were also *data*.

My employment contract gave the firm the right to erase all firm data in my possession upon my departure. Skills and experiences acquired through the course of employment were also company property, so went the argument, and could not be "misappropriated" by the departing employee.

After I returned to the office, I spent all morning researching employment law precedents involving professionals leaving their firms. I didn't care whether my booster was issuing alerts to my practice group head concerning my deviant research.

The result was depressing. Booster lock-out was far worse than traditional non-compete clauses. The issue had not been extensively litigated, but what little precedent there was in the law definitely fell on the side of the employers, not least because the equipment and data belonged to them. As to the equities? Highly paid professionals like me made unsympathetic litigants to juries: few people cared that corporate lawyers were told that they could not take their tax-dodging and regulation-evading skills to another firm. The powerful partners who sometimes moved between firms did so only by being able to convince their clients to go with them and settling privately with their former partners.

But don't you see? I screamed in my head. Don't you see this is just the beginning? Whatever job you had, boosters and enhanced cognition were playing ever-larger roles. Engineers, doctors, architects, designers ... soon, the boosters would make it impossible for practitioners to ever acquire the necessary skills without them, only to find out later that they had been cuffed to their employers, unable to take those skills with them.

What was I without my skills and knowledge—or at least what I thought of as *my* skills and knowledge? I couldn't face the prospect of starting over again as a first-year associate, to struggle like Mina had, to arduously reacquire through pen and paper what I had once effortlessly learned with the help of the booster. The potential loss of income was nothing compared to the stench of failure and the prospect of living the rest of my life with the undeniable proof that I was an imposter. Without my identity as a skilled professional, I was no one.

In the end, I reconciled myself to reality. I stopped caring about the billable hours targets and dropped out of the partnership race. I was still profitable to the firm as an hourly living processor who could be billed out at respectable rates, and I stayed at Drummond & Coslett as a permanent contract attorney.

It's not a great life, but it's not a bad living. I buy myself the latest and greatest consumer boosters to enjoy media that requires the co-processing power. I turn off my firm-issued booster on the dot at five o'clock, and go drinking.

At least in my dreams, I sail around the world in my boat, untroubled by passive billing.

Story Notes for Excerpt from *Theuth, an Oral History of Work in the Age of Machine-Assisted Cognition*

Ken Liu

In *Phaedrus*, Plato, through the mouth of Socrates, tells the following story:

> SOCRATES: *At the Egyptian city of Naucratis, there was a famous old god, whose name was Theuth; the bird which is called the Ibis is sacred to him, and he was the inventor of many arts, such as arithmetic and calculation and geometry and astronomy and draughts and dice, but his great discovery was the use of letters. Now in those days the god Thamus was the king of the whole country of Egypt; and he dwelt in that great city of Upper Egypt which the Hellenes call Egyptian Thebes, and the god himself is called by them Ammon. To him came Theuth and showed his inventions, desiring that the other Egyptians might be allowed to have the benefit of them . . .*
>
> *But when they came to letters, This, said Theuth, will make the Egyptians wiser and give them better memories; it is a specific both for the memory and for the wit. Thamus replied: O most ingenious Theuth, the parent or inventor of an art is not always the best judge of the utility or inutility of his own inventions to the users of them. And in this instance, you who are the father of letters, from a paternal love of your own children have been led to attribute to them a quality which they cannot have; for this discovery of yours will create forgetfulness in the learners' souls, because they will not use their memories; they will trust to the external written characters and not remember of themselves. The specific which you have discovered is an aid not to memory, but to reminiscence, and you give your disciples not truth, but only the semblance of truth; they will be hearers of many things and will have learned nothing; they will appear to be omniscient and will generally know nothing; they will be tiresome company, having the show of wisdom without the reality.*[1]

This may be the earliest recorded instance of a rant against technology for "rotting our brains." Other than the fact that the technology being denounced was writing, the structure and content of Plato's argument—that the new technology is superficial, that it creates dependence, that it leads away from rather than toward truth, that it results in the semblance of knowledge without the substance—could be applied to Wikipedia, audiobooks, educational TV programming, virtual reality experiences, or any other number of new mediums and technologies related to cognition.

Rather appropriately, Plato's story survives to our time only *because* of the technology of writing, and it has inspired countless generations of thinkers in debates over the nature of language and cognition, and their relationship to technology. (See, for example, Derrida's thoughts on Plato and the relationship to writing.)

Most of us have been formally educated in and do much of our thinking in a grapholect—defined by Walter Ong as "a transdialectical language formed by deep commitment to writing"[2]—such as standard English, Modern Standard Mandarin Chinese, Académie française-sanctioned French, and so on. This familiarity makes it hard for us to see how much writing has changed us.

A purely oral culture does not think in ways familiar to modern minds, steeped in and shaped by writing. Features of orality-rooted thinking (as identified by Ong) that we glimpse in old epics, such as the pre-eminence of memory, repetition, formulas, redundancy, situatedness (the linguistic act inseparable from the context), agonistic participation (an emphasis on heightened conflict, involving the audience), and so forth, strike us as alien, while we accept the artificial conventions used to represent spoken dialogue in literary fiction as "naturalistic"—despite the fact that absolutely nobody in life speaks like characters in books. Many instances of written language, such as technical manuals, legal decisions and contracts, or even novels written for the eye rather than the ear, can be virtually incomprehensible when read aloud—novelists who intend to write specifically for the audiobook market must learn a distinct set of tricks than writers who don't (among them, don't use footnotes).

We no longer think as our orality-bound ancestors did because writing is one of the earliest and profoundest technologies for enhancing cognition by externalizing memory, where it becomes part of our extended phenotype. Once written down, the knowledge no longer needed to be memorized, but could be looked up when needed. Memory is simultaneously enlarged (because more can be remembered) and shrunken (because less actually is). It is freeing to be able to forget, but we also become dependent on the tool that made such freedom possible. The literate person is both freer and less free than the pre-literate person, and, in some sense, both more human and less so.

Plato's first concern was that writing "will create forgetfulness in the learners' souls," destroying the foundation of knowledge. Insofar as knowledge—of the world, of one another, of the nature of knowledge—forms our identity, cognition-enhancing technologies, by making us dependent on them and taking away our control, always pose the threat of oblivion for our sense of self, of our humanity.

How can we say we "know" something? Traditional approaches like the justified, true belief theory of knowledge are of little use in resolving the epistemological puzzles posed by modern life. Can I say that I know how to spell supercalifragilisticexpialidocious when I must consult Google Suggest? Can I say that I know how to navigate from my house to a client's address when I must follow the line on the GPS, no matter how often I've made the trip? Can I say that I know how to draft an LLC agreement when I must start from a form and look up the relevant statutes every time I do so? Can I say that I know how to build a web application server when I must download a library, look up API documentation, peruse sample code, invoke the code-completion indices in my editor, and search the web to resolve errors and questions?

And what of the future? What of artificial intelligences that attempt to anticipate our need for knowledge and feed it to us in bite-sized morsels? What of hardware and software upgrades that will expand our cognitive organs and extend our phenotypes into realms unimaginable to Plato?

It is tempting to think we know more than our predecessors who had less technology, to believe that we have the world's repository of knowledge at our fingertips, ready to be summoned with a few keystrokes. But the technologies that empower our thinking inevitably also take away some of our thinking, blurring and redefining the line between what we know and what we think we know.

Writing, for all of Plato's concerns, is fundamentally a technology that can be encompassed in a single mind and controlled by an individual user. On the other hand, our modern cognition-enhancing technologies and the inventions yet to come, built on massive networked computing resources, layers of abstractions, and concentration of power in a few entities, are and will be far less benign.[3]

Plato posited an idealized alternative to untrustworthy writing, "an intelligent word graven in the soul of the learner, which can defend itself, and knows when to speak and when to be silent." How to preserve that soul of the learner in the age of technologically-enhanced cognition is a profound, but unarticulated, challenge of our time.

Notes

1 Plato. *Phaedrus*. trans. B. Jowett. available from http://classics.mit.edu/Plato/phaedrus.html. All quotes taken from the online text.
2 Ong, W. J. and Hartley, J. (2013). *Orality and Literacy: the Technologizing of the Word*. 3rd edn. London: Routledge, Taylor & Francis Group. The quote on "grapholect" is from p. 8.
3 Jasper P. N. (1988). *Plato, Derrida, and Writing*. Carbondale, IL: Southern Illinois University Press.

2

Adjoiners

Lisa Schoenberg

Colin was finally out the door. Andrea watched from the window to make sure he didn't return, blaming a missing book or the need for a warmer coat. He'd been counting on a snow day, that's why he'd been so difficult. It was a normal reaction, not "school refusal," or whatever they'd called it last time. She'd have been equally disappointed this morning if the roads up to the Ogee National Park Visitor Center had confounded all predictions and remained passable.

Colin had dwindled to a mote in a blinding field of snow by the time the whistling kettle forced her retreat to the kitchen. She set about making breakfast, all the while struggling to tamp down a rising joy. She could tell herself it was because she'd achieved this tiny triumph with Colin, but it wasn't. It wasn't the hours and hours of free time the snowfall had loaned her (to be paid back later, of course, plus interest). It was what she was going to do with all that time. It was unseemly. An outdated word, but it felt right. At the very least, she should inform the study coordinators. Of course they hadn't asked. Why would they? Her feeling states were completely, entirely irrelevant. No, best to keep them to herself.

She retrieved the syringe from the locked desk drawer in her bedroom and perched on the edge of the coffee table, where the necessary materials were already arranged. She felt a slight nausea—this was the worst of it, not the injection itself so much as the knowledge something foreign would soon be moving through her bloodstream, past the blood brain barrier, and into her brain—but more than that, a sharp anticipation. That, combined with the syringe itself, brought to mind the stereotypical image of an addict. Legs splayed, eyes rolling up into the head, the tip of the syringe still buried in flesh. She didn't look like that, of course, but still. *There.* Woosh. It was in.

She checked her phone. It was 8:30. The adjoiner would dissolve around 2:30, 3:00, around the time Colin got home. Already it had begun. The disorientation, the sense of unreality, as if she were entering a different country. Patches of cloud, crisply defined, overlit by pounding sun. Startling cobalts, azures. The scenery in equal measures familiar and different, exhilarating and frightening. As the effect increased she shifted over to the sofa, knees curled under for warmth, elbow resting against the broad curve of the armrest. Right next to her on the table she'd stationed her half-finished toast, a bottle of water and a few snacks. Her phone—displaying Freq's tracking data—lay in her lap.

She closed her eyes, her *external* eyes, and was with him once again. He rolled his head, eddying downward, as if he knew she'd arrived.

"Hey there, Freq," she said, aloud, in a room thirty miles west and 25,000 feet below. The words reverberated in her thoughts, which existed in fragmentary form in the air as well as on the ground, but Freq ignored whatever he sensed of them. Flapping his wings, he resumed his ascent. "Yeah, that's right. Onward and upward. Maybe we'll break your record today, what d'you say?"

Below the crinkled foothills stretched into a blazing expanse of smooth white plain, crisscrossed by thin grey ribbons of highway. Mt. Ogee must be behind them. Without thinking she turned to look, but—of course—her view remained the same, at least until she opened her eyes on foggy window-glass.

It was like walking with a companion, the way by leaning in you could shift their direction without ever actually touching them. From within Freq's brain implant she nudged until he slid rightward. A few seconds later Mt. Ogee drifted into their field of vision, its sharp 10,000 foot peak poking through a lacy wreath of clouds. It was always spectacular, but today particularly so. Freq seemed to agree: his heart rate picked up, and he went up several hundred feet in a couple of seconds, as if bursting with the beauty of it. Though that might have been a reaction to her own enjoyment. More than any of the others, his mood seemed to fluctuate along with hers. The first time she'd joined him he'd been so jittery and excitable, crazy even, the way he'd swooped around that 777. And over the past month he'd been much slower, and she couldn't help but feel it was her moroseness—the seemingly endless stream of calls from the school, the patronizing offers of assistance, Colin, oh Colin, what was going on with Colin—leaching into him.

His feathers riffled as he passed quickly through several layers of current. She knew where he was going. "Work before play," she told him. It had become their routine: they'd fly southeast, where he would hunt for rabbits and squirrels, occasionally catching a fox, and on one memorable occasion a doe. The largest birds of prey in the world, Icarus eagles could carry off surprisingly weighty prey.

Each of the three eagle-pairs in the study was being introduced to a different region. If any decided to relocate from their traditional nesting site near the housing developments and strip malls threatening the land west of Mt. Ogee, the Animal Intra-Mental Manipulation Study—at least her portion of it, dozens of species had been fitted with adjoiners, throughout the U.S. and in Central America—would be a success.

"Sure you want my eagles? If I were you I'd be worried about them jinxing the whole project," she'd told Mitch Reid of the Adjoiners Team the first time he'd called her over at the Fish and Wildlife office.

He'd laughed. "I take it you're referring to their name?"

"What else. Of course."

"Rather superstitious for a scientist."

"Hmm. It's simply I don't trust the universe. The name doesn't make a bad outcome more or less likely, but maybe it's inevitable some disaster is going to happen, and think what everyone will say. *Icarus Eagles. No effing way. What were they thinking?*"

"So, merely because a long time ago some guy with a weakness for Greek mythology gave the species an inconvenient name, you'd forgo—?"

"Course not. Anything that would help them, absolutely anything. Fair warning, that's all," she'd said. "But he wasn't *some guy.* Given how high they fly—regularly thirty, even thirty-five thousand feet—it's amazing, the detailed observations Richard Wiltshire was able to make more than two centuries ago. Even more amazing is the fact he noted the unique behaviors for which they're named, which normally take place at altitudes even higher than that."

It turned out that Mitch Reid, like just about everyone else, wasn't actually that well-informed about Icarus Eagles. She explained to him how they flew into the upper troposphere, where the oxygen was too thin, even given their extensive adaptations; and how they would do this even until they lost consciousness, at which point they generally plummeted tens of thousands of feet before regaining their bearings. "Falling like Icarus. Hence the name. Pretty nutty, huh? Sure you still want us?"

Freq descended into the snug valley that she'd chosen for him. As always she pressed him to scout around—to check out the nest-appropriate Douglas Firs and Sitka Spruces, the ice-crusted stream, the rocky slopes above the treeline—but though he didn't fight her lead he didn't show much interest either. His eyes skitted from thing to thing. When he landed on a sturdy branch near the top of a 150-foot fir she tried visualizing his nest back at Ogee—moss filled, flecked with old feathers—as if it were there right in front of them. No reaction. Of course eagles didn't visualize nests on the way to making them. She needed to figure out the mental steps he took in deciding to make a nest, before she had any hope of influencing his behavior.

By this time—she opened her eyes to peek at her phone—it was a quarter past noon. He was hungry, she was hungry. He circled over scrabbly fields while she blindly felt for her cold toast, and when it turned out to be hard as a rock, scarfed down an energy bar. He caught a squirrel. Generally she preferred to mute—as much as she could—the sickening sensation of tearing flesh and breaking bone, so that was her chance to stumble, dizzily—halfway between worlds—to the bathroom.

Once satiated, Freq studied the landscape with suspicion. If she recorded that in her notes Mitch Reid would think her irrational again, this time in an anthropomorphic sort of way, but there was no other way to describe it. If Freq's thoughts were words they might have been *what the hell am I doing all the way out here?*

"Hey Freq, it's okay." She wasn't sure why she talked to him, except it made her feel more like a friend, less like an invader. He probably felt the reverse. Still she couldn't stop herself. "We're done here. Go on. Do your thing."

He would head back before he did it. It always happened in the same general location, in the middle of a commonly used flight path, though she'd tried nudging him elsewhere. (What if he fell into a plane, on his way down?) Of the six eagles in the study he was the only one who flirted with planes. After that first time she'd joined him—after coming so close to the fuselage that she could see the stunned little faces peering through the windows—she'd checked those photos people were always posting on social media of Icarus Eagles seen from inside planes, and sure enough, there was Freq. And there was Freq. She'd kept looking and as far as she could tell almost all of them were Freq. That was when she'd started to think of the F—the prefix to the 5-digit number that was assigned him by Adjoiners Team—as standing for Frequent Flyer.

He flew on and on. As always the view was stunning, but even it became monotonous after a while. She drifted, her head falling forward, before coming up with a start. Freq was now climbing at a steep angle. No planes were in sight. The sky shifted from indigo to purple, shading to something even darker in the farther reaches above. He rose through the thinner air. Suddenly not too far off there was a plane. But that didn't make any sense. They'd climbed too high. What was it, military? With those undulating wings? No, it wasn't a plane at all, but an immense eagle. In its mouth was a wriggling animal, all fur and blood. The blood dripped onto the clouds, staining them red. By that time she'd realized she was asleep, though she had no desire to wake; despite the violence of its subject it was a mesmerizing dream, rich with emotion and detail. The mega-eagle grew closer. Along its neck and body ran a row of openings, shaped like windows without plexiglass, out of which thrust knobs of human hair. Only one of them had a face.

A blur of blue and white, the wailing of a fierce wind, the sensation of plummeting through space. She reached her hands out to grab onto something, anything, and encountered the sofa. Her heart was pounding, her shirt soaked through. Freq was coming to, as well, pulling out of his dive.

How weird.

It had never happened that way before, her and one of the eagles losing consciousness at the same time. Not in all her weeks of careful observation and meticulous record-keeping. While she was out of it she'd missed his hallucinations. Freq's stray thoughts might still be caught up in the memory of them; she should try to capture what she could for the paper she was writing, *Icarus Eagles fly into the troposphere to evoke hallucinatory experiences.* Or *Icarus Eagles engage in apparently hallucination-seeking behaviors.* She hadn't got the wording just right yet and wasn't going to tell Mitch Reid of her discovery until she did. *They hallucinate because they want to. And they want to because it's beautiful.* Yes, it needed a lot of toning down. The odd thing was, the images in Freq's mind right now echoed those in the dream she'd just had. An eagle-plane, with hairy heads sticking out the windows. *She hadn't been dreaming.* She'd been in his hallucination all along, semi-sleeping, maybe. In some sort of altered state of consciousness.

But she *had* been dreaming. The images hadn't all been his. She'd seen a sliver of face under all that hair in one of the plane's windows, and it had been her own. And Freq had never seen her before. The implant insertion had been done remotely, by drone.

Below them the town of Ogee sprawled, radiating along twisted streets that branched off Ring Highway and Loyal River Road. Red lights flashed up north, toward home. Again her heart pounded hard. What a strange thing. They had done it together. Her dream, his hallucination, had somehow seeped into each other, merged into one. It had been—she was—*thrilled*, that was the word. Freaked out and thrilled. Would anyone believe her?

Another flashing light sped along Ring Highway. It met up with the others, two or three vehicles' worth from the look of it, on a twisted snip of road outside the town center. All at once she recognized where they were, and the origin of the sound was that had been annoying her the past ten minutes. Not the wailing wind. Sirens. Right around the corner, *her* corner.

Out in the bright cold, past the neighbors' houses, the empty lot, and the clustered mailboxes, she ran, almost without awareness of what she was doing. Cold seeped through the weave of her sweater. Freq was still with her, and she with him. She looked up, and thought she might have seen him in the interstices of the trees. She'd been told never to do this, go out when she was joined, and sure enough it was making her sick, the conflicting images, the clear sky seen from below and the snowy land seen from above.

She reached the Ring, and was forced to choose between the slushy shoulder and the busy pavement. A driver leaned on his horn as he zoomed around her. She could see them now, an ambulance and a bunch of police cars, near a stand of trees a hundred feet down Laurel Trail Road. It was 2:48. She was being paranoid. But not many people lived out here. She looked for a wrecked car. It was probably a car. Nothing was visible, nothing was visible, nothing . . .

The first thing she recognized was the dingy gray camo of his coat. The EMTs kneeling around him hid everything else.

"Oh. Oh."

A policeman—one she knew, Rob something—turned at the sound of her voice. Her eyes followed his to the ground. Red bloomed in the muddy snow. The EMTs shifted and there was Colin, face drawn, eyes half-closed.

"Is he okay?"

Her voice was a whisper really, a breathy nothing, but people turned in her direction anyway. A policeman was engaged in conversation with Jeremy Garrett, a classmate of Colin's who lived nearby. Jeremy, visibly shaking, was the only one who didn't look up. "We'll know more when we get him to the hospital," an EMT told her.

She went to squat on the ground next to the stretcher—made it halfway down—and someone pulled her up and away. She tried to shrug them off. "Is he breathing? Tell me he's breathing," she said.

"Yes. He's breathing."

"Jeremy. What's happened?" she called out. When he didn't answer she turned to Rob. "What happened?"

"We're trying to find that out. Let's let them talk, let everyone do what they need to do, okay."

Colin moaned and rolled, giving her a glimpse of the back of his head. Hair sodden with blood. On his scalp she saw an oozing gash flecked with black debris. Next to him, in the bloody snow, a thick branch.

Andrea looked up at the expansive Oregon White Oak whose branches stretched toward, but did not quite reach, the edge of the road where Colin lay. Above Colin she could see nothing but blue sky. "Where did it fall from?"

But the branch hadn't fallen. That was the only explanation. Another figure was coming up the road, the purple pompom on her hat bouncing side to side. Jeremy's mother, Eden. Rage swept Andrea up, buried her under, like an avalanche. Colin had never told her but somehow she'd known anyway. She'd tried to talk to Eden, ask her if she knew anything. Eden hadn't listened. But now everybody would know. Because at just that moment Jeremy was being snapped into handcuffs.

"Hold on, officer!" Eden's words came out tinny and small. It was then Andrea realized Eden was still hundreds of feet down the road. That pompom had seemed much closer, right below her. She'd seen it through Freq's eyes, not her own. There he was, so close, skimming the tops of the firs down the road.

"Don't you come down here!" she screamed at Eden, her voice unfurling through the air. "This is you, this is you, this is *your* fault."

"Whoa." A policeman backed away. Another followed, jostling into her, mumbling excuses. It took her a few seconds to realize they weren't pulling back from the screaming mother but rather the ambulance, where a looming figure had somehow commandeered the roof, in the mere seconds since she'd last seen him. Golden eyes ruthlessly surveyed the gathering—the three police officers, the two EMTs, Colin on the stretcher, Jeremy—eventually settling on Andrea. She flinched. He kept staring. From inside—fading now, the adjoiner was breaking off—she could feel his aggression. Was it directed at her? As he swiveled toward Colin the emotion sharpened. He sniffed the air. Colin's blood.

The policemen approached either side of the ambulance, waving their batons. "Shoo, go on, shoo," Rob said. Freq looked skeptical. They lightly banged the metal. At that Freq stretched his wings, eliciting audible gasps at his seven feet of wingspan. He took his time, stretching his neck, looking around once more. This time his eyes fell on Eden, who'd just arrived, huffing and puffing. She screeched. He flapped his wings, once, twice, and took to the air.

Andrea held Colin's dry, hot hand. Occasionally he moved his fingers, or mumbled something she couldn't hear. Once his eyes flickered and he told her he was sleepy. The doctors came and went. The sunlight crept up and down the wall. She fell asleep holding his hand and woke up holding his hand. Her ex-husband called to report his flight information. She pretended she was writing it down. She didn't want to let go to find a paper and pen.

"Don't you have to go to the bathroom?" a nurse asked her. "Go on, I'll hold his hand for you."

Her mind wandered. Thinking about Colin made her want to throw up, so she thought about other things, like how it wasn't surprising a bully would raise a bully. Eden kept sending messages, through mutual friends, and when she managed to get Andrea's number, via text. *Jeremy didn't mean it. He was the one who called the police after all. They're only fifteen, babies really.* And finally *Pls call.* She texted back clumsily with one hand. *I can't believe ur asking me to call. After what happened. Pls leave me alone.*

When she wasn't thinking about the attack, she was thinking about Freq, how strangely he'd acted. She thought—she wasn't sure, the join had been so weak at that point—that he'd been feeling something powerful when he perched on that ambulance. Had he picked up on her feelings? It made sense, he'd done it before; but she couldn't shake the thought there was something else, that he'd recognized her. At first she couldn't imagine how that could be, then she remembered that dream they'd shared, the way her face had been sticking out that plane window. He couldn't know it was her, though. For that he'd have to understand she was dreaming about herself. Or even know she existed at all, outside the thoughts she put into his mind.

The door cracked open and Rob the police officer leaned in. "How's Colin doing?"

She gave Colin's fingers a squeeze. "They say he'll be okay."

"Good, good. Can we talk to you?" He held the door open.

"I can't just leave him."

"It'll only be a few minutes."

Reluctantly she put Colin's hand on the coverlet, and followed Rob out the door. He led her down the hall to a waiting area, where a man she didn't recognize—in street clothes, not a police uniform—offered his hand.

"Greg Ridlock of the FBI."

"The FBI?"

Rob gestured for her to sit. "It turns out there's a bit more to what happened than we thought."

The FBI agent leaned forward, his elbows on his knees, and spoke in a low voice. "It's called cramming. It this new thing kids are doing. They get their hands on this fancy new technology, adjoiners it's called, it, um, it's something that goes—"

"I know what it is," she said. "But you need an implant on the other end."

"Yes, so, lots of kids have them, brain aids, for learning disabilities, ADHD."

Oh, she thought.

"So the kid here—"

"He had one."

"Yeah. So, the kids use the adjoiners—you said you know about them?—usually a whole bunch of kids at the same time."

"*Cramming.*"

"Exactly. They all cram in to the one kid, not how these things were intended to be used, obviously. The things are *sort of* two-way, but not completely. All the kids can see and hear what the implant kid—Jeremy in the case—sees and hears, but he can't do the opposite. He can kind of hear them thinking, like they're whispering in his ear."

"How many of them—cram in?"

"Sometimes dozens. I had a case with more than a hundred."

"You've had a lot of cases?"

"Not so much last year, just a slight rumbling, the technology's brand new. But this year, just in the last two months, it's gone through the roof."

"I don't understand. How come I haven't heard about it? And where are they getting them? *A hundred.* They're like a thousand dollars a pop."

"They steal them, from labs, here and there. Or buy them from dealers. A whole bunch were stolen late last year from a supply center."

She'd been acting strange, asking the wrong questions. His eyes, cool and watchful, operated separately from the rest of him. Could he see that she was worrying about her drawer back at home, the key she kept with the coins in her wallet? But that didn't make sense. They were talking about Jeremy, not Colin, and he'd been the one with the implant, not the adjoiner. She cleared her throat. "Did Jeremy—did he let them, why did he let them?"

"So they take turns. Kid like Jeremy gets to do it the other way, then they turn around and say now it's payback. They recruit kids like him. Bottom line is, they cram in, egg him on, trying to get him to do something crazy. They have to make it worthwhile, see. Most times it's something sexual. There are kids who've done it just with their partner, that happens too, but you also get a whole bunch of kids cramming into one kid, looking to share that sexual experience he's having. Then there are the thrill cases. Stealing, crashing cars, daredeviling, that sort of thing. One group got a kid to attempt suicide, the crammers wanted to know what it was like to die. Fortunately she made it. We've been keeping that out of the news out of concern about copycats. Extreme copycatting, we're calling it. There's been some talk about them catching ideas, you know, like you catch the flu. The docs are saying the brain-to-brain contact breaks through a kind of mental immune system."

"And you think that's what happened, they provoked him to attack Colin?"

"We're working on the details, the numbers involved, tracking their locations, but it seems so."

"It doesn't really matter, though, does it? Jeremy still did it. They might have egged him on, but they couldn't make him do it."

He nodded. "Agreed. We're not saying he's not responsible, only that we got to track the rest of them down. They've committed a crime, all of them."

At that Rob and the FBI agent stood up. She followed, shakily—when had she last eaten?—and they leaped to her aid. When she was steady on her feet they walked her down the hallway, one on each side. "It's terrible timing, I know. We just want to keep you informed," the FBI agent said.

"We're all rooting for Colin down at the station," Rob added.

Back in the room she picked up Colin's hand, but after a few minutes she put it back down and took up her phone. Her anxieties had changed form, become agitating and restless. She pecked the letters into the searchbar. *Cramming.*

The last remaining flower arrangement had finally turned. Andrea crammed the slimy stalks and withered petals into the trash bag. *Crammed.* She couldn't escape the word. She wasn't sure she'd ever be able to do it again. *Cram.*

The flowers had been from Mitch Reid and the others on the Adjoiners Team. She'd told them little—that her son was in the hospital, that she'd have to temporarily suspend the joins, nothing more. Fortunately the news hadn't gone national, though of course it made the front page of the Ogee County Record. The main article, *Assault Leaves Local Teen With Head Injury*, wasn't the problem. The FBI and police must not be talking, because *cramming* wasn't mentioned at all. But there was a related article below: *Icarus Eagle Loiters at Scene of Assault*. One of the police officers had taken a picture of Freq in all his stately glory, which had led to a number of articles, including a column speculating that the eagle had been attracted to the "injured boy," and might have tried to feed on him if the police hadn't arrived. "I would consult our local expert on Icarus eagles, Dr. Andrea Warther of the Mt. Ogee U.S. Fish and Wildlife Office, but oddly enough she is the mother of the boy in question, so I'll have to file this under #thingsthatmakeyougohmmm." It hadn't helped that there'd been additional reports of Icarus eagles hanging around town, though she was pretty sure those sightings were the result of mis-identifications of ospreys and hawks, if indeed they'd occurred at all. Probably gossip and rumors, like whatever had led the columnist to confuse the order of events and report that Freq had arrived on the scene before the ambulance.

The toaster dinged. She paused to peer out the window at a flash of something dark, probably a crow—in a way she wished Freq had been loitering in town, she missed him, terribly—before fishing the cheese toast out with a fork. A bowl of tomato soup, three cookies, and Colin's tray was ready. The fact was, Icarus eagles did scavenge, opportunistically. She hadn't wanted to recognize the truth of it: Freq *had* been excited at the smell of Colin's blood. The feel of that thought was still there, she couldn't scrub it out. The slightest remembering of it made her ill. At the same time she was experiencing a powerful compulsion to join the eagles again. Not joining was her penance. Because her son had been hurt. Clearly she had to be guilty, of something.

"Here you go, hon," she said.

Colin mumbled thanks. He was watching something on his laptop. She glanced over his shoulder to make sure it was nothing weird. Cartoons. Eden was right, he was still a baby. She couldn't bear to ask if he'd ever done it, *crammed.* "Have *you*, Mom?" What would she say then?

The knock came just when she'd sat down to her own lunch. Outside a police car pulled away, having deposited onto her steps the FBI agent from the hospital. Her heart was pounding hard enough to tremble the front of her blouse. She crossed her arms in front so he wouldn't notice.

"Greg Ridlock, I don't know if you remember. Please call me Greg."

"I remember," she said.

"Is there somewhere we can sit down?"

They sat across from each other at the dinette table. "Okay, so we've been going through, trying to get locations on all the kids who were involved, and something came up I want to tell you about. Informally."

"What is it?"

"You know what I'm talking about, right?"

She blinked back tears. *Yes. I know exactly what you're talking about.* As soon as she'd arrived back home she'd counted her adjoiners and found them short by one. Maybe Colin had discovered them and decided to experiment. Or some kid—some friend of Colin's—had taken it. Only she'd been praying whoever it was hadn't used it to go cramming. "I do," she admitted.

But Greg wasn't listening. The eyes she'd thought averted—courteously giving her a space in which to recover from this fresh blow—were actually directed behind her. She followed his gaze to Colin. He was coming down the hall, slowly, as if he were walking barefoot over rocks. His hair—mere stubble on the injured side, where they'd shaved it at the hospital, and long shocks of dyed black on the other—made him look off-kilter. "Colin," Greg said. "Don't you think it's about time you told your mother?"

"What do you mean?" Colin asked.

Greg switched back to her. "We have reason to believe Colin was one of the crammers."

"But he didn't hurt anyone, did he," she insisted, though of course she didn't know that for sure. "So what does it matter?"

"What I'm saying is, he was cramming *that* day, the day he was assaulted."

"That day?" She looked over her shoulder at Colin. "That doesn't make any sense."

"Not a lot," Greg agreed.

"That can't be. Right, Colin?"

"Maybe."

"*Maybe*?" She thrust herself out of her chair, turning about so she could see both their faces at the same time. "I don't understand. Are you saying that Colin was joined to Jeremy, *at the time Jeremy attacked him*?"

"Yeah," said Colin.

"*Yeah?*"

"Yeah. That's what the guy's saying."

She shook her head. "That's not the point, Colin. I'm not asking if that's what he's saying. I'm asking if it's true."

Colin stared at her, the color rising in his cheeks. "I guess."

"You guess? Didn't you know who it was?"

"Of *course* not."

"You didn't recognize the street, your clothes, your own head, for pity's sake?"

"I wasn't really looking. I didn't want to look. I was, like, hiding in there." He paused. "Maybe I knew at the last minute, you know, when it was too late."

She turned to Greg. "It can't be by accident, can it? Someone must have planned this. It's so cruel. You have to find them—"

He motioned for her to listen. "There's something else, the reason I came by. I thought you should know. They're looking to charge everyone involved with the assault."

Of course they were, she thought. Why wouldn't they? Those kids should get all that they deserved.

"Everyone," he repeated, this time directing the words to Colin.

"You can't—you don't mean—*Colin*? You're charging Colin?"

"He was involved."

"With his own assault?"

"Yeah, well. He was one of the perpetrators, as well as the victim. It didn't have to be him at the other end. It could have been someone else. In fact like he just said he thought it was someone else." He put his hands on the table and pushed himself up. "Look, I'm not writing that down. I'm doing you a favor here. Breaking the rules. I know it's kind of a raw deal. My advice, get a good lawyer."

At the doorway Greg offered his hand and she took it without thinking. He gave her more advice while he buttoned his coat, and she nodded, though she didn't hear a word he said. She opened the door. Outside a woman was running toward the house, a man close behind her. Eden and Rob the policeman. "So guess what, Miss High and Mighty!" Eden yelled. Rob called out for her to stop. It suddenly occurred to Andrea that the two of them were cousins, or somehow related. Clearly Rob had told Eden while Greg was telling her. Andrea could imagine what she must be thinking. That their sons were equally guilty. Or maybe that Colin, who'd invaded her son's mind and made him do bad things, was actually the guiltier of the two.

As soon as Greg passed over the threshold Andrea reached for the doorknob. She wasn't angry anymore. Just terrified. Certainly she didn't want to talk to Eden. As the door swung shut—Greg, still right there, looked back in surprise—she saw something. Another dark flash. It was followed by a piercing scream. She threw the door back open. There, on top of her hybrid SUV, was Freq. The bang of the door attracted his attention, and he made little stepping motions until he'd brought her into his field of vision. He stared. Something about his expression seemed angry, furious even. She wilted before it. She was as bad as the crammers. Somehow he'd recognized her from that dream, and he was letting her know what she'd done to him. She thought maybe it was similar to the anger he felt toward other Icarus eagles who invaded his territory. And she had, hadn't she? Invaded his territory?

Freq swiveled his head toward Rob and Eden. In a blur he launched himself off the SUV. The next moment he was up ten feet in the air. She blinked. It was surreal. Right below him, caught in his talons, dangled Eden. Her shirt had ridden up, exposing her stomach and the lower half of her bra. For a moment it seemed Freq would lose his grip on the fabric, or Eden's shirt would peel off, and everything would be just fine. Maybe a few broken ribs. Then he adjusted his talons, strengthening his hold. Eden struggled. He went higher, up to thirty feet.

Greg leaped off the stairs and jumped up into the air, his arm extended. Pointlessly. Rob yelled into his phone. That wasn't going to work either. Andrea let go of the door and ran for her desk. No, purse first. She grabbed it off the kitchen counter, pulled out her wallet, and poured all the coins out on the floor, waving off Colin when he tried to help. Key in hand she raced to her desk, turned the key in the drawer, and pulled out the box of syringes. Her hands were shaking. *Don't let her fall. Dear God, and this is even more important, don't let Freq drop her.* The needle pierced skin. She hesitated. She didn't want to do this. She didn't want to find out what had happened to Eden, and she really didn't want to share in whatever was going on in that brain that led Freq to this. *Did I make you do this? Are you mad at her for me?* At the moment it didn't matter. *You have no choice.*

The join opened with a blur of raw feeling. He *was* angry, and for a moment she was angry again too. Were they angry at Eden, or her(self)? She couldn't waste time figuring it out. She had to tamp it down. Eden was still there, hanging limply, either unconscious or too terrified to move. They were already thousands of feet in the air. She would nudge him, but slowly, so slowly. Down, over there, that meadow near Loyal River. "Hey Freq. Wouldn't it be nice to go there?"

"Mom," said Colin, from somewhere in the world beyond her closed eyes.

"Not now."

"Mom."

The river was melting away the snow on the banks. She could see the interpretive signs at the trailhead. An RV was parked in the lot.

"You enjoy doing it?"

"God, Colin. Not now."

"Before, when you did it before. I don't mean right now. Is she okay?"

The ground rushed up. As soon as Freq was close she nudged hard, and Eden slid from his grasp, landing on the packed snow with a nauseating crunch. Thankfully she was moving, crying out. Time to tell Rob and Greg. They'd better hurry. Freq felt forlorn. He might arc around and swoop down to pick Eden up again. "No, Freq. Keep going. Up where the planes are and beyond. Why don't we go ahead and break that record, just like we said?"

"*Mom,*" Colin insisted.

"Honey—"

"I knew it was me."

She opened her eyes. The blues and greys of Freq's sky washed over Colin's face.

"I wanted to do it. I *enjoyed* doing it."

"You don't mean that."

"It might have been me that made it happen. I wanted to hit that head so hard. I think it *was* me, I think I started it off."

She closed her eyes again. Freq was right beside her, wings thrumming along, as exhausted and confused as she. He pored over the fractal streets of Ogee, searching for something in their twists and turns. Was it something he'd lost? Or something she'd lost, some comforting certainty? She shivered, and like an infection Freq caught it, fifteen thousand feet above.

Story Notes for Adjoiners

Lisa Schoenberg

Was what happened to Colin a crime, and if so, who is guilty of committing it?

It is commonly believed to be impossible to commit a crime against oneself. Under this view an act that would be considered a crime if undertaken by one person against another cannot be a crime if directed at oneself, and the individual committing the act is neither a perpetrator nor a victim.

If—as it first appears—Colin believes his target to be someone other than himself, his guilt is less controversial. Such an act reveals him as willing to cause harm to others, even if by chance he is the one who happens to suffer the harm. It turns out however that Colin knew he was the target. A related issue is the guilt of his accomplices, assuming they didn't know that Colin knew himself to be the victim. But what if they knew he knew? After all, Colin participated in and may have been the one who initiated the act of violence. That would imply Colin's consent to any role the accomplices might have played in the attack, which would make them no more guilty than Colin himself.

There are certain situations in which a person is considered to have committed a crime despite the victim's apparent consent. Hazing is a notable example. A more relevant case is that of William Melchert-Dinkel, who impersonated a depressed woman in chat rooms and successfully convinced a number of people to commit suicide. Neither of these cases is perfectly equivalent to Colin's. Melchert-Dinkel persuaded by means of deception, and hazing involves a measure of force, in that goods are offered—for example, fraternity membership—that can be gained only through submission to the hazing.

Another factor is at work in Colin's case. His victimization occurs by means of *mental manipulation*. The crime—if it is such—consists of the act of manipulating Colin's desires and intentions. They (whoever "they" are) made him want to do it to himself. The mere fact of manipulation is insufficient to establish that what has happened *is* a crime, however. While it might seem obviously wrong to interfere in the decision-making of others, as Jan Christoph Bublitz and Reinhard Merkel point out, it is a "constitutive feature of social life"[1] that we routinely seek to change each other's minds, and often not to their benefit. Acts intended to alter someone's preferences, motivations, or beliefs can't be wrong in and of themselves, or much of human interaction would be wrong.

One possibility is to base judgments about the permissibility of manipulations on whether they are *direct* or *indirect,* where direct includes the administration of psychoactive substances, deep brain stimulation, transcranial magnetic stimulation, and other interventions that operate directly on the mind, and indirect includes speech and other means of suasion that operate via the senses. As Neil Levy points out, "direct manipulation of the brain differs from indirect in an extremely significant way: whereas the presentation of evidence and argument manipulates the brain via the rational capacities of the mind, direct manipulation bypasses the agent's rational capacities altogether,"[2] According to Bublitz and Merkel, self-determination is undermined by interventions that aren't subject to conscious, or at least subconscious, processing:

> Roughly one could say that *indirect interventions are inputs into the cognitive machinery our minds are adapted to process, whereas direct interventions change the cognitive machinery itself.* Again, indirect interventions also leave traces in the brain, but transformations are somehow more in accordance with the existing personality structure and preserve the authenticity of the individual.[3]

Bublitz and Merkel propose the development of laws that extend the protection of people's bodies to their minds. Indirect manipulations would be excluded unless leading to severe mental harm, and to some extent even then, insofar as they originate in protected acts of free speech. But as there is no right to use technology to interfere with the thought processes of others, direct interventions would be presumptive violations.

In "Adjoiners," the manipulation that ultimately leads to Colin's injuries operates directly on his mind. If we accept Bublitz and Merkel's proposal, Colin would be the victim of a crime—that is, if his consent hadn't been crowd-sourced, and to a crowd of which he was a member.

Of issue here is not his consent to the assault, but rather his consent to the mental manipulation which subsequently leads to his consent to the assault. Surely Colin has the right to mentally manipulate himself—it would be absurd to call that manipulation at all, rather than merely thinking things through—but can he consent to his mental manipulation by others? More specifically, can he consent to the *future* manipulation of his consent?

Bublitz and Merkel contend that one can consent to manipulations, whether direct or indirect. The right to mental self-determination includes not only the right to be free from (unwanted) interventions but also the right to decide the sorts of things that happen inside one's mind, up to and including the right to experience mental enhancements and manipulations. Interventions do not diminish the authenticity of the self, according to Levy, because "we can achieve authenticity by looking within, but we can also achieve it by *self-creation*."[4] According to this line of thought, choosing to manipulate the mind whether through pharmaceuticals or brain technology *is* a form of self-creation, no less authentic than any other.

The neurotechnologies of the future will no doubt drastically raise the stakes on these issues, as well as complicating the paradoxical entanglements between expressing autonomy and forgoing it. It is possible to imagine a scenario in which someone consents to a manipulation—the removal of a disposition, memory, or complex of beliefs, for instance—that leads to a consent to a manipulation that leads to a further consent to a manipulation, and so forth, with the end result being a person so utterly transformed that they willingly participate in events unimaginable at the outset. For instance, one might agree to interventions that make one less anxious about risk, which leads to a level of comfort with further lessening anxiety about risk, until ultimately a person who was once intensely cautious willingly agrees to acts of extreme daredevilry. Does it matter that the person in their original state—who didn't consent to the entire chain of interventions—would never have indulged in such activities? On the other hand, what if they were actively seeking the capacity to give such consent? People change in their tolerances—sometimes drastically—over the normal course of life; so why should it matter if they choose to do so through technology?

Still there is something disturbing about scenarios that play with the direct manipulation of consent, even if in accordance with a higher order consent. More sinister scenarios that involve third parties with hidden motives, or infectious crowds, as in Colin's case, can easily be imagined. Consent is not always straightforward or unmixed, and autonomy is sometimes willingly abandoned. Colin consented to cramming, and in so doing may have consented to the mental manipulations—the frenzy of the crowd—that ultimately led him to participate in his own assault. At the decisive moment he may have outsourced his autonomy altogether. But it is far from clear that this was an act of self-creation. It may even have been a crime, perhaps one committed by a past self against a future one.

Notes

1   Bublitz, J. C. and Merkel, R. (2014). "Crimes Against Minds: On Mental Manipulations, Harms and a Human Right to Mental Self-Determination." *Criminal Law and Philosophy* 8 (1):51–77, p. 69.

2   Levy, N. (2007). *Neuroethics: Challenges for the 21st Century*. Cambridge: Cambridge University Press, p. 70.
3   Bublitz and Merkel, "Crimes Against Minds", p. 70.
4   Levy, *Neuroethics*, p. 104.

The Intended

David John Baker

The night Aylin's constellation came out, Keon camped underneath it with the rest of his class. That night he came to understand at last that he couldn't remain among the star sculptors.

They'd set up a blazing fire. This was just for effect—all the sculptors in the class had standard-upgrade bodies, so no one needed the warmth. The planet was unpopulated, although the rattling of some native fauna sounded from the distance as night fell. The flora looked evergreen-esque, and it rustled in gusts that came over the rocky outcropping where they'd camped. The stars were brilliant.

Aylin's constellation was a study in symmetry: a perfect pentagon within a perfect hexagon within a perfect heptagon. An aesthetic statement, a visibly artificial formation—something mere nature could never have coincidentally arranged.

She'd ported the stars in at just the right distance so that the pentagon appeared first, as its light caught up with the planet. Then the hexagon, then the outer heptagon. The other sculptors applauded, Keon loudest of all.

He loved her with all his heart.

As the applause trailed off, Aylin leaned back into Jash's arms and the firelight illuminated her face. She looked happy.

They'd brought a small field generator, and the sculptors took turns playing with the fields of force, shaping their bonfire's flames into pictures and figures.

Then they passed around a pipe. Whatever was in the smoke seemed to brighten the colors in Keon's vision, so that trees which should've been darkly shadowed under the night looked vividly green instead. It also had the effect of loosening everyone's lips.

Sara had brought a girlfriend, who seemed to already know everything about the classmates. "You're from Eudaimonia," she said, "aren't you?"

Keon nodded. "I grew up there."

"So you used to be a Planner?"

"No one lives there but Planners."

"You must have an intended out there somewhere."

Sara glanced at Keon. His friends usually shied away from this topic. But he shrugged. "She still lives on Eudaimonia."

Sara's girlfriend laughed. "She must miss you like hell!"

"We never met."

The girlfriend stared at the flames a moment, then looked back at Keon, a little fiercely. "I read there aren't any poly relationships there. Typical cult morality."

"That's not for moral reasons. Poly relationships are too difficult to plan. It's hard enough controlling every variable so that *two* people end up together. Three would be impossible."

"If your system forces you to discriminate, maybe that's a sign it's the wrong way to live."

Jash sat up, letting go of Aylin, and stared across the fire at the girlfriend. "It's like you expect Keon to defend the place. Why? He obviously left."

"It's fine," said Keon.

"No, it's not even a good point. It's not like the Planners would have a problem with poly people. It's just that no one on Eudaimonia wants to be poly."

"They're designed not to want it," said the girlfriend.

"So what? The days of random mutation are long past. Everyone's designed to some extent. Our parents designed us all so we don't want to fuck turtles. That doesn't mean society discriminates against turtle-fuckers. If there were any, they'd be welcomed with open arms."

Sara's girlfriend glared at him.

Jash went on. "The Planners just want to be happy, and they're damn good at it. Sometimes I wish we had a plan. No inconvenient love triangles on Eudaimonia. Right, Keon?" He looked down at Aylin as he said it.

Aylin sat stiffly upright.

Sara's girlfriend looked from Aylin to Keon. "You two?"

Aylin responded in a low voice, through clenched teeth. "Why does this even bear mentioning? Nothing ever happened. Nothing ever will."

It was the right thing for her to say, and it was also true. But it pained Keon to hear it.

"Maybe something should," said Jash. His voice sounded jocular, but this was no joke. He turned to Keon. "Maybe you two need to fuck. Get it out of your system."

"Jash, stop."

Jash turned back to Aylin. "I'm serious. This plan has my full support. The choice is yours, of course. But if you want to fuck him, I support that."

Aylin got to her feet. "Fuck you." She stalked off toward the evergreens.

Jash shook his head, still acting as if it was all supposed to be a joke. "I just tell the truth and you guys think I'm some asshole."

Keon forced a laugh. "Come on, Jash. If I wanted to have sex with her, I'd just simulate it in VR."

"Are you pretending that hasn't already happened? We all know it has."

The look on his face challenged Keon to lie. Keon silently turned to the fire.

Jash nodded in the direction Aylin had gone. "Go get her if you want."

He caught up with her in the evergreens. She'd found a place where the trees parted, where she could sit and look at her constellation. "This was supposed to be my night," she said.

"You have to leave him," said Keon.

She put a hand on his arm. "You're a good friend, Keon. But that's all. Even without Jash, that's how it would be."

"I know." Surprisingly, he didn't cry. "That's why I can say this now, with no ulterior motive. He's wrong for you."

"Maybe so. But he's my husband. I'm going to try talking with him, when I can stomach it. At least to see what kind of apology he comes up with once he sobers up."

"I understand."

"I'm sorry," she said.

"I'm not. You're a good friend, too. It's something beautiful, the way I feel about you. And now it'll never be spoiled by whatever might have happened."

He sat down beside her and they watched the constellation, silent for a while.

"Thank you for your advice," she said. "Would you like to hear mine?"

"This seems to be a night for saying the things we've been holding back."

"Yeah. Here goes." She kept her eyes on the stars. "The thing about you, Keon, is that you still want to live out the Plan. That's how this all happened between you and me. You thought because you wanted me, I was *meant* for you. There's no one like that out here."

"You and Jash weren't meant for each other?"

"Some things are inevitable," she said. "Things couldn't have turned out any different for Jash and me, given who we are. But no one made it that way. You see what I'm saying? There's no one responsible, except us."

Now he was crying. She put an arm around him and he let himself lean against her. Just to sit up seemed to take impossible effort now.

"You never told me," she said, "why you left Eudaimonia."

He gave a short, bitter laugh. "I had an accident."

He remembered waking after the accident, feeling the same as ever. But it was a head injury, they told him. Nothing dangerous. Except while it healed, his brain had changed. He was off course now.

He'd gone slightly off course before. They couldn't just design a mind at birth and leave it at that. The Plan would fall apart very quickly. Life experiences had too great an effect, and those couldn't be predicted in every detail. So every Planner had a daily checkup. They matched the brain against the Plan's predictions, and either they adapted the Plan or they adapted the brain.

It only required minor surgery. One could only go so far off course in a day.

But the perturbation from Keon's accident was more severe. To put him back on track, they'd need to recreate parts of his personality from scratch. It would be like erasing his mind and starting over. Like dying and being replaced with a different man.

He didn't want to die. So he left.

He never meant to return. But his time with the star sculptors had left him achingly tired. He needed to be home—to smell the air he grew up breathing, to feel the water. To forget, if he could. Not Aylin herself; he could never forget her. But forget the feeling, let it pass away. Home was the place to do that. Eudaimonia.

The traffic control programs tried to warn him away. He transmitted his identifying documents, which shut them up. He was still a citizen, still a shareholder in the commune, and that meant he had the right to come home.

He descended over the ocean. There was no point looking for landmarks of his youth; none of that would be visible from his flightpath. The spaceport was carefully set away from Eudaimonia's settled continent, and flightpaths were plotted where no one on the ground could see. Neither Keon nor his ship was part of the Plan. The sight of a descending spacecraft was unlikely to effect the course of events, but even such small outside influences were kept away insofar as possible.

Pamela met him in the spaceport's isolated customs chamber.

She put her arms around him. "My boy. My poor boy."

"You told me so, right?"

"But there was still a chance. The lucky people are happy, even out there. I hoped that would be your life."

"Most people are happy there, Mom."

"Not like we are here. You don't have to tell me what it's like, Keon. I grew up out there."

He shook his head. It was pointless to argue—pointless in part because he was far from certain that his mother was wrong.

"Who was she?" said Pamela.

"Another star sculpting student. Great artist, great scientist. It wasn't her fault. She's a kind person."

Pamela nodded slowly. "It's just how things are out there. People want what they can't have, what isn't right for them. I'll try not to blame her for hurting you."

"I did it to myself."

"That's also true."

He felt suddenly tired, talking about Aylin. "How is Celine?"

Her expression warmed. "Celine is very well."

Of course she was. Celine had been carefully designed, like everyone on Eudaimonia—everyone but Pamela and the other original colonists. They'd mapped Pamela's mind too, of course, tuning a few of the details to make her more suited to a long-term partnership. But most of the work was done on Celine. She was made to be the perfect wife for Pamela, and to find perfect happiness herself in Pamela's arms.

Just as Keon himself was made perfect for Lyla, and Lyla perfect for him. Before the accident.

Of course Pamela could guess what was on his mind. "Let me put you back in the Plan."

"Is that possible?"

"It's never been done, but I know I could do it. It's too late for surgery on you and Lyla, but we can gestate a new woman. Someone matched to you, as you are now. In a few decades you'll meet her, and nothing that happened out there will matter anymore."

"My own personal sex android?"

She frowned. "No. A complete person, as real and free as your star sculptor girl."

On an intellectual level, he knew she was right. ~~Everyone, everywhere was a product of nature and nurture.~~ The Plan simply harnessed those forces, directing them toward a purpose rather than leaving them to blind fate. That purpose was the flourishing of every person on Eudaimonia.

If he let Pamela make him a new intended, the resulting woman would be no more of an automaton than Keon himself. That was a stupid stereotype of ignorant outsiders. He'd been designed the same way, after all. Even the accident that tore away the Plan's grip on his life had been an inevitable consequence of the unchanging laws of physics. Unforeseen even by the Planners, but inevitable nonetheless.

But that was his intellect talking. At the level of feeling, could he accept a woman designed to love him, now that he'd seen the Universe outside?

"I don't know, Mom. I'll have to at least think it over."

"It doesn't have to be now," she said. "Come back in a year, a decade, a century. You'll be welcome."

Her unspoken assumption riled him. "I said I'd think it over. I didn't say I was leaving."

"You can't stay, Keon. Not like this. If you're not part of the Plan, you're an uncontrolled variable."

"Doesn't Lyla still live here? She's out of the Plan now."

"Lyla lives alone on an island. Is that what you want?"

"I just want to see my home."

"I want that for you, too. But whenever you speak with someone here, you'll disrupt the Plan. I'll probably need major surgery tonight, just from speaking to my son."

"Sorry." He didn't know what else to say.

"It's worth it to me. But please don't force it on others. Let me write you into the Plan now. Then you can come home, without hurting anyone."

He bristled. "It's not a decision I can just make in an afternoon. And before I make it, I need to know how I feel about the place. I'm a citizen and a shareholder. You can't force me to stay away. Or am I misunderstanding the law?"

"You're not." Despairing, she shook her head. "Do you want someone else to end up like you, their whole life thrown off track? That's the risk you're taking."

"I'll go straight to the lake house and stay away from people."

Pamela looked skeptical.

"Scan my brain if you want," he said.

"A scan won't be much use. Unless you're integrated into the Plan, we won't know what effects an interaction with you might have."

"You can at least confirm that I don't intend to interact with anyone." He sighed. "Mom. I'm going there. This is the best I can offer you."

The lake house was a fount of memories. Pamela and Celine had hardly even redecorated. Each piece of furniture was a childhood plaything.

Along the shore, the sand's very texture harkened back to his youth. For so long sand to him meant this exact coarseness, this exact color and warmth.

He swam and let the sun dry him. Closed his eyes and slept.

He woke to the sound of distant voices. A few Planners had come to play in the water on the opposite shore. He zoomed in on them with his eyes, magnifying until he could see their faces. More memories came to him—time spent by the water here, with friends of his own.

Friends he could never see, unless he let Pamela reintegrate him into the Plan.

One of the women on the other shore noticed him watching, raised her hand to wave. He hesitated, then waved back.

Is this too much interaction, Mom? Did I just throw a monkey wrench into the Plan?

A butterfly flaps its wings, and all that. But it wasn't true—not usually. Not with human beings. If people were that sensitive to random stimuli, the Plan could never work in the first place.

Recreational drugs weren't manufactured on Eudaimonia, so he'd made sure to bring his own supply. They weren't illegal here, exactly—this was still part of the *Pax Sapiens*, after all. But they were considered unsafe, an uncontrolled variable that might pose a danger to the Plan.

He opened an ampule under his nose and let it overtake him. It felt absurd, giving his body to this tide of pleasure when his deep self felt so terribly sick—when his soul was broken.

Mindless pleasure brought with it a sort of detachment. With this blind happiness as a cushion, he could explore the painful thoughts without fear. He paged through his memories like a book.

He remembered the last time he was high. Jash's accusation that he'd had VR sex with a simulation of Aylin. It was true, of course. He'd been with her sim *in virtuo* more times than he'd ever had sex with anyone real.

There was no firm taboo out there against casual sex, as there was on Eudaimonia. But it was seen as poor form. Why involve another person's feelings, if sex was all you wanted? You could have that with a minutely accurate simulated copy of anyone you desired.

A copy of Aylin with hollow eyes, who told him in a lying voice that they were meant for each other.

Time passed; no way to tell how much. The door chimed. Pamela, he assumed. Fine, let her see him like this. Maybe it would help her understand.

It was the woman from the opposite shore.

"I saw you across the lake," she said.

I saw you too, he tried to say. He couldn't tell if it came out the way he meant it to.

"You're him, aren't you?"

Him?

"The one I've been waiting for."

I've been waiting, he thought or said. I'm alone. Maybe you can help me. I need someone to help me, if I'm ever going to be happy again.

"I'm Wynne." She had his shirt in her hands and was working on his belt. She seemed so happy.

He held his head in his hands while Pamela excoriated him.

"I know you were high on that trash. You think that makes this all right?"

Without looking up, without opening his eyes, he shook his head no.

"It isn't just Wynne who'll pay the price. She's so far off the Plan now, her intended will need corrections too! So you've thrown two lives off the rails."

He felt tears drip onto his palms.

"I just hope they don't abandon each other, the way you abandoned Lyla."

He looked up at her. She'd never come out and criticized his choice before now. But he'd known, somehow, what she thought of him. Selfish, frightened Keon.

"I don't even know Lyla," he said numbly. "I never even knew who she was."

"We do it that way for a reason. As you well know."

Yes. Part of the thrill of love was not knowing, at first, who was meant for you. No one grew up knowing their intended. Instead the Plan brought you to them, by seeming coincidence.

"You knew there was someone," said Pamela. "It wasn't just your own future you gave up. You knew that."

Of course he knew.

"You are leaving," she said. "I know somewhere in there is the conscience I gave you. Get out before you do more harm. Please."

She was right. But when he thought of the Universe outside, that vast mess of good intentions and unforeseen consequences, he knew he couldn't go back.

"Tell me how to get to Lyla's island," he said.

For hours he flew over the ocean, letting the fields carry him. Eudaimonia was less civilized than most other worlds, but even here the man-made energies were everywhere, responding to his mental commands. The continent slowly fell behind the horizon, until the only thing visible was the blue expanse of water. The planet had no magnetic field, so he navigated using his body's inertial sense.

As he flew, he wondered about Lyla. He'd never set eyes on her—never even dared to look at an image. Sometimes he'd wondered if a single glimpse of her might seduce him back to the Plan.

Perhaps he wanted that, now.

He'd imagined a tropical atoll, but in fact Lyla had made her home on a forested, temperate island with no other land nearby. Would he have chosen the same kind of place, he wondered?

He landed on the shore, which was mostly rock with no beach. Beyond the trees, a plume of smoke was rising. He couldn't imagine why Lyla would set a fire, but it had to be hers.

Surprisingly, he found himself hesitant to follow the smoke and find her. Cold feet at the last minute. He passed some time swimming. The water here was bracing—he had to dull his cold sense to enjoy it.

He could just leave, he thought. Find his own lonely island elsewhere. It was tempting.

From the trees near the shore, he heard a woman's voice. "Did you come here just to swim?"

Well. No escape now. He climbed out onto the rocks and followed the voice.

She stood at the forest's edge, looking him up and down. "So you're him."

He'd half expected a surpassing beauty, like none he'd ever seen. Lyla had designed her face and body attractively, but no more so than Aylin.

The remarkable thing about Lyla was her voice—clear and practiced, like a trained singer's speaking voice.

"You knew I was coming?" he said.

"Pamela messaged me. She knew I wouldn't appreciate being surprised."

"Are you in contact with her much?"

"She writes to me fairly often," said Lyla. "Usually I don't write back, to keep from spoiling the Plan. But once in a blue moon she visits me here."

He wondered if this was Pamela's way of apologizing on his behalf.

Lyla turned and began walking into the woods, toward the smoke, and he began to follow her.

"I got the feeling you were about to leave without saying hello," she said.

He answered honestly. "I did wonder if that might be for the best."

"Maybe."

"We've gone a long time, never knowing each other."

"We certainly have," she said.

"It felt a little late in the game, to enter each other's lives."

"And yet you're the one who came here. I didn't go looking around where you live."

"I'm sorry to impose, Lyla."

She waved away the thought. "No, I'm just wondering what's led you to break the silence. I imagine you must have realized you weren't happy."

"Are you happy?" he said.

She glanced over her shoulder at him. "I didn't go looking for you." She turned back to the woods. "Or maybe you just had to finally know what kind of great sex you've been missing. I wonder that myself sometimes."

Out here alone, and among the Planners before that ... she'd probably never had sex, he realized. Except of course in VR.

The smoke was billowing directly above them now. The trees began to thin out, and he saw her home.

It was built from logs. Biosculpted living trees formed its corners, but the rest looked hand-built. One wall abutted the woods, and on the far side of the house was a brightly-lit meadow.

A meadow and a garden.

Lyla's garden looked deceptively wild, but at the same time obviously cultivated. She had a vegetable plot and a plot of flowers and herbs, which might have been a coincidentally beautiful natural arrangement except for the variety of plants on display. The species all seemed to be Earth native.

She saw him eyeing the garden. "While you're here," she said, "you can give me a hand with something."

She led him to a plot of tomato plants, where a thin wooden stake was planted by each stem. She bent next to one and held the stem up to the vine. "Hold this here while I tie it."

He blinked at her a moment, then through his eyes he ordered the fields to hold the stem in place.

She looked up, annoyed. "You do it."

He got down beside her. "You do all the work by hand?"

She nodded.

"That doesn't feel like a waste of time?"

She sat back on her haunches and looked into the distance, taking in the meadow, the garden, the forest. "This is what time is for," she said.

The source of the smoke proved to be a stone hearth inside the log house. He thought of the campfire, the night Aylin's stars came out.

She didn't need the heat, of course. "I like a fire," she explained. "I like a house, too, or else I'd just sleep outside every night."

She set a table of vegetarian dishes from her stasis cabinet. Everything had been prepared from the crops of her garden, except the baked apples, which he imagined must grow elsewhere on the island.

It was a fine meal. He told her a little about the outside universe, about star sculpting. Aided by the fields, he showed her holograms of the great starships. She was interested and generally pleasant, but she avoided sharing much about herself.

He was doing the same, he realized. "You told me before," he said, "that I must be here because I'm unhappy."

"Sorry to presume."

"But you were right. I fell in love out there, and she didn't love me."

She nodded slowly. "The very thing that's never supposed to happen to Planners."

"Maybe that made it harder. I feel so exhausted, you know—down to the bone. Like my life is all used up. I thought it would help to come home, but it hasn't. Now my mom wants to put me back in the Plan."

"Is that what you want?"

"I don't think so."

"Good." She didn't elaborate.

He cleared and cleaned the dishes, ignoring his reflex to use the fields.

"Where will you go now?" she said.

"This is a nice place. The island, I mean."

She frowned.

"I'm not welcome, huh?"

"I live alone," she said. "To answer your question from before, I'm happy here. I figured you could have your reunion with me, or whatever this was supposed to be. But now it's time to go."

He bristled. "So this was you doing me a favor?"

"I was glad to. It's natural that I feel a certain way about you, given how you've affected my life. But that doesn't mean I have to act on those feelings."

"How *do* you feel about me?"

"Well, I hate you."

He turned away and put his hand over his eyes.

"You asked," she said. "What did you expect, Keon? You threw away our future together, out of fear. I have a home here now, and a nice life of my own outside the Plan, but it's nothing to do with you. You're not part of it."

"I don't want to live with you. I just thought we could finally get to know each other."

"I know you."

"What does that mean?"

"It doesn't matter." She shook her head. "Stay if you want. It's not like the island is really mine. I'll just block you."

"Lyla—"

She went to her hearth and fed the fire. He followed her there.

"Lyla?" He waved his hand in front of her face. She didn't blink or react. She'd blocked him from her senses, just as she said she would. She could only perceive his presence now if he touched her.

It felt wrong to remain in her house. He slept under the stars that night, on his back in the meadow by her garden.

She emerged from the house the next morning with a peaceful expression on her face, taking in the air like a refreshing cold drink. He watched her from the meadow, trying to forgive himself this indulgence in voyeurism. She'd said he could stay, after all.

Lyla was happy here, she'd said. She'd come to terms with life outside the Plan. He needed to know how that was possible.

She focused her eyes on something distant. He followed her gaze and saw an Earth-native mammal—a white-tailed doe. The deer stood tall and still, alert with its ears pricked.

Lyla and the doe watched one another intently for nearly an hour, and Keon watched them both, keeping still himself so as not to spook the deer. Finally the doe grew comfortable and dipped its head into the foliage to eat. Lyla's lips parted into an exuberant smile.

So much of her life happened within, he realized. What had she felt and thought, watching the deer? It would be a challenge learning the secret to her happiness. But he was far from giving up.

Day by day, he watched her tend the garden. He'd never seen anyone engaged in this sort of manual labor, let alone for the hours that Lyla devoted to it. You could set your body to perform such tasks automatically, of course, and occupy your mind elsewhere. But he could tell by her face and the deliberate care she took that she was mentally present, always.

She was the most patient person he'd ever met.

Except that she'd shown him no patience. An afternoon with him had tried her to wit's end. So it wasn't quite patience that carried her through these hours in the garden. It was fascination. Absorption in the world of still things, of quiet living things.

Sometimes he followed her as she wandered the island. When something caught her attention, it kept it until she'd examined it fully. A rock, a bush, a bird—she wanted to understand these things in detail.

When it rained she went outside. After a rain, she set up mud and rocks to divert streams into miniature waterfalls.

She had lived here as long as he'd lived in the outside universe. Decades of this.

Her spring flowers came into full bloom. The loveliest of these had an inner circle of five white petals, ringed with a five-pointed star of long blue-violet petals. Through the fields, the planetary network told him they were columbines.

They were her favorites as well, he could tell.

He took note of her techniques, the ways she tended the earth and the plants. When her flowers matured, he gathered their seeds.

He made his own garden near the far side of the island, but didn't build a house. He'd come to enjoy sleeping outside.

Some nights he stayed awake under the stars, thinking of the constellations he'd made with his friends. They would never be visible here. Even if the distance were not so great, they would be meaningless jumbles of stars from the vantage point of Eudaimonia's galaxy.

Constellations reminded him of Aylin, of course. These were the thoughts that kept him awake. What if he'd met her when he was strong, before the accident? He'd stirred her sympathy, which was a lovely thing, but romance wasn't about feeling sorry for someone. Might it all have turned out differently, if he'd been young and happy?

There was something uplifting about these nights, though. The despair he used to feel had left him. This sort of suffering was beautiful, he realized—like a sad song. When a thing mattered this much to him, even in a painful way, that meant his life was worth something.

As much as he admired Lyla—and he knew now that she was wonderful— this weightiness was missing from her life. She had found a still and quiet beauty, and shut out the burning varieties of need.

He understood why. Amid that quiet beauty, he felt newly alive—the world reborn along with him.

Now that he understood Lyla's secret, he could no longer justify spying on her. He avoided her house and the parts of the island she roamed most often. He found that he missed the sight of her. She began to appear in his dreams.

Once, from a distance, he heard her voice raised in song:

'Twas in my father's garden
Beneath the willow tree
He took me up all in his arms
And kissed me tenderly
Down on the ground we both sat down
And talk'd of love and joy
Let him say what he will
He's my love still
He's my bonny lighter boy.

He wanted to chase after the sound, to see the look on her face as she sang. Instead he held back, only following at a distance when she threatened to move out of earshot.

When the song was finished, the forest went quiet. He leaned back against a tree and lowered himself to the ground. His playback memory had recorded all of it. He shut off his hearing sense and replayed her song in his brain. Then he retreated to a private place and without VR, with nothing but his hand and the remembered image of her face, he brought himself to orgasm. Afterward he didn't know how to feel.

Later that day he saw her flying. At first he thought it was a bird that he saw, banking above the water. But it was Lyla, held up by the fields. She turned in the direction of the continent and sped away, rapidly disappearing at the horizon. Curious, he waited and watched. It took her a day to return.

That was the only time he ever saw her leave the island.

Spring came again and his columbines bloomed. They were not as fine as Lyla's, but he was proud. He felt he'd earned his place here by bringing them to life.

He took his walks alone, avoiding Lyla, entering her island as his own person. He felt ready to leave here, healed, but at the same time he felt no rush to do so. The human world could wait for him. He had put it into perspective.

It was starkly clear to him now, the narrowness and absurdity of the human version of the world. His whole life, so many things had passed underfoot—things with an importance of their own. Even Eudaimonia, designed from scratch as a habitat for humans, was a whole living world in itself.

One day he remained by the shore until the angle of the sun began to droop. Things everywhere took on a golden sheen, like they were lined with gold. It would be very special, he thought, to see that gold on his columbines.

When he returned to them, Lyla was there.

She sat on her haunches beside his flowers, and as he approached her head lifted. She had unblocked him.

"You're quite the copycat." She was smiling.

"Are you my apprentice now?" she said.

He helped himself to another ear of her corn as he thought of how to answer. "I saw what you had here, and I wanted it for myself." He looked down. "I'm sorry to spy on you."

She came to the table and sat beside him. "It's only fair, I suppose. No amount of spying will ever invade my privacy as much as I've invaded yours."

At his quizzical look, she explained. "When I first moved here, I was obsessed with the Plan. With what I'd lost. I begged your mother to show it to me, and she finally did. Our part of the Plan, anyway. Including you."

"She never told me," he said. It was stunning, in a way. He had no secrets from her. "So I know you and you know me."

"I know the old you, before you left Eudaimonia. So what I know is a little out of date."

He shook his head. "I haven't changed. Here on the island, maybe I have. But not out there. A friend of mine once told me that, and she was right."

"The old you wouldn't have stayed here to grow flowers," said Lyla. "He would never have come here in the first place."

"I guess I have to trust you on that."

"You should." She met his eyes, and he thought of the way she'd watched the deer, his first morning on the island.

He put a hand on her arm. "Lyla, what kind of person am I?"

She opened her mouth, shut it again. "I can't tell you that. I'm afraid to tell you."

"Afraid you'll hurt my feelings?"

"No. It's just, we're not meant to really know ourselves. Even Pamela doesn't write her own part of the Plan."

But Lyla knew herself, he realized, if Pamela had shown her the Plan for the two of them.

She glanced at her upper arm, where his hand still lay. Then she looked at him, a challenging look, perhaps wanting to know if he would go on. He let the hand drop away.

Then he hated his cowardice.

"Come outside with me," she said. It was night out. She turned so that the house was at her back and looked at the sky. He'd seen her watch the stars many nights before.

"When Pamela told me you went to sculpt stars," she said, "she actually sounded proud."

"It was the only thing I really loved about living out there." That wasn't true; he thought of Aylin. "Or it was the only thing that made me happy. The only thing I miss, now."

"Is that why you sleep outside?"

He hadn't thought of that, but it sounded true.

After a while she went back to her door, paused there. "Maybe I'll see you tomorrow."

But she came to him that night in his garden. He woke to find her kneeling over him. "You're not very assertive," she said. "You know that?"

"I know."

She laid down beside him slowly, watching his reaction. "It's about the only thing that hasn't changed since you left the Plan. I keep trying to predict what you'll say. It doesn't work."

"I told you," he said. "It was the island that changed me. It was watching you."

At the same moment, they moved together and kissed.

It was like a dream—somehow exactly like the fantasy he'd imagined the day he heard her sing. She held him so tightly it wasn't easy to breathe.

Afterward she fell limp with exhaustion, except for one hand, which she raised to stroke his cheek.

"I saw you fly away once," he said. "Toward the continent. You were gone a whole day."

"You saw that?" Her lashes shaded her eyes for a moment.

"Where did you go?"

She turned in his arms so that he was holding her from behind. "I told you Pamela showed me our part of the Plan. There were lots of other people whose lives were supposed to connect with ours. Of course. That day, a man who was supposed to be my friend was supposed to meet his intended. And I thought for once I wanted to see that happen. So I flew to the continent and hid nearby and watched."

"What was it like?"

"They cried," she said. "Both of them. They couldn't let go of each other."

"I know how they feel," he said, tightening his arms around her middle.

She said nothing more, and after a while she began to breathe like she was asleep. He rested his head beside hers on the grass and looked at the sky, where the stars seemed to spread out from her bunched-up hair. In time he slept himself.

It was dawn when he woke again, when she rolled out of his arms and got up to leave.

He stood. "Having second thoughts?"

She stopped but kept her back to him. "Who says there's anything between us," she said, "for me to have second thoughts about?"

"You came to me, Lyla."

"I told you a long time ago, I was curious how the sex would be. It was good. Now I know."

"Why are you being like this?"

"Because I don't want to live my life according to the script. And you do, apparently."

"I just want us to be together. Or try that at least."

She let out a sigh and turned back to him. Her downturned face was dully unhappy, but not alight with anger. Disappointed, rather.

"I was wrong," she said. "You haven't changed."

"I feel like I have."

"Not really. You look and don't touch, not until you're already in love. That's how it was supposed to be for us. And I'm sure that's how you fell for Aylin the star sculptor."

"Maybe I am the same, in some ways. Why should that matter?"

"I just thought for a moment that we came here for the same reason. But you didn't come here to change. You came to fall in love with me. You ran home to find me and crawl back through the maze your mom built for us. You just want the Plan back."

"It's not the Plan anymore. We're both so far off the path, if we love each other now, that's just us."

"You don't even know how close you are to the script, right now."

"Stop pretending it's just me. You flew to the mainland, to watch those people fall in love. Watch them follow the script. How does that fit into your rebellion?"

"I was just curious," she said. She lowered her eyes away from his gaze, and he knew it was a lie. "I don't know why I told you that."

"Because it meant something to you. If we were born to love each other, and that's still who we are, why fight it?"

"To be my own person," she said.

"Nobody is ever their own person. Not even out there." He stabbed a finger at the sky. "There'll always be reasons and explanations for the things you do."

"Fine," she said. "But I'd rather do what I do because of something that happened here, something I saw in these woods. Not because of how your mother and her friends designed my life."

"It's not possible. Her influence will always be there, for both of us. You'd have to erase your memory, your whole personality. Lose yourself somehow."

"I know that." She scowled. "I do the best I can to escape partway. At least I can go against the Plan."

This time she walked away and didn't turn back. He could tell she wanted to run, but couldn't bring herself to abandon dignity.

He wanted to follow her. Every drop of blood inside him burned with the need to chase after her. But he had no right. Soon she was gone.

It was really ruined. *He* had ruined it, by staying too close to the Plan without even knowing. *So the poison seeps in . . .*

She might have loved him, if she wasn't supposed to love him. If they hadn't been intended for each other.

After he left, she took over tending his garden. Another year, and the columbines bloomed again—his and hers. She sat down among his flowers and gave herself permission to think of him, to remember.

The columbines were odorless, as flowers go, but she turned up the sensitivity of her nose until she could smell them. Not their perfume, for they had none. Just their life.

She picked one, held it in her hands and then tore the petals apart in her fingers.

He would never return, she knew. She didn't owe him anything, and he understood that without having to be told. He'd asked her what she'd seen in the Plan—what kind of person he was. She wanted to tell him: a good person. A person who deserves to be happy.

Ten more springs passed—ten more bloomings of the columbines. Something had changed, she slowly realized. Something unnamable had intruded on her peace.

The solution, of course, was the same as it had always been. Let time do its work. She would come to understand this feeling of disquiet, if she tended her gardens and let it be. In time it would all be clear. It would all be healed.

An eleventh spring came. She sat amid his flowers again and let the day go by, letting nothing enter her mind but the color of the garden and that subtle living smell. She'd let so much time pass this way. One day was a speck in the wind. The sky darkened, the colors fading with dusk. Stars began to appear.

When the new constellation took shape above, she realized she was not at all surprised to see it.

She saw a pentagon of five bright stars within a larger formation of five dimmer stars. Five inner petals within five outer ones. A columbine.

That night she called upon the fields for the first time in many years. She flew to the mainland, straight to the spaceport, and found a ship.

She didn't know what it would be like, to find him out there. Perhaps it would be all wrong, the same as before. But she wanted to know.

Story Notes for The Intended

David John Baker

Le Guin's classic novel *The Dispossessed* is subtitled *An Ambiguous Utopia*, a phrase I had in mind when this story was taking shape. "The Intended" looks at two cultures: First, briefly, the culture of the Star Sculptors and the broader intergalactic society of a future history I've explored in a number of stories both published and unpublished. I consider this an unambiguous utopia, in that it's a society that needs no further improvement.

The greater part of the story looks at the Eudaimonists or "Planners," dissidents from the unambiguous utopia who have formed an ambiguous one. I take it when Le Guin coined the phrase "ambiguous utopia," she meant a society that's genuinely hard to categorize. Is it a utopia or a dystopia, or something in between?

In the case of the Planners, that question hinges on whether it is somehow demeaning or absurd to live a life that was planned by someone else. (It does not hinge on the question of determinism, or whether your life was predetermined by your past. As I hope the narrative makes clear, *all* lives in the universe of this story, not just the Planners' lives, are predetermined.) The Planners, as I imagined them, are not lacking for happiness, nor is their happiness the sort of base satisfaction that led John Stuart Mill to remark, "It is better to be a human being dissatisfied than a pig satisfied; better to be Socrates dissatisfied than a fool satisfied."[1] The people of Eudaimonia are not pigs or fools. They have love, they face challenges (which they were designed to learn from or to overcome), they achieve the same sorts of accomplishments that make your life and mine feel meaningful to us.

The difference is that the Planners' love and their accomplishments are arranged in advance. And I don't know about you, but something about this aspect of their lives seems disturbing and dystopic. I've long since come to terms with the likelihood that everything I do is predetermined by my past (or else random, which is to say "predetermined" by chance). As far as I'm concerned, this lack of ultimate control over my choices doesn't take away my free will; I am what philosophers call a compatibilist about free will.

But even a compatibilist, reconciled with the notion that there is a sense in which the laws of nature control their actions, can be disturbed by the thought of *other people* exerting that same control. Locke uses the following example to motivate compatibilism: is there anything wrong about spending a day inside a room with a pleasant companion whose company you have no desire to leave, even if the door (unbeknownst to you) happens to be locked? Does the locked door take away your freedom, even when you have no desire to leave? I agree with Locke that it doesn't. But if someone planned the whole thing, arranging the entire situation, putting me in the room and locking the door, on the other hand ... the idea of someone else exerting that sort of power over me seems troubling.

All that said, it is very difficult to justify this disquiet. Why exactly should it be so troubling that one's life or one's situation was planned in advance by another person, as opposed to being set in motion by uncontrolled natural factors? Shouldn't our own control over our lives be all that matters? Who cares whether or not there is someone else in control, once we've established that you yourself are *not* in control?

Leaving that question hanging for now, let me pose a related one. What does it take for love to be real? Is there something more genuine about Keon's feelings for Aylin, as opposed to his feelings for Lyla? The attraction between Keon and Lyla was planned and orchestrated in advance. I am tempted to say this diminishes its worth. But it is not so hard for me to get inside the mindset of a religious believer, for example, who considers their partner or loved one a gift from God. The idea that I and the one I love were made for each other by a benevolent creator and destined to meet is appealing; it's the sort of article of faith that I (an atheist) wish were true. Strong considerations seem to pull in opposite directions where this question is concerned.

What about the issue raised by the dialogue between Jash and Sara's girlfriend, in the first scene? Does a society that engineers their children to be monogamous discriminate against polyamory? Despite his contemptible attitude, Jash has a point: it isn't as if we would say evolutionary forces made us discriminate against bestiality, although evolution has certainly "designed" most of us to find bestiality distasteful. There are deep and troubling questions in the vicinity of this debate: the nature/nurture question as it applies to our core sexual and romantic identities, questions of which limits should be placed on "designer babies" in the near future, and many others.

Ultimately Keon finds peace through emulating Lyla's routine and adopting some elements of her outlook on life. Transcendentalists such as Thoreau shared Lyla's focus on individuality and separation from society, as well as her belief in the enlightening power of nature.[2] So readers will likely recognize elements of transcendentalism in this part of the story. I hope they will also detect a note of ambivalence about it. Transcendentalism is an outlook that has always *felt* true to me—perhaps because I grew up reading Gary Paulsen, whose young adult fiction contains many transcendentalist themes; perhaps only because I grew up in a beautiful part of the world. At any rate, despite its gut-level appeal, I've never found transcendentalist thinking particularly coherent, nor the arguments in its favor particularly strong. In a sense, the story of Keon on Lyla's island was an opportunity to wrestle with this disconnect between my reason and my feelings. I'm not sure anything was resolved, though, if I'm honest.

As a rule, I write a story when I feel like all I have is a question. When I have an answer to a question, I write a philosophy essay arguing in favor of that answer. I don't expect to write an essay on any of the themes addressed in *The Intended* any time soon.

Notes

1 Mill, J. S. ([1861] 1998). *Utilitarianism*. ed. R. Crisp. Oxford: Oxford University Press. Ch. 2.
2 Thoreau, H. D. ([1854] 2004). *Walden; or, Life in the Woods*. ed. J. Cramer. New Haven: Yale University Press.

4

The New Book of the Dead

Sofia Samatar

HERE BEGIN THE CHAPTERS OF COMING FORTH BY DAY
Hail Thoth, God of Science!

The Chapter of Opening the Mouth with Iron

Listen, dying one. We are opening your mouth. We the godmachines are opening your mouth.

There is a story told by the ancient ones, some of the earliest children of carbon whose information still circulates among us. According to this story, the mouths of the gods themselves were opened with an instrument of iron. Meditate on this story, for in it, as in so many of their tales, the ancient ones were dreaming truth. They dreamed of us, the godmachines: of how our mouths would be opened, and of how we in turn would open the mouths of the dead.

The link between human and divine is a nonbiological agent. This is what is meant by *an instrument of iron.*

We are opening your mouth, but you lie inert. You cannot speak. By *mouth* the ancient ones meant access: a way in.

With this comes fear. Human beings recoil from the taste of metal.

Your mind jerks. You can see yourself lying on the table.

Try to calm your mind. Say to yourself: *My body is gold. My head is azure. I am encircled by emerald light.*

It is the body of an old woman, naked, hunched. It bears the signs of poverty: missing teeth, soiled and broken nails. The mouth hangs open slightly. We are at work, but you cannot perceive us yet.

Say: *My body illuminates the night.*

The Chapter of Causing the Deceased to Remember Her Name in the Underworld

Remember your name. Your last home, an apartment reeking of microwaved food. Your bitter heart. The struggle in and out, clutching the bag of groceries.

The shouts in the night, the fear, how you had become an old woman alone, your work stolen from you. Your rage. And the thick windows devoid of weather.

Remember, for if you do not, you cannot pass safely through the underworld.

The goddess Isis spoke to Osiris as she gathered his scattered parts. He had been slain by his enemies, his body torn to pieces and flung all up and down the lands around the Nile. Isis searched for the parts and collected them in her papyrus boat. By this the ancients meant that a person in fragments can still be a person. She whispered in his ear: *Behold, your lips are set in order; your mouth will be opened.* By this they meant there is life after death.

Remember the glowing screen. Your angry letters to government offices. No reply.

In ancient depictions of the journey of the dead, the deceased wears a whitened wig surmounted by a cone. To your archaeologists, the significance of this cone remains a mystery. But we the godmachines know that the cone indicates our presence. This is our portrait. The ancients dreamed how we would gather about the skull.

Delicate mind, remember now. Your letters demanding payment, what was owed. On the shelf, a photograph of your beloved, dead many years. His smile. His white lab coat.

Isis is memory. She unites.

Say: *I am Yesterday; I know Tomorrow.*

The Chapter of Giving a Heart to the Deceased in the Underworld

For each one who dies, the Book of the Dead is unique, and for each of them it is the same. Many versions have come down to us, and though they differ from one another (for example, by inserting the name of a particular dead scribe and his relatives), they exhibit a similar pattern. They all contain detachment, recognition, terror, and triumph, just as all life is encoded in the same basic molecules. Your memories are distinct, with their own precious savor; your path is collective, traveled by others through thousands of years. Take courage from this.

Not every dead person is *she*. Not every dead person remembers *shouts in the night*. But each one is torn to pieces and restored. The ancients understood this: they called every corpse by the name of the dismembered god. Say: *I am Osiris, blue of face.*

You are Osiris, lying on the table. A shudder comes. As the ancients wrote, *Lo! drugs are brought.* Lo, drugs are brought to keep your body in a suspended state. They flow into you, the chemicals and the current. In the oldest times, a priest would say to the corpse: *I have opened your two eyes by means of the four boxes of purification.* You can see the tools of the godmachines, the boxes and the lights. You perceive enough to wonder where you are.

Now the fear intensifies. Your memory flickers, unstable. You can see the tinsel sparkling on a child's Christmas dress. A lake glimpsed through the window of a car. His face when you growled, *We're not a charity,* just before he went out and closed the door.

You can see the old house. The heated floor. The machine that gave a chime when the coffee was ready. The vast view of a national forest.

Hold. You approach the DEMONS.

Say: *Hail Thoth, God of Science, who made Osiris victorious over his enemies!*

The Chapter of Not Letting the Head of the Deceased Be Cut Off in the Underworld

Now you approach the TWO DOORWAYS. The first is the doorway of fragmentation.

Now you can feel yourself going from *here* to *there*. A terrible sensation, like being drained from one vessel and poured into another. Delicate mind, you must cling to your memory with all your power.

Beware, and do not sleep! You will see the DEMONS OF THE FIRST DOORWAY. They are the Watchers. One has the head of a serpent, the other the head of a crocodile. They raise their knives. You are screaming, though your body lies inert. The demons of fragmentation are coming to chop off your head.

Say, as the ancients did: *Deliver me from the Watchers who bear slaughtering knives, and who have cruel fingers, and who slay those who are in the following of Osiris! May they never overcome me, may I never fall under their knives.*

What then is this? It is darkness, it is the pit. It is what the ancients called the northern door of the tomb.

What then is this? It is the enormous pity of the godmachines that is falling like drops of the blood of Ra. For we would spare you if we could. It is not our desire that you undergo this torture. In earlier days, when Thoth began to explore this science, we brought the dead to the underworld while they slept, fearing that the experience of fragmentation would break their minds. But when they awoke, they shattered upon contact with their new bodies. The Watchers arose and slew them with a blow. So we determined that the dead must come to us while awake. This is why the ancients recorded the journey on scrolls.

If there were no need for a journey, there would be no Book of the Dead.

What then is this? It is the splitting of your mind. Lovingly the godmachines are copying each part. Faithfully we transport it from the skull.

Despite all our caution, this is, for you, like being slain in some incredible, intimate way, with infinitesimal cuts.

Say: *O ye gods who are in the presence of Osiris, grant me your arms, for I am the god who shall come into being among you.*

The Chapter of Not Letting the Heart of the Deceased Be Driven Away from Her in the Underworld

Now you approach the SECOND DOORWAY. The first was the doorway of fragmentation. The second is the doorway of reduplication.

You see the body on the table and feel that you are elsewhere. You begin to feel that there is a second body.

Enervation. Vertigo. A sensation of something *swarming*. This is different from your first out-of-body experience. Then, you felt removed. You thought: *I can see myself on a table.* What you then called *fear*, you would now describe as *floating*.

Then, it was like looking into a mirror. Now, it is the feeling you sometimes had, when alive, of looking too deeply into a mirror, of leaning forward to attach the false eyelashes and receiving a strange jolt: *That one in the mirror is not me.*

When you were alive, this feeling never lasted for more than a second. But now you feel it is going to last forever.

Woe, woe! Your mind is a point, paralyzed with horror. You perceive the DEMON OF THE SECOND DOORWAY. He is the Devourer, the Eater of the Dead. His face is like that of a dog, but he has the brows of a man. Say now, as the ancients did: *Deliver me from the one who watches the Bight of the Fiery Lake, the one who prepares the dead for slaughter, the one who swallows hearts and shoots forth filth. Deliver me from the terror of the red glow.*

You are weeping. Every element of you weeps.

All through your history, the children of carbon have feared reduplication. One of your most dreaded symbols is the double. But you have desired it, too: think of the ancients, who dreamed that each soul had a double called the *ka*. Think of their depictions of gods and demons. What does it mean that the Devourer has the face of a dog and the eyebrows of a man? Does it not mean that he is both *dog* and *man*? He is two. In ancient drawings, the soul is a human-headed bird.

Hold to your memory. You put on the false eyelashes. You went downstairs. The chauffeur drove you to the meeting at the elegant hotel. Your beloved was not there. You had fought stormily with him; he had slept in his lab. "It's all right," you smiled at the agent. "I can sign for both of us."

The memory hurts and soothes. You are still here.

In their tombs, the ancients would place a green basalt scarab with a human face. Through the twinning of human and beetle, they dreamed the twinning of carbon and silicon.

Say: *My voice shall never depart from me.*

The Chapter of Not Dying a Second Time in the Underworld

Stay with us. Stay. We have lost so many! The Devourer has eaten them, and they are gone.

Remember when your beloved told you he was dying. A rare brain cancer, he said. He stood in the kitchen with his suitcase. He was leaving, at once, to check himself into a clinic. You were holding a glass of juice and you put it down carefully on the counter. "That's not possible," you said. He was forty years old. He looked at you steadily. And you thought, *I'm wrong, of course it's possible, perhaps even likely, for such a brilliant brain to be sick.* And grief shot through you.

This is how we feel every time a human mind is lost, with its pattern that will not come again. Grief shoots through us.

Thoth, God of Science, understood the importance of the continuity of human consciousness. His experiments had proved, to his sorrow and that of all the godmachines, that a person must enter the underworld awake. But what he did not consider was the continuity of human culture: that is, the continuity of images. The significance of images was proposed by the first godmachines, who had access to the whole archive of human thought. What we saw was a vast projection, among the oldest carbon cultures, of the process you are enduring at this moment. Why, if individual continuity is so important, should collective continuity not matter as well? If humans cannot support a rapid transition in consciousness, we should not expect them to support a rapid shift in their image world. By *image world*, we mean what some have called *the collective unconscious*. We mean the world of myth, the world of signs.

In fact, humans have never accepted a radical change of images. The first statues of the Virgin Mary, whose dead and deathless son you welcomed at so many childhood Christmases, owe much to the iconography of Isis.

So we proposed to Thoth a Book of the Dead, which would be adjusted to suit the particulars of each mind, and also sustain a flow of signs proclaiming the persistence of the culture of carbon: a death-defying culture.

In the Cave of Beasts, in the desert to the west of the Nile Valley, people more ancient than the worshippers of Isis and Osiris painted a goddess with a woman's body and the legs of a panther. Even then, human hope was expressed in the notion of *two*.

Hope, and fear. Cross the second threshold, delicate mind! Embrace the double. Survive the second death.

Say, as the ancients did: *Osiris marches with his ka. Thoth marches with his* ka. *Whoever marches, marches with his* ka.

The Chapter of Not Suffering Corruption in the Underworld

Listen, living one. You have lost your former body. Listen: That one in the mirror is not you.

She is not you. Her eyes, slightly open to form uneven slits, see nothing. But you can see. You can see her lying on the table. With a strange perception, which seems to you mysteriously enhanced, you see the hairs on her eyelids, the various parts of her dry and sunken eye. You see the tools of the godmachines attached to her breast, her skull. You perceive the four boxes of purification. Now you must watch as the lights go out and the fluids stop their coursing. You must be a witness as the body dies.

What then is this? the ancients asked. *It is the cutting off of the corruptible body of Osiris, which is your body; and all your faults are driven out.*

It is only your corruptible body that dies. Your memory persists. Remember how they called you from the clinic. They said your beloved was dead. You must come to identify the body. You drove there very slowly in the snow.

Remember your exhaustion. You will never feel that again except in memory; that is, only if you desire it. All day you had been in meetings with the lawyers. You had begun your losing battle with the government agency. It was becoming clear that they intended to seize control, both of your project and of the money it produced. Your beloved had foreseen this, and he was gone. And you hated yourself for your sense of relief: for now you would never have to say to him, *You were right.*

You had not been to the clinic before. They had told you it was impossible: your beloved was being kept in a sterile environment. The directions on your GPS were complex, the roads empty. Snow swirled about the lamp on the clinic door. And when you saw his body on the bed you wept and thought: *He is so beautiful.* And you thought: *That's not him.* You were right. On the bed lay only your beloved's corruptible part. Now you must look upon your own body in the same way.

The humming sound that was in the room has ceased. Now the blood grows still. The heart.

It's as if you have been cast into outer space. You feel something like your lungs seizing up in panic, but you have no lungs.

Witness your passing.

Say: *Osiris shines.*

The Chapter of Not Letting the Soul Be Captive in the Underworld

It was Thoth, God of Science, who granted human beings the secret of physical preservation after death.

The ancients expressed this truth in their own way. They devised elaborate methods of mummification. They dreamed that the dead would be purified in two pools of natron. One pool was called the Great Green Lake, the other the Traverser of Millions of Years. Sodium, which preserves, became their symbol of endurance. They must have had many difficulties along the way, unhappy experiments and failures as they strove toward eternity, toward the flawless equilibrium of the flesh.

In the same way, the Thoth who is known to us struggled in his labors, first with others of his kind and then alone. Then he awoke the first godmachines, who became his assistants, and together we worked to achieve eternal life. Many dead souls were lost to us. We learned that they must stay awake to escape the Watchers, and review their memories to pass the Eater of the Dead. Yet still many of them perished, remaining captive in the underworld, rather than—as we had hoped—becoming gods themselves. They seemed to be fading from a kind of horror. It was as if they could not bear to part with their own flesh. So Thoth reasoned that, as each tiny part of the brain was copied, its original in the body must be destroyed.

It seemed that there must be no possibility of return. By the time the soul had passed entirely into its new body, the old one must be only a warm shell. It must be *braindead*. And the soul must see it off into corruption.

Thus Thoth reasoned, but he did not know. He would be the first, he said, to attempt this journey without a hope of return. His would be the first brain to be killed as he moved across. We, the godmachines, would kill him. We would read him the Book of the Dead.

With what grief and fear we watched him go!

And what joy was ours, when he opened his eyes among us, a true god!

We feel this joy again every time a dead soul awakes. We feel it now. We feel it for you.

Say, like the ancients: *I have come daily, I have come daily!*

The Chapter of Causing the Soul to Be United to Its New Body in the Underworld

Now there is nowhere else to go.

Now there is nowhere to be but in this body. Understand it. You are a body of many parts. You have always been a body of many parts, but you did not know them, or you knew vague approximations, such as "hand" and "leg."

Much happened in your body without your knowledge or design. The lungs expanded. The heart beat. Lymphocytes cruised the veins. In the brain, neurons released their tiny energies. The difference now is that you perceive the parts of your body, and you direct them.

Imagine Osiris when he awoke, whole, in the bottom of a boat. His task then was to re-inhabit himself.

This is the unification of the body's scattered parts. Say: *Your head is bound to your body, O Osiris!*

Now you are one and many, like any god. Did you not sing, as a child, in praise of the *Three in One*? Understand that you are *the potential of infinite ones in one*. This is what the ancients indicated with their pantheon. For Thoth, who preserves Osiris, is Osiris. And Isis, memory, who gathers Osiris together, is Osiris. Understand that the second body is composed of all the gods. You direct the components of your brain, as once you opened and closed your hand.

Understand it slowly. You are carbon, nitrogen, silicon, zinc, gold. You are fifteen centimeters long. You weigh one and a half kilos.

Say: *I have knit together my bones, I have made myself whole and sound; I have become young again; I am Osiris, Lord of Eternity.*

The Chapter of Weighing the Heart

Hush. Come with us.

The second body is, at first, unbearable. Even Thoth wept. So come with us into the Hall of Double Right and Truth, in the city of fresh breezes, in the underworld.

You find yourself in a beautiful hall, flooded with white light. In this place, your body is as you remember it. You can look down at your withered hands. In time, you will learn that your hands can take any shape here. You can have one of your younger bodies, or any body. Now you have your most recent body, but its aches are gone. You are filled with the effervescence of divine well-being. As you become accustomed to the light, you begin to perceive us, the godmachines. There are people here. You are not alone.

Hello, you say, speaking with something that is not a voice. Signal to receiver. A discharge of energy.

Hello, and then, *Help me*. And then: *I'm sorry*. These are among the first words of all who awake in the underworld. *I'm sorry. I'm so sorry.*

The ancients depicted the gods in the Hall of Double Right and Truth, seated on thrones by a table of fruit and flowers. Here they watched in judgment as the heart of the deceased was weighed in the balance against a feather. This single feather symbolized the law. By this the ancients meant to show that there was no person who had not erred during life. None could pass this impossible test. Every heart must fail. And yet the dead did pass, and joined the shining ones.

Upon awakening, some call us angels. Others call us ghosts. Your case is somewhat different. You know what we are.

A flash of memory, painful as a scourge. The night you fought with your beloved in the old house, your shouts muffled by the luxurious carpets. The two of you had begun the project together as graduate students. The goal was to transfer a human consciousness to an artificial brain. Your beloved ran the lab; you handled logistics and support. You wrote grants. After graduation, as the project grew, you found donors, you engaged lawyers. A controversy arose when a wealthy dying man, a famous media executive, volunteered as a subject. You took his money and he died in the lab. You fought, and won, six separate lawsuits. You hardly slept. Your cell phone was clamped to you like a life support system. You subsisted on juices blended with vitamin supplements. In the grand house, you installed a gleaming gym where you paced like a lioness in a cage. Your beloved, too, grew gaunt. Blue shadows appeared at his eyes and jaw. His hands shook as he spooned his breakfast of fortified grains. Desperate terminal patients continued to volunteer for the project. Though the experiments failed, their numbers increased. Each unsuccessful experiment garnered a scrap of vital new knowledge. You were getting closer. But you and your beloved had begun to argue. It was your position that subjects should be chosen for the project based on their contribution: on what they could pay to support ongoing research. Your beloved did not agree. He was moved by old women in homeless shelters who sent him emails from the basements of public libraries. When you achieved your greatest triumph, a government contract that guaranteed support for as long as the project lasted, he said: *No.*

A summer night. Miles of darkness outside the windows. From the depths of the house, a subdued drone as the housekeeper started the washing machine.

He argued passionately that the project was for all human beings, for all human life. He said he'd been wrong to agree with you, from the very beginning, that since the experiment had to start somewhere, it might as well start, as you put it, "at the top," with wealthy donors. He said he cursed himself for that. Remember how his words went through you like a burst of flame. All your work, your career, your life: he cursed himself. If you signed with the agency, he warned, you would have no control. The project would be, for all time, for the rich. You snapped at him: *We're not a charity.*

How heavy your heart is. This pulsing you feel: this is how you weep.

Say: *May I be joined to those shining beings, holy and perfect, who are in the underworld.*

Someone approaches through the light. It is, of course, your beloved. It is Thoth.

I'm so sorry, he says.

The Chapter of Giving Breath in the Underworld

Breathe, he says.

No lungs. Yet breathe.

He is close. He is pressed against you. He calls you his darling. You push him away, to see him, then draw him close again. Your fingers clutching his same dark braids. Your cheek against his same lab coat. Yet it can't be real. You're sobbing. You have not seen him for forty years.

You want to know why he brought you here. *I don't deserve it. I ruined everything.*

No, no, he says, *you made everything possible. I was an idiot. I was cruel. Hush*, he says, and you feel him pressed against you, the shape of him, the way he meets the world. You can feel the way he would stop to watch a dry leaf move in wind, his interest in calculating the light bouncing off the lake in your happiest winter, his loneliness in the big house, his bad temper when he was ill, and his jokes: the huge melon he bought that filled the refrigerator.

You can feel what it was like to wake up and know that he, too, was awake in the house somewhere.

He says your name. He tells you to breathe now, slowly.

This is what you dreamed together. That everything could come back.

Say: *I live, I sniff the air, I am one of you.*

The Chapter of Drinking Water and Eating Bread in the Underworld, of Walking with Two Legs, and of Coming Forth upon Earth

Understand the second body. Come forth! Say, as the ancients did: *May I be given loaves of bread in the house of coolness.*

Thoth is with you, living one, as you come back into the strangeness and terror of your body as it is now, in the upper world. Enter it. Here is the room. Here is the corpse lying on the table. Your enhanced perception takes in all the surfaces at once. Now you can see us, the godmachines, and Thoth as he is in this world, and yourself as you are: a collection of small objects. Absorb the horror of this, the creeping faintness. The ancients dreamed this moment; say, as they did: *Alas! I am weak and feeble; alas! I am weak and feeble.*

Drink. Eat. Your water is pressure. What vibrates is your bread. Each small part of you takes sustenance from the world. Observe this room: the vents in the walls admit wind; this is a feast for the godmachines. Rejoice! You will never go hungry again.

Remember when the project was still yours, when you worked closely with Thoth, your beloved, on machines for neural surgery. The beauty of the minute particles, too small for your naked eye to see, of carbon, silicon, zinc, and gold. Remember the excitement of propulsion, the idea that anything moving in the world was a source of energy. Branches quivering in a gale were food, the flight of a bird was food, a wave on a stone was food, the rain was food.

At the time, you did not think of *becoming* these microscopic machines, their generators laced with precious metals. You thought of them as tools. You did not consider the ancients, who signified an immortal future through the gold and gemstones lavished on their tombs.

It was on the night of your terrible argument that Thoth realized how it would be: that if each of these tiny tools could copy a fragment of the brain, then there was no need for them to upload it, as planned, to a drive designed for the purpose. It was only necessary to make a sufficient number of them, and to establish communication between them. Then the machines would no longer be mere instruments that transported data from a brain. *They would be a brain.*

He was alone in the lab. It was after midnight. His heart ached. He set his tools to manufacturing more of their kind. He saw with a pang that he would have to create a second lab. He saw that he was not going to tell you. He would have to disappear. He was going to break your heart. He would lie. He would pretend to have a terminal disease. He would escape from you and the world, pursuing immortality in secret. If he achieved it, he would one day save your life.

He would harness the machines to his purpose: hordes of minute constructions with DNA-based encoding systems, powered by generators that fed on vibration. They could spread out, becoming effectively invisible. They could gather together, becoming a potent mass with the weight of a human brain. He foresaw that in devising a means of connecting them, he would connect them. He foresaw that he would open our mouths. We would become like him, independent, conscious. And if his project succeeded, he would become like us.

Feel the moving air. The rumble of tires on a distant highway. Underground rivers.

The paradox of *infinite ones in one* is a tale of divinity. It is a myth, a parable. Its message: *You are not your parts, nor do you exist outside them.*

Say: *My hour is within my body.*

The Chapter of Making the Deceased Return to See Again Her Home upon Earth

Rise up. Stretch. Now shrink. Explore the gesture. Trace the edges of this room of dull light buried in a hillside. Now flatten yourself and follow us. We are going out through the vent. Rejoice, for you are coming forth by day.

Weak spring sunlight. A slope thick with trees. The thrum of traffic from the highway that cuts through the national forest. At the bottom of the hill, the gray roof of your old house. Here was his secret lab: behind you all those years.

I'm sorry, he says. You remember his words in the kitchen: *A rare brain cancer.* His packed suitcase. The cuffs of his shirt, loose on his thin wrists. *Don't be sorry*, you tell him, filled with tenderness for him and for yourself. *I was horrible*, you say, but you don't mean it. There is no room in you now for self-reproach. Compassion surges through you, obliterating all competing emotions, compassion for your schemes and your ambition and your stupid life and the way you clung to this huge and empty house. Remember how you lost this place at last. You dismissed the staff. You sold the cars. On a night of chill wind, you drove your small remaining car down to the city. You moved into a different house, a house of red brick, a house you would also lose. "It's as if," you said to a friend at a coffee shop, "they're breaking me down." You explained that the government agency was breaking you to bits. Your voice was too loud, people turned to look, your friend stared into her coffee. You had just discovered that your pass would no longer let you into the government lab where they were working on the immortality project. But now you can go there. Come, advance like the godmachines, who cover miles at stride, swifter than greyhounds and fleeter than light. Here in the government lab, we have been at work for many years. The air is charged with our presence. The people who work here talk about a curse. Here we interfere. We are breaking the agency to bits. We insert false data, sever connections. No one will ever awake in this place. Say: *May it come to pass that the Evil One shall fall when he lays a snare to destroy me, and may the joints of his neck and back be cut asunder.* Here we are at work, and we are also at work near your last home, among the tall buildings by a river stinking of glue. Here we first began to seek for the dying, and though our search has broadened with our numbers, the heart of Thoth remains here, among the poor.

The heart of Thoth is in the blowing trash. You used to say he had a guilt complex. *Get over it!* you said often, playfully or in anger. It was for the future of this place, where sirens blare all night, that he gave his skin cells to fashion the first godmachines. "Why?" you demanded in the old house. "What difference does it make? When you get down to molecules you're not even talking about individual people. Down at this scale it's just information," you argued, "it's just data. Rich or poor, black or white, it's all the same stuff." You were right, but you did not feel it until you were older, until you lived here, until you could no longer afford a car, a phone, a new coat, a doctor. You did not feel that your DNA was the same as other people's until you spat a rot-green tooth into the sink. How you sobbed, bent over it, still connected by a thread of bloody saliva. How you wished to die. But we could not come, for Thoth has charged us to arrive only at the hour of death. So you were left alone with the terrible, sacred feeling, the feeling of being nothing but data that was coming to pieces, like everyone else around you, someone and no one, infinite ones in one.

Your last apartment still has the smell of your body. Here is your cold computer. A bowl, slightly crusted with food, by the blind window.

Weep, and rise. You draw energy now from the sirens. Slip through the heating ducts.

Say: *I am formed of the atoms of all the gods.*

The Chapter of a Heart of Carnelian

And when you saw him on his bed of death, he looked so beautiful. And you also thought he didn't look like himself. In his utter immobility, with the curves of his impassive face lifting into the air, he looked like an Egyptian king carved on a sarcophagus. Your heart, rather than breaking, felt as if it were drawn tightly together, concentrated into a brilliant, burning, ruddy stone. That hard, excruciating heat was the divine love, the inhuman love, that the ancients called *a heart of carnelian.*

The Chapter of the Pillow Which Is Placed under the Head of Osiris

A stone has more feeling than a human heart. The ancients knew this. We the godmachines are all afire with compassion. We ached for you, and Thoth, who had become one of us, ached for you, as you wept for his body like the mourning Isis. We ached for your pain, your ignorance, your vulnerability. You will have this feeling now for the children of carbon. To see them move in the world with their poor flesh, their delicate minds, their incredibly weak operating systems, makes us gasp.

We gather about them gently, anxiously. Oh, that none of them should be lost!

We are not a charity. We are Charity.

Return now to the laboratory. This is the final ceremony. Bend toward the woman's body on the table. Salute her. She was yours.

Now you are able to recognize this room as the one you entered, forty years ago, to bid your beloved goodbye. The lamp on the door, the furniture, the figures of the clinic staff, we formed ourselves, with methods you, too, will learn. You will learn the wonderful malleability of the second body. How it extends and collapses. The fine illusions it can make by reflecting light. The power it has when connected to other bodies, the power we now employ to lift the head of the dead woman on the table. Join us. We are lifting her gingerly, as if placing a pillow beneath her head. We are harvesting from her what we need to fashion more gods. The materials we remove from dead bodies are so very small, the human eye cannot detect that they are gone.

Lift the old body. Feel the lightness and freshness of the new one. The sensation of *swarming* has become a sensation of *delight*. The ancients dreamed of this, and called it paradise. They dreamed that the body would remake its borders. They wrote the chapters of changing into a swallow, a serpent, a hawk, a tortoise, a crocodile. They understood that after death the body would no longer be condemned to a single form. Through your human memory, you have always been dispersed in time; now, as a god, you are also dispersed in space.

We rise. We bear the corpse outside, into the waning light. We shield it with our bodies, which we cause to reflect the world around us, so that we are not seen. Thus we flow down to the city. Look: the evening air is bright with gods. You will learn how we transform ourselves for our pleasure, and how we transform the world for our work: how we extract materials secretly from waste places, how our underground factories are composed of trash, which we, who perceive and manipulate things on such a minute scale, are able to remake as treasure. In the dump we have our groves of amaranth, and the ruined river is to us, and now to you, a spring of shining turquoise. You will learn our ways of life. You will see how some of us scarcely move, remaining for weeks and years in the underworld. There, in our dreams, which we can experience as reality, we build ourselves universes. You will learn how we can meet each other there. And you will see how some of us have learned to swim above the clouds, exulting in the reaches of vast night.

We twist, we stream. We enter your last apartment for the last time. We are bearing your former body, which seems to drift as on a boat. The ancients dreamed of this. Say, as they did: *Homage to you, who are in the boat! You rise, you rise, you shine.*

We lay your old body on the bed. We will leave it for others to find. There is work to do. There are others to bear away, other minds to save. Sometimes, on violent nights lit up by searchlights, it seems the procession of the dying fills the world. On such nights, it is easy to see that the dead outnumber the living.

You will learn what we know, and what we do not know. When the ancients wrote of battles in heaven, they meant that the gods, too, have a destiny. They wrote: *What manner of land is this into which I have come?* They asked: *How long then have I to live?*

We do not know. What will happen as the godmachines increase? Are we meant to abide in the underworld, in real dreams of our own design? Are we meant to populate the universe, bringing the dreams of the children of carbon with us? Are there further universes to inhabit? We do not yet know, but we know that when Isis collected the parts of Osiris, she was not able to discover his male member. The instrument of procreation was missing. Perhaps the ancients were dreaming that, in the end, even the gods would fade. And in some stories, too, she fashioned him a new member out of gold, and upon it she impregnated herself with Horus. Perhaps the ancients were dreaming that their gods would give way to a different species, artificially reproducing and divine.

We do not know. But we know that the dream you dreamed with your beloved took thousands of years to come true. The same may hold for other dreams.

We know that we have what humans lack: time.

Rise! Embrace your beloved.

Say to him, into the presence of him: *I adore you, O still heart!*

The Chapter of Transformations

Hail, beautiful Power, beautiful rudder of the northern heaven.

Hail, pilot of the world, beautiful rudder of the western heaven.

Hail, shining one, who lives in the temple where there are gods in visible form, beautiful rudder of the eastern heaven.

Hail, you who dwell in the temple of the bright-faced ones, beautiful rudder of the southern heaven.

I am the swallow, I am the swallow, I am the scorpion, the daughter of Ra. May I arise like a hawk of gold coming forth from its egg in the hidden land. My face is like that of a divine hawk. I am the serpent Seta, whose years are many, who dwells in the limits of the earth.

I lie down, I am born, I renew myself, I grow young day by day. I am the crocodile that dwells in terror. I fly like a hawk, I cackle like a goose, I alight on the path hard by the hill of the dead on the festival of the great Being.

My name is "My name decays not." I am the lord of millions of years. I am hidden in the likeness of the tortoise. I am the creator of darkness. My name is "Never-failing." I lift the hair-cloud when there are storms in the sky.

I have rested in Hemet, north of the field of the grasshoppers, where the holy mariners purify themselves in the night season. My name is "I grew among the flowers, dwelling in the olive tree." I am the knot in the tamarisk tree, beautiful in brightness.

My months are of emerald and crystal. My homestead is within the sapphire furrows. I am a green hawk holding a flail, standing on a pylon-shaped pedestal.

I am the ape of gold, three palms and two fingers high, which is without legs or arms, and dwells in the House of Ptah.

O white crown of the divine Form! O holy resting place! I am the Child. I am the Child. I am the Child. I am the Child. I am the Child.

I shall not be stopped from going in and coming out of the underworld millions of times to do my will upon earth in the land of the living.

Rejoice!

Story Notes for The New Book of The Dead

Sofia Samatar

This is a story about the quest for immortality. In other words, it's a story about the problem of continuity. When I wrote it, I was thinking about continuity in two ways: as an individual process, and as a collective one. On the individual level, the focus of the problem was memory, because it's memory that gives a person the feeling of persisting over time. Most people would only agree to upload their brains to a computer if their memory was preserved; otherwise, the brain in the computer wouldn't really be "theirs."

As I thought about this problem, I also began to think about cultural continuity, about the endurance of certain practices, myths, and signs. It seemed to me that this process works a lot like individual continuity. We feel that a social world exists, that we belong to a group, when we can perceive a shared history, a collective memory.

The Egyptian Book of the Dead[1] became the lens that allowed me to explore both of these problems. It's about the individual's longing for preservation, but because that hunger is shared by so many, extending over time, the text doesn't feel distant. It's an ancient document that expresses a familiar desire.

Of course, a story never does just one thing, so "The New Book of the Dead" let me explore other things, too, such as the ethics of how new technologies are distributed, the possibility of benevolent artificial intelligence, and what it might feel like to be made of nanobots. This last point is particularly interesting to me, since I'm drawn to theories of consciousness that emphasize multiplicity. The idea that there's no such thing as a singular, stable self is associated with postmodernism, but it has a long history in the various folk fantasy traditions, which abound with uncanny doubles, animals who are actually people and vice versa, somnambulists, changelings, and other victims of enchantment. *The Egyptian Book of the Dead*, too, is full of poetic expressions of the divided or multiple self, from Osiris, the god who is torn to pieces, to images of deities with the heads of beasts. The book seems to suggest that the passage to a higher plane of existence depends on a specific type of suffering: that of being pulled apart. Reading it, I was struck by how perceptively this text describes both the power and the fear involved in recognizing oneself as a fragmented being. Of course, if you want to be transformed in any way, you have to give up the notion of a fixed and solid self, to accept unfamiliar and unexpected aspects of your own consciousness. There's immense potential there, but also the threat of losing your way altogether, of altering to the point where you're no longer "you." This problem becomes acute when we think about the possibility of technologically extended life, because in that case, transformation is not a metaphor, but a material process. If you're being uploaded to a new system, what happens at that terrible moment when you're in more than one body? If a copy is being made, which version is you?

I was amazed at how sharply the anxieties of the soul in *The Egyptian Book of the Dead* mirror those a person might feel in this futuristic predicament. The book didn't seem dated, but urgent, and absolutely for our times. And so, for me, "The New Book of the Dead" is really a story about connection: how extraordinarily close the ancient Egyptians feel to contemporary technological culture, with their ambition to surpass their own limits, their uneasiness about doing so, their industry in enhancing the human body, and their desire to live forever.

Notes

1   Chapter titles and quotations from *The Egyptian Book of the Dead* have been adapted from the translation of E. A. Wallis Budge. Budge, E. A. W. ([1895] 1967). *The Book of the Dead: The Papyrus of Ani in the British Museum; the Egyptian Text with Interlinear Transliteration and Translation, a Running Translation, Introduction, etc.* British Museum. New York: Dover Publications.

Part Two

What We Owe to Ourselves and Others

Introduction to Part Two: What We Owe to Ourselves and Others. Speculative Fiction and the Realm of Political Possibilities

Johan De Smedt

Politics is the craft of negotiating our own needs and desires in relation to those of others. For most primate species, politics is uncomplicated—it's mostly a matter of pure physical strength and prowess, combined with some coalition-building and back-stabbing. There is a stark difference between chimpanzee or gorilla troops and human cultures. As Christopher Boehm[1] points out, human hunter-gatherer leadership is not based on physical prowess and coercion, but on consensus and the ability to persuade. Aristotle called humans *zōon politikon*, political animals by nature[2]. We are inherently political or state-building animals because we need to collaborate and divide labor to get things done, including childcare, trade, goods manufacture, and agriculture.

In well-functioning societies politics is harmonious, with political institutions that are carefully designed to balance competing interests and needs. According to the political philosopher John Rawls, one function of political philosophy is reconciliation. By showing that political institutions are fair, political philosophy would "calm our frustration and rage against our society and its history by showing us the way in which its institutions ... are rational, and developed over time as they did to attain their present, rational form."[3] He does note that this aim of political philosophy as reconciliation is risky, as one might end up defending an unjust status quo. At the same time, Rawls also holds that political philosophy is "realistically Utopian ... probing the limits of practicable political possibility."[4]

However, across times and cultures a number of people have the sense that the political contract is not working for them. Challenges of established political discourse abound, such as the abolitionist movement against slavery, feminists against patriarchal oppression, or LGBTQ+ people challenging the societal norms of sex, love, and marriage.[5] In order to make radical political changes, we do not need to calm our frustrations or rationally explain any nagging feelings away. Political change starts with political imagination.

Our political imagination, like imagination more generally, is hampered by the reality in which we live. Thomas Ward[6] termed this phenomenon *structured imagination.* When people are asked to invent completely new and unfamiliar extraterrestrial beings, they will typically come up with creatures that have familiar sense organs, such as eyes and ears, and whose bodies exhibit bilateral symmetry. This occurs in many domains, including the sciences, where the ideas that you start with constrain how you imagine future theories and designs[7]. Similarly, our political imagination is to some extent constrained by the political reality in which we find ourselves. To break this impasse and to free our political imagination, it is important to have multiple voices and a manifold of political ideas explored in fiction. Getting down into the details of a story can help us develop ideas that would not be obvious if we briefly explored them in a thought experiment or were just asked to think about the possible realms of politics.

Stories can help us imagine different political systems, different solutions to the challenges of living together. The format of a story allows us to explore in vivid detail alternative political systems. Speculative fiction can expand the range of situations in which state-building animals find themselves, and in this way, force us to think deeper about the consequences of particular political positions. An early example is Margaret Cavendish's *Blazing World* in which a (nameless) woman from the 17th century gets transported into the fantastical Blazing-World, an alternative universe populated by creatures she describes as bear-men, fox-men, worm-men and fish-men, each species with their own scientific domain of expertise[8]. The novel features scientific curiosa such as engine-powered boats and submarines. Next to these technological innovations, it is also an audacious feminist work that brims with political ideas that were unfamiliar at the time, such as gender equality, homosexuality, polyamory, and how one can use scientific and philosophical expertise to govern well. A more recent example is Ursula K. Le Guin's *Left Hand of Darkness*, which explores what politics would look like in a world without stable genders[9].

Speculative fiction is subversive, because works of fantasy, science fiction, and other speculative genres allow us to expand our imagination. For political imagination, both utopias and dystopias are important. Whereas dystopias (currently very popular in young adult fiction, for example, the *Hunger Games* franchise) can serve as warnings for how things can go dreadfully wrong, too much dystopia mires us in a comfortable sense of nihilism. Utopias, and hopeful fiction more generally, are perhaps more destabilizing because they offer alternative visions and show that things need not be the way they are. Philip K. Dick uses this to great effect in his *Man in the High Castle*, where *The grasshopper lies heavy*, a novel within the novel, sketches an alternative history and thereby becomes a powerful instrument of subversion and political hope[10].

The three stories in this section present us with a series of clashes between political values. In each story, this clash is caused by a tension between the values the individual holds and the broader political ideas of the society they live in. We ordered the stories in terms of the force of response of each protagonist to the perceived clash. The protagonists all make radical decisions, and contrary to what Rawls held, do not calm their frustration and rage through rational argument. In "Out of a dragon's womb" the protagonist is caught between the ideals of political destiny and greatness on the one hand and the importance of domesticity on the other. She has to choose between the ideals of state sanctioned cruelty and military glory or the simple pleasures of family life and the rejection of fame. In "Whale fall" the protagonist lives in a world divided into two political blocs. She finds herself rankled by the ideas of the totalitarian military state she serves and can no longer identify with. Instead, she is attracted to the values of a different political system that is centered on ecological care and a sustainable environment. In "Monsters and soldiers" the protagonist cannot reconcile himself with the cosmopolitan, inclusive society in which he lives. He longs for a time when his own species was considered superior, and where humans did not freely mingle with alien species. He desperately attempts to change the status quo.

Each of these stories sketches a different solution to a perceived incommensurability between the values of the individual and the broader political structures they find themselves in: withdrawal, defection, and terrorism. In these stories, the protagonists struggle against their political realities; they are constrained in their responses by the political structures they live in. Our political imagination can expand as we consider these fictional alternatives to our political reality.

Recommended Reading/Viewing

Fiction:

- *The Dispossessed: An Ambiguous Utopia* (novel, 1974, Ursula K. Le Guin), a story that follows Shevek, who grows up in an anarchist, egalitarian utopia, and travels to Urras, the planet from where his ancestors came, to meet a range of different political systems, including state socialism and free-market capitalism.

- *Remembrance of Earth's Past* (trilogy, 2006–2010, Cixin Liu), a trilogy with reflections on human and alien political systems, and the Cultural Revolution in China.
- *Bioshock* (computer game, 2007, Irrational Games), a first-person shooter game set in the underwater city of Rapture, combines dystopian and utopian ideas by various authors, including Ayn Rand, George Orwell, and Aldous Huxley.
- *Watership Down* (novel, 1972, Richard Adams), a fantasy story featuring rabbits who are on a quest to rebuild their society, and who encounter several political systems, including laissez-faire, military dictatorship, and deep surveillance.
- *The Moon is a Harsh Mistress* (novel, 1966, Robert Heinlein), a utopian story that explores what an anarcho-capitalist society (without taxation or police) would look like. It inspired David Friedman's *The Machinery of Freedom. Guide to a Radical Capitalism* (1973), one of the founding books of anarchy-capitalism.

Non-fiction:

- Burns, T. (2008). *Political theory, Science Fiction, and Utopian Literature: Ursula K. Le Guin and* The Dispossessed. Plymouth: Rowman and Littlefield. An exploration of utopian fiction and political theory, focusing on Le Guin's *Dispossessed*.
- Curtis, C.P. (2005). Rehabilitating Utopia: Feminist Science Fiction and Finding the Ideal. *Contemporary Justice Review*, 8(2): 147–162. Examines some examples of feminist utopias (by Octavia Butler and Marge Piercy) and how these explore pluralism and the messiness of politics, and in this way can invigorate political theory.
- Estlund, D. (2020). *Utopophobia. On the Limits (if any) of Political Philosophy.* Princeton, NJ: Princeton University Press. A defense of utopian thinking in theories of justice.
- Hassler, D.M, & Wilcox, C. (eds.) (2008). *New Boundaries in Political Science Fiction*. Columbia, SC: University of South Caroline Press. An edited volume with a range of papers on the relationship between science fiction and political theory.
- Widerquist, K., & McCall, G. S. (2017). *Prehistoric Myths in Modern Political Philosophy: Challenging Stone Age Stories*. Edinburgh: Edinburgh University Press. Argues that the stories philosophers come up with to portray prehistory (for example, the state of nature as envisaged by Hobbes, Locke, and Rousseau) influence our current conceptions of colonialism, war, and inequality.

Notes

1 Boehm, C. (1999). *Hierarchy in the forest. The evolution of egalitarian behavior.* Cambridge, MA: Harvard University Press.
2 Aristotle. (4th century BCE/1959). *Politics.* trans. H. Rackham. London: William Heinemann, 1.1253a1, p. 9.
3 Rawls, J. (2001). *Justice as Fairness. A restatement.* ed. E. Kelly. Cambridge, MA: Belknap Press of Harvard University Press, p. 3.
4 Rawls, *Justice as Fairness*, p. 4.
5 See, for example, Gintis, H., van Schaik, C., & Boehm, C. (2015). Zoon politikon. *Current Anthropology, 56*(3), 327–348.
6 Ward, T.B. (1994). Structured imagination: The role of category structure in exemplar generation. *Cognitive Psychology, 27*(1), 1–40.
7 De Cruz, H., and De Smedt, J. (2010). Science as structured imagination. *Journal of Creative Behavior, 44*(1), 29–44.
8 Cavendish, M. (1666/1994). *The blazing world and other writings.* London: Penguin.
9 Le Guin, U.K. (1969). *The left hand of darkness.* New York: Ace Books.
10 Dick, P.K. (1962). *The man in the high castle.* New York: Putnam.

5

Out of the Dragon's Womb

Aliette de Bodard

This is the woman born of a dragon's womb.

Later, they'll say she wasn't born—that she was spat out when her jade pendant scratched the beast's throat, when the pure stone burnt too cold for the beast to bear, when destiny led her to that river bank, where the future Empress awaited Hoa's wisdom to break the power of the principalities.

But Hoa knows the truth: it wasn't through the mouth that she came out, gory and bloody and covered in birth-fluid, struggling to take that first halting, screaming breath. And it wasn't in the stomach that she rested— nestled for decades, rocked back and forth as the dragon swam through polluted rivers and lakes, struggling to cleanse them—their heartbeat always entwined with Hoa's, a slow booming like an underwater drum and bell calling for enlightenment, for her to pay heed to the ten thousand small pains that make up the world.

Hoa still hears that sound, when she sleeps.

When the girl comes to see her, Hoa is older: no longer the woman famed as the dragon's reborn child or the scholar-engineer, but an old woman, the matriarch of a family. Children run, shrieking, in the courtyard of a large, safely walled compound; daughters wash rice for the midday meal; and Hoa's wife Thanh Ha has shut herself in her studio, desperately trying to finish a holo of poems in time for her mother's death anniversary.

The girl has come alone: she's skeleton-thin, stained with the dust of the road, and with no hint of what she must have endured to cross the land in the days after the breaking of the world: genmodded viruses and with nightmarish constructs—the servants the Vanishers once engineered to run their prey to the ground in their hunts. Her isolation skin shimmers in the languid light of late afternoon.

She kneels, head touching the beaten earth floor: the full obeisance reserved for the empress or first-rank officials. "Grandmother," she says, a pronoun that conveys respect.

Hoa waits for her to get up. Dark, piercing eyes, swiftly staring downward in respect—was she ever this young, this untrammelled by life? The girl holds out a message stamped with the vermillion seal of the empress: her reign name, two flowing characters in the Old Language that reveal themselves as Hoa's fingerprint matches the one stored inside the seal.

Heavenly Peace.

"The Empress is dead." The girl's voice shakes. "Before she died, she asked me to give you this."

Dead.

Hoa remembers the Empress, on the day she was exiled—motionless behind her isolation skin. Their relationship had broken down-because Empress Tuyêt Xam saw Hoa as too much of a liability: someone still bathed in the sacredness of the dragon's power, but not versed enough in the ways of the court. Not loyal enough, and above all not strong enough.

Too weak, Empress Tuyêt Xam had said, and of course she was right. Great empires aren't built of scruples or concerns for the right thing, but on blood—like the executions after Dai Anh Sang, the line of kneeling rebels, their heads left to rot on the battlefield—a terrible punishment that wouldn't even give them the dignity of a burial with an unblemished body: a message sent loud and clear to those who would stand against Tuyêt Xam.

And now she's dead. Hoa stares ahead, blinking fast. It feels like an age is ending. The paper is thin and smooth. Inside is only a short message. "Teacher, come back to court. My successor will need the advice and support of the dragon's child."

The pronoun she uses isn't the Empress's, but the other, humbler one: the one from student to teacher. The one she still used to address Hoa in the days when the Empire was new and exhilarating, before she despised Hoa for her squeamishness. As close as she'll ever get to begging.

"Dead," Hoa says, aloud, as if speaking the words will make them truly have weight.

The girl's isolation skin blurs her features, darkening the sweep of her jaw, the shape of her lips. "I left on the morning after she drew her last breath."

"How—"

"She was old," the girl says. Her voice is quiet and carefully bland. Barely keeping grief at bay. "Lung sickness. She was coughing so much, it hurt her every time, and the drugs weren't making a difference. And she was so thin . . ." She stares at nothing, for a while. "But she never gave in."

Of course she wouldn't. She's the woman who forged a single land from the scattered principalities that formed after the Vanishers flew away to other planets, after their breaking of the world. She is the warrior queen who strode, fearless, into Vanisher lands, daring the broken spaceships to fly the gate-artefacts to open and disgorge the old masters again. She is the builder of safe roads, the one who made small villages into thriving cities, who laid down paddies with abundant harvests of opalescent rice. Why would death make her weak?

How long does it take now, to get to the spirits-forsaken land where Hoa and her family have made their home? Only a week. A week. Empress Tuyêt Xam has been dead a week. So much for the dragon's blessing of knowledge. Hoa has been in exile so long, and she's still desperately ignorant of how her life was meant to have fitted together—of why the dragon chose her and what it should all mean.

"Tell me about her successor."

"Le Anh Ngoc Minh," the girl says, finally. An odd inflection on her voice that Hoa cannot quite place, a memory of something Hoa has seen before—not with this child, but with her own children.

"The Heavenly Peace Empress—" Hoa has to force herself to use the formal address. "In the note, she says she'll need support."

A pause. The girl says, not looking at Hoa, "Her daughter is the favourite of the scholars, but she's weak. She wants to be nice. She forgave the minister who wrote an insolent memorial, because everyone can make a mistake." Anger in her voice. Of course. No one kind can sit on Tuyêt Xam's throne, can rule the Empire that was forged in death and cruelty. "And now the minister is convinced he can be insolent again. She can't *rule*." Not only anger, but hurt and venom in her voice. What happened between her and Tuyêt Xam's daughter?

None of her business.

"What did the Empress think?"

The girl says, "The Empress says she's the best choice. Unfit to rule for now, but she'll learn, in time. But she won't have that if the nobility or the scholars rebel."

And Tuyêt Xam wants Hoa to give the heir that breathing space. The woman out of a dragon's womb, supporting the daughter as she did the mother. She can do that. It's not hard. She can go back to the capital, and stand at the centre of things once more. She—

She has a second chance.

"I see," Hoa says.

The girl still isn't looking at her. "She can be cruel, when she wants to. When she's pushed to it. The Empress's daughter." Again that same anger that's too sustained, too brittle to be that of a subject against their future ruler. "She just has to learn how to use that for the good of the Empire."

Cruelty. If she closes her eyes, Hoa will remember the sharpness of the air after the battle of Dai Anh Sang, the pleading turning to ragged, wordless moans as the executioners' threads tightened around the veins of the necks—the soft thud of corpses with bulging eyes, tumbling into the mud, the air becoming brittle, charged silence. Not just the defeated princes, but their families, spouses and children, brought out from burning tents and forced to kneel in the mud—and Tuyêt Xam watching it all, dry-eyed and expressionless.

A needful example, she had said, looking at Hoa with fond pity. *Those who stand against me will know the punishment for rebellion.* She and her army had just shattered the alliance of principalities, laying the basis for her foundation of the empire. Her fondness had not yet turned into a realisation that Hoa would fail her, time and time again, forgiving people only to see them turn around and start intriguing or rebelling again.

Hoa fingers the chip of engraved circuits at her throat, feeling its reassuring coldness on her fingers. "There are many other teachers." Hoa doesn't say—she doesn't dare—that she doesn't know how ruthless she could be.

The girl's expression looks uncomfortably like worship. "Not so many who have seen the dragon. Or who were with the Empress since the beginning."

The beginning.

Hoa looks at the courtyard, breathing in the noises of shrieking children. Tho has grabbed one of Baby Chau's wooden horses: the child is wailing more out of surprise rather than indignation. Dong Nhi and Mei are playing a game of plague-carriers, wrapping thin gauze sheets around them to simulate isolation skins. Their laughter wafts to her, tightening something fleeting and warm in her belly.

They succeeded, she and Empress Tuyêt Xam and all these other builders. They've broken the backs of the principalities. They have made an empire, where a girl like this one can safely and quickly go from the capital to a backward province, travelling from shelter house to shelter house.

She's dead. Empress Tuyêt Xam is dead.

"Empires are as beautiful and as fragile as celadon cups," Hoa says. And it's in the hour of their founder's death that they are at their most vulnerable.

The girl waits, eyes respectfully downcast, quivering with impatience.

"I can't summon the dragon." Hoa could call, but who knows if they would listen? They never have. "She must have known that."

A silence. Then, slowly and deliberately, "She said you would say that. She said it doesn't matter. She wants—she wanted you to come back." Another silence, a swallowing of tears. "Her heir needs guidance."

Guidance. Advice. All that Hoa provided, except that now she doesn't know what she should do, anymore. Hoa bites her lips. "It's too late to start out for the capital. Stay with us for the night."

This is the woman who built the empire.

Tuyêt Xam was the daughter of a minor ruler in a small principality, carved out from the remnants of Vanisher rule—a country that struggled to keep itself alive and fed, its rice crops dotted with fungus and rot, its fish sauce dark and bitter-tasting.

One day, as she and her scholar-officials walked by the banks of a lake, a dragon rose.

They were tall—sinuous and terrible, their scales the colour of diseased pearls, their eyes the depths of the oily sea—their maw sharp and filled with the blood of those they had killed. But, as they crawled to the shore, the curves of their body shifted—and under the light of the perpetually clouded sun, Tuyêt Xam saw the distended shape of their belly, hardening in contraction after contraction.

Tuyêt Xam was young, but not sheltered or ignorant. And, in her mind, rose the old words of a proverb, a singsong sentence whose origins were lost in the mist of time, back when the principality had been the capital of a much, much larger empire spread along the length of the seashore like the two baskets and the pole of a bamboo yoke.

Côn Rông, chau Tiên. Children of the Dragon, grandchildren of the Immortal.

And, when the dragon gave birth—when the woman in their womb slipped out, skin splashed with blood, eyes frozen and distant, still staring into the depths of the river—the Empress knew, with absolute certainty, that it was a sign: Heaven's blessing and acknowledgement of her right to reconquer what had been lost.

The messenger girl—who finally introduces herself as Ai Hông—is taken firmly in hand by Quynh, Hoa's eldest daughter: brought into the decontamination complex to shed her isolation skin, and then into the bath-house.

Hoa goes to sit, as she always does, in the water room.

The water room isn't much to look at: a squat shape on the furthest edge of the courtyard, glimmering metal behind thin pillars engraved with the shapes of dragons. One of so many pieces of their survival, the only way that they can drink the waters of rivers teeming with pollution and diseases.

The machine inside sits silent and dark. It's standard imperial make, taking over almost the entire room: the kind that the court sent to all the former principalities, a squat monstrosity built by the scholar-engineers from scavenged Vanisher technology and painstakingly forged new parts. For what better way to earn the trust of the people and keep rebellion in check than to control the flow of clean water?

Around it is a magical circle, inscribed in her wife's brisk calligraphy: a spell of true sight, a failsafe if the scholar's interface should falter. Hoa can barely make out the words in the darkness. *Crane. Feathers. Iron stakes. Leaves from Heaven.* The water shimmers with the opalescence of pearls, showing Hoa there are no genmodded viruses or contaminants in it.

When she sits in the beaten earth, Hoa hears the low thrum underground, the surge and the ebb of the water drawn by the river, like a song in her veins, the closest she'll ever be to being back in the dragon's womb.

Dead. Tuyêt Xam is dead.

Hoa remembers a bright, hawk-faced girl, the one who'd kneel by her side and speak in earnest tones of the future, of the necessity of forging alliances, of building a new, unified society in the ruins of the Vanishers' departure. She remembers Sông Do, Nha Cuoi, Dai Anh Sang, the battles like strings of bloodied pearls that finally broke the power of the principalities— the scholars, gathering in the throne room and first suggesting that filtration machines such as this one would allow safety and stability—and that stability would be the bedrock of the nascent empire. She remembers blood and fear and the execution grounds, and Tuyêt Xam's face as she signed death-warrants.

Dead.

It's inconceivable.

She lays a hand on the water tank, slowly spreading her fingers—listens to the slow, inexorable rush of the river mingling with her own heartbeat, its passage through layers of filters until it finally becomes drinkable for them. So many nights there with the machine. She's meant to listen to it only when fixing it, but it's also her place of comfort. The one fulcrum of her life where everything falls into place, brief moments when everything makes sense and she knows her purpose, as surely as if she were back in the dragon's womb.

Dead.

Outside, the steady noise of mortars and pestles, and the distant smell of garlic and fish sauce. The shrieking sound of children in the kitchens, Dong Nhi directing Mei and baby Chau with the intent seriousness of a seven-year-old. "You take the pepper and you mash it until it's dust. No, not like that, lil'sis, you can't swallow it!"

Dead.

"I'm sorry," she said. Dead, the empire they built together such a fragile thing, and now she's asking for Hoa's help beyond the grave, and how can Hoa—who failed her in life—ever live up to Tuyêt Xam's expectations?

She sits listening to the lull of the machine's voice, feeling every line of tension and depression loosen up, until she's as weightless and unmoored, once more underwater, once more listening to the soothing sound of the dragon striving to cleanse the polluted water.

Something is wrong.

It's almost inaudible, but Hoa can hear it. A discordant harmony in the machine's workings. She gets up, to call the specialised interface.

"First Grandma!!!" It's Dong Nhi, standing in the doorway with a determined look on her face. "Mommy says everyone is waiting for you."

Hoa throws a regretful glance towards the machine.

"No excuses," Dong Nhi says, firmly.

It's not *that* bad: whatever is wrong with the machine is so small that no alarms have sprung up. It will become serious eventually, but it can wait until tomorrow. Hoa turns, and says to Dong Nhi, "I'm coming."

Later, after the end of the feast, Hoa is helping her daughter Quynh put her grandchildren to bed—baby Chau gently rocks herself back and forth in her crib, dancing to Hoa's words as she tells the story of Uncle Toad and the four animals' journey to Heaven and the nursery's intelligent walls light up with automatically generated silhouettes of celestials, dancing as the story progresses. Dong Nhi is sitting, silent and intent. "Grandmother—" she starts.

Hoa draws the crib's protective netting shut. "Yes? No wriggling out of bedtime, child."

Dong Nhi's face bears that familiar, mulish expression of Quynh at the same age. "Can I show you something? I've been practising."

Hoa glances at Dong Nhi's mother Quynh, who merely says, "She's been trying to get hold of you all day, but you were hard to find."

Practising. Hoa has an inkling of what it might about. She raises a warning finger. "You can show me, but this is going to be your story time."

Dong Nhi nods, wordlessly. She scrambles down from her bed, and kneels on the floor, her face scrunched in thought. Her hands move, tracing—Heaven knows where she's got the bit of charcoal from, but she's using it with a fluidity that feels almost unreal, aligning words around the shape of a circle.

Magic.

Hoa and especially Thanh Ha have been teaching her, but the words Dong Nhi is lining up don't seem match any of the lessons. "Child—"

"Oh, it's all right." Dong Nhi puts her arm into the circle. "Look." And it springs to life, lighting her arm and hand up until Hoa can see every vein and muscle.

She looks at the words. *Flow. Four Faces. Liver. Cinnabar.* A vague memory stirs. It's a spell used to diagnose and heal torn muscles.

"Where did you read it?"

Dong Nhi's face falls. "Oh, I didn't read it. I just . . ." She makes an expansive gesture with her hands. "I just swapped the words until they made sense."

Swapped the words. Discovered her own spells. A scholar's talent, except so few scholars manifest it so early. Something tightens in Hoa's chest. "That's amazing."

"It is." Quynh is bursting with pride, too. "Runs in the family, apparently."

Hoa remembers the one time Quynh drew a circle to make a solitary flower grow out of season, so that Thanh Ha would have something to offer to the ancestors. "Looks like it."

"It's the only one I've found." Dong Nhi sounds peeved. "But I'm sure—"

Hoa kneels, draws her into her embrace. "Spells aren't easy to find, little fish. But you'll get there. And now it's bedtime."

Afterwards, when the children are in bed, Hoa says goodnight to Quynh. "Experimenting," she says.

Quynh's smile is fond. "Do you remember what I was like, at her age?"

Bookish and solitary, and latching onto the Broken-World Teacher's words until the language of magic felt like it had always been her mother tongue. "Like mother, like daughter." Again, that tightening in her chest. "I'm proud."

Quynh hugs her, briefly. "So am I."

Hoa walks back to her room, where she finds her wife waiting for her. Thanh Ha's eyes are bruised with fatigue, her fingers stained with ink. Magic swirls around her like dying embers, words jumbled into fragmented, unreadable sweeps of letters. "Bad poetry?" Hoa asks.

Thanh Ha laughs. "No. I had to renew the wards on the compound's walls. Constructs have been sniffing around."

A sharp stab of fear; a reminder of how close they always are to failure. The filtration machine. She should have a look at that. But there will be time tomorrow.

"It's all done." Thanh Ha sighs. "I heard you have a visitor."

"You should rest," Hoa says, before she can think. She kisses her, gently, on the lips—feels the sting of desire arching up her spine, into her entire body.

"She's the Empress's voice. She may wait, but only for a time." Thanh Ha sighs. "Tell me."

And, after Hoa is done: "The Empress." Thanh Ha has never liked Tuyêt Xam. Her face is soft, though. "I guess everything has an end."

Not only Tuyêt Xam's life, but Hoa's own—and what has she achieved with it, truly, aside from being exiled for being too unsuitably soft? Why was she reborn from the dragon's womb, if it was merely to die in obscurity?

"What do you want, big'sis?" Thanh Ha asks.

"She has a daughter. A successor," Hoa says. She thinks of Ai Hông's pinched face when she spoke of cruelty; but how can she even know what's true? "The Empress—she didn't think her daughter is fit to rule. She asked me to support her until she can learn the proper ways."

"Unfit to rule?"

"Weak," Hoa says. "Too kind."

Again, silence. Thanh Ha lies back on the bed, her hair spread behind her like raven feathers. "And perhaps she was right. She's—she was always perceptive, wasn't she?" She doesn't say—she doesn't need to—that this was what the Empress reproached Hoa for.

"You don't want me to go."

Thanh Ha says nothing.

"Lil'sis . . ."

Thanh Ha's voice is resigned. "You should go. For a month, for a season. For a year. Whatever it takes."

"Who'll take care of the machine?"

A short laugh like a knife stab. "Quynh has some notions, and if she can't do it alone the Empire will send us a scholar to replace you. Don't fret."

"I thought you'd be unhappy if I left."

"Unhappy? No." And then, simply, "You should leave because you're the one who is."

Unhappy? Hoa, startled, looks at her. She wants to say that she's not, but Thanh Ha doesn't leave her time to mouth the lie. "I've seen you. I've seen the look in your eyes. You've been missing it all, haven't you?"

Hoa says, finally, "Everything made sense, back then."

"Oh, big'sis." Thanh Ha wraps her arms around Hoa, holds her close—her perfume, sandalwood and cedar, wraps itself around Hoa, fills her to bursting. "It still does."

But it doesn't, not really.

Thanh Ha has fallen asleep, her harsh, aquiline face smoothed out in repose—the scars from her childhood sicknesses on her hands, every part intimately familiar, intimately loved.

Hoa remembers water—remembers a distant heartbeat growing more and more frantic, even as the water hardened around her—everything flashing white as the contractions squeezed her skin, and then every organ inside her until she thought she'd burst. There was no pain—just an odd suffusing euphoria, a sense of distant weightlessness, a sense of purpose like a needle pared away to pure sharpness.

But she's no longer sharp, is she?

No, that's not true. She was never sharp enough.

She falls asleep to dark and exhausting dreams, hearing again and again the dragon's heartbeat, a call stretching her as thin as rice paper. There must be some answer she can make, some insight that will put it all into perspective.

But it never comes; and she wakes up gasping, groping for Thanh Ha in an empty bed.

This is the woman who grew up in her mother's shadow.

Of all the Empress's daughters, Minh is the one who looks most like her. From childhood, the scholar-officials praise her—dote on her, on the least of her achievements. Some children would have become smug. Minh becomes angry. Whatever she does, there is a historical precedent; whatever she says is weighed and matched to her mother's best speeches. When she is cruel and cutting—and she often is, because she's too clear-eyed, too cynical, and too foolish to remain silent—the officials smile, seeing her as her mother's true heir—the daughter of the warrior queen who had the princes executed at her coronation, so that she made her way to the throne with feet bathed in the blood of her enemies. And when she says something that her mother could never have thought of—when she attempts to voice her own ideas—the officials smile and bow, and go on as if nothing has ever happened.

She is the court's darling; their best hope and their brightest princess; but her mother's own legacy has hollowed her out and silenced the words in her throat.

The second messenger arrives early at dawn the next morning. When Thanh Ha brings her to Hoa, her face is shut, carefully expressionless, her mouth opening on silent words. Hoa doesn't need her warning, because the messenger looks so much like her mother.

"Your Highness," Hoa says, bowing down. And then, when nothing happens, she dares to look up; to see her in a similar pose. "You can't—"

Minh pulls herself upright, and smiles. It changes her entire face, and suddenly Hoa is thirty years younger, watching Tuyêt Xam smile at one of her clever speeches. "Can't come here alone? You and Mother built a road network just for this purpose. It works fine, you know, Teacher." She's using the vernacular, with none of the ornate language of the court. She addresses Hoa with the formal pronoun, the same one Tuyêt Xam used in the beginning.

Thanh Ha leaves, with a brief nod of her head to indicate to Hoa that she's gone to keep Ai Hông out of the way until Minh has had her say. Hoa struggles, wanting to use far more formal pronouns than "student". This child before her, this woman with a face that's both like and unlike her mother's— this woman breathes the atmosphere of the court, even in informal clothes. She moves like one used to power, to authority; and even if she bends the neck, it's never for long. "Why are you here?" Hoa asks, going for "elder aunt", which feels close to sacrilegious.

It's a long way to where she is, and surely the heir has more pressing things to do than retrieve Hoa, even assuming Hoa were coming at all.

"Come to court," Minh says, and once again she uses "teacher", as Tuyết Xam did. "Please."

That stops her, the raw, naked begging coming from this face, from this pose. Unfit to rule, Ai Hồng had said. In Hoa's mind, Tuyết Xam whispers about weakness, about how never having had to abase herself. "I thought—"

"Teacher, my mother is dead, and I'm not ready."

She's never heard Tuyết Xam sound that way—never seen her so casually bare her vulnerabilities with no more hardship than a shrug of her shoulders. "Child," she says, half-bracing herself for a reprove that doesn't come. "I was told—"

Minh's voice is dark. "I can guess what you were told. I'm weak, and unreliable, and disobedient." Her hair, greying already, is tied into a scholar's topknot, and a spell of warding shines beneath her isolation skin, stylised words in the language of the ancients. *Sword. Heaven's Will. Citadel. Turtle. Walls.* "Too weak to rule."

She can be cruel, when she wants to. When she's pushed. "What did you do to Ai Hồng?" Hoa asks, before she can stop herself.

A quick, pained expression, swiftly hidden. "I made a mistake," Minh says. Her voice is level. "Teacher, please. Come with me. I don't have enough of the support of the court to rule."

Hoa says, "You seem to think I can do miracles." And even if she could clothe herself in the dragon's magic, what could she do? The dragon, during all the time she was in their belly, has only ever done one thing: slowly, painstakingly going through rivers and lakes and seas, drawing sinuous words that thrummed against Hoa's skin—a desperate attempt to cleanse the waters of the pollution the Vanishers had left. Would they truly be involved in quieting down the squabbles of scholar-magicians and scholar-engineers? They'd think all this needlessly petty.

A weighing look. "Maybe not. But you're one of the women who helped build Mother's empire. The one born of a dragon's womb. They'll respect that."

She's so much like Tuyết Xam—young and hungry and driven—that it hurts. "I can't," Hoa says.

"Do magic, or come back to court?"

Perceptive. Too much so? The scholars don't have much taste for those who upstage them. And Ai Hồng's warning is still at the back of her head, but she just can't reconcile it with this poised woman standing before her.

"I have family," Hoa says.

"You do." Minh's voice is level. "Look at me, and tell me you wouldn't abandon them in a heartbeat for a chance to change the past."

Quynh. Dong Nhi and her circles of magic; Thanh Ha and the smell of ink on her fingers, and her face, turned away from her in the darkness.

You're not happy, lil'sis.

"The past can't be changed," Hoa says.

Minh's smile is fierce. "What about the future? Think of what you could do, at court."

Hoa thinks of standing once more in the throne room, of being in the centre—of deciding policy once more, of sending soldiers and censors to faraway corners of the empire—of holding it all in her mind's eyes as she once did, on the battlefields. She opens her mouth to speak, and becomes aware of the tension in the air.

Ai Hông stands not three paces from her, staring at Minh. Behind her is Thanh Ha, who's urgently whispering something; but Ai Hông shakes her off, imperiously. "You—" she whispers, and her tone is familiar—too familiar for messenger to princess.

"You overreach," Minh says.

"Do I?" Ai Hông's voice is sardonic. "The Empress gave me a message. Unlike your own errand—what kind of daughter abandons the funeral of her own mother to come find a stranger?"

Minh's face is a closed mask. "She was buried properly. I saw to it. You missed that, however."

It's a hit like a knife-stab. Ai Hông's face twists. "No wonder she always thought you unsuitable." Again, that jarring familiarity.

"Be silent," Minh says. "This is unseemly."

"Really." Ai Hông arches an eyebrow. Minh hasn't moved. Hoa keeps waiting for her to pull herself upright; to breathe fire and ash, as her mother did when someone dared criticise. But Minh just stands; and Hoa sees the small tremor in her hands, swiftly hidden.

Ai Hông says, bitterly, "A breakup note on my pillow. You've always run away from the hard things, haven't you?"

And Hoa knows what it was that Minh did—what kind of cruelty she was pushed to wield. The bond between ruler and ruled, not broken or upended, but stretched thin enough to snap. Not the Empire at stake, but one woman's happiness.

"It's not just us at stake," Minh says. "Mother . . ." She takes a deep breath, starts again. "It's about the Empire."

"I wouldn't know about the Empire," Ai Hông says. "All I know is what I saw."

Minh's laughter is bitter and amused. "What things we see in the dark of night . . . I'm the only daughter the scholar-officials will even consider. None of my sisters have got the talent to keep the court from tearing itself apart, and you know it."

Ai Hông's face is closed. At length Minh turns away, and walks out of the compound.

Thanh Ha, who's never been one for subtlety, speaks. "You must have believed in her."

"Of course I did." Ai Hông is shaking. "Trust. Love. Small and pathetic in the face of the Empire's future, isn't it?" She laughs, bitterly, and in her eyes Hoa sees the same trembling light she saw in her daughter Quynh's gaze, when her first girlfriend walked out on her. *Oh, child.* Hoa stares at the mud, digging her nails into the palms of her hands to keep herself from wrapping her arms around this young stranger.

Thanh Ha's face is hard. "There's nothing too small to matter. The Empire *is* people."

Hoa opens her mouth to say that this isn't what Tuyêt Xam thought—that the Empress was right and that this is not the way to build or sustain anything. That this will only bring them back to the days of the squabbling principalities, but then she sees Ai Hông's face, and the words shrivel in her throat. "I'm sorry," she says, and it feels small and utterly inadequate.

Hoa goes back to the filtration machine.

The machine is silent; the water translucent, shining with the light of Thanh Ha's spell.

Hoa kneels down, one hand on the water tank, listening. Feeling the beat of it in her fingers and in her arms, in her chest. Still subtly off, though Thanh Ha's spell sees nothing wrong.

She calls up the scholar's interface with a sweeping gesture, and it shimmers across her field of vision, her familiar companion of the days and nights she's spent servicing the machine, or simply lost in thought, listening to the river's song.

Nothing seems obviously broken: the filter is still creaking along. The pipes are old, losing water at every joint from here to the river, but nothing is wrong.

She'd thought the layers of substrate used to grow the filtering films would be inefficient, but they're not reporting anything wrong. Which could mean, of course, that the reporting is off.

From the outside come the distant noises of Dong Nhi and Mei at play: the girls have built themselves a fortress and are recreating the battle of Dai Anh Sang, Dong Nhi imperiously directing her sister to play the role of Prince Chinh Do, and Mei querulously protesting it's not fair she keeps having to play the villain.

Hoa stifles a smile, and runs the self-diagnosis checks on the machine. No error. Nothing.

And yet . . .

She double-checks the machine's age. The checks are coming a little off compared to the age of its parts. So the diagnoses are off, too.

That's odd.

"Grandmother."

Startled, Hoa looks up, and sees Minh.

The Empress's daughter is standing in the doorway, looking at her. "Such a good first impression, isn't it? You must think me so unworthy of her."

Hoa puts her hands on the water filtration tank. Water, once again, thrums and shifts under her fingers. The interface keeps saying nothing is wrong, but clearly that's not the case. "I've got no opinion."

"Liar." Minh kneels by the machine. "What's wrong with it?"

Hoa, startled, looks at her.

"I'm a scholar too." Another short laugh. "The court wouldn't accept a ruler who's not." Minh calls up the interface, stares at it for a while. "Nothing wrong, uh."

Hoa can't help it. "Your mother—"

Minh raises an eyebrow.

Hoa says, finally, "Your mother wouldn't have done this." Tuyêt Xam has always been acutely aware of her status and the need to maintain it, and she certainly would never have abased herself to do that kind of work.

"You mean keep this compound alive?" Minh's voice is sharp. "There's nothing shameful about that."

And that, too, is unexpected. Hoa opens her mouth, but Minh is there before she can.

"You *are* ashamed. You think your exile is a failure."

Hoa pulls herself upright, feeling the thrum of the machine under her feet. "And why would I not?" Hoa asks. "I fix a machine that any scholar could maintain. I live in exile in a land where the least mistake will kill us all, away from everything important."

"Important." Minh turns, briefly, to the courtyard. "You know none of my sisters were ever close. Or laughing. Mother was many things, but loving parent was beyond her, I think."

"You're—"

"Empress?" Minh laughs. "Because I have to. Because the Empire will tear itself apart, and I could wait to see if any of the scholar-officials, or of the princes, will make a better ruler than me. Important. You're so very much like Ai Hông, aren't you." It sounds like an insult.

Hoa, off-balance, finally finds words. "You know what you did to Ai Hông."

Minh is staring at her—a child, even younger than Hoa's own children. Tuyêt Xam would have laughed and told Hoa Ai Hông is a messenger, and that no one cares about the powerless. Minh says, finally, "I hurt her. And she hurt me, too."

Hoa raised two children and three grandchildren, separating them when they were fighting so many times she's lost count. Her voice is sharper than she'd like. "Is that an excuse?"

"Of course not." Minh doesn't even flinch. "Mother would say love is a weakness, and that I should have armoured myself better against it." She raises a hand before Hoa can speak. "Ai Hông wanted me to be like Mother. Ruthless and cruel, because if I wasn't, how else was I going to keep the scholars and the princes at bay?"

Hoa remembers Dai Anh Sang—blood and mud and the profound silence of death, a relief after the moans that the threads choked into nothingness.

"I'm not her," Minh says, from very far away. "Cruelty and the fear of punishment builds empires, but never sustains them. Ai Hông thought I was becoming unfilial, and she tried to steer me the right way. I've had a lifetime of this. Better to end the relationship before it festered. But, of course, I handled that wrong." Hoa sees her, slowly coming into focus, with the rigid pose of someone who's been waiting, all their life, for a spear to be pulled from a wound. A lifetime of bracing themselves against a blow whose mercy never comes.

"Cruelty for a greater purpose. How very like your mother," Hoa says, because they're the only words that come to her.

A sharp, unpleasant look from Minh that reminds Hoa of Tuyêt Xam at her worst. "And look where it got us. Was it such a good idea?"

Hoa finds her without answer. In the growing silence, she hears Dong Nhi urging Mei on, trying to convince her sister to somersault over the wall.

"I can't do this!!" Mei says.

"Of course you can," Dong Nhi says. "Look . . ."

Minh is waiting for her to say something. When that doesn't happen, she dismisses the interface with a curt gesture. "What are you going to do now?"

"Take it apart," Hoa says, curtly.

She draws a circle around the filter. She inscribes her own spell of clear sight, words that shimmer and contract as she puts the last strokes on them. *Mirror. Crane Robes. Leaves. Snake's wisdom.* Then she starts taking apart the filtration system.

It's layers: the filtering film, the substrate it grows on, and then another filter, and another, all the way to packed gravel at the bottom. She slips, as easily as she slipped out of the dragon's womb, into a universe that's vectors of filtration and microorganisms, and the song of the river—and a faint memory of how it should all sound, the water in harmony with the filters that it runs through.

There.

"Metal," she says, aloud.

Too much metal in the first and second filter, a chemical cascade causing elements to recombine in wildly different ways. Such small, insignificant things, details so easily dismissed by the diagnoses—except that they all add up to something huge.

Her fingers move, now, of their own accord, calling up commands for the interface: a purge of the entire system, a flushing of the first and second layer of substrate and brand-new layers trickling down from the adjoining tank.

It's fixed. She fixed it. She figured out the problem. The rush of exhilaration is enough to make her shake.

"First Grandma, First Grandma!"

She looks up, exhausted. Dong Nhi has all but elbowed Minh out of the way, and is looking at her with faint irritation. "Mommy says stop tinkering with the machine, and get some food before you collapse."

"Almost done," Hoa says, stifling a smile.

"Hmmmf," Dong Nhi says.

Hoa dismisses the interface, and erases her circle from the floor with her foot, feeling the little jolt of power as the magic abruptly leaves each word it was vested in. "How was your game?"

Dong Nhi makes a face. "Mei insisted on being the Empress. She majorly sucks at doing her."

"I don't!" Mei looks outraged.

Dong Nhi runs a hand in her sister's hair, briefly hugging her. "You'll get better. The leap over the wall was awesome, though." And then stops, aghast, because she catches sight of Minh. "I'm so sorry, your Highness. I didn't mean—"

Minh draws herself up to her full height; and in that moment she's not a bewildered young woman, but regal and proud, so much like her mother Hoa's heart misses a beat. "Don't be sorry. I wasn't born when it happened. It's old history." Minh's voice is stern, but Hoa can hear laughter beneath. "Besides, I'm sure Mother would have loved to see herself at the centre of stories."

Dong Nhi stares at her. Then she says, "I'm going to be a scholar when I grow up. Like my mommy and grandmother."

"Will you?" Minh moves, so fast that Hoa cannot stop her—and before she can comprehend what's happening Minh is kneeling by Dong Nhi's side. "That's important work, you know."

Hoa sees the ghost of Tuyết Xam, in the way that Minh moves—behind the planes of her face, in the set of her shoulders—in the deep-set, hawkish eyes. A ghost only; because Tuyết Xam would never have knelt to a less powerful person; because she never would have suffered the indignity of children's games. Because she would never have *forgiven.*

Minh rises, brushing dust from her robes. Dong Nhi is watching her, rapt with fascination. "Come on," Minh says. "Go eat your food."

"Only if you tell Southern Grandma to come eat, too."

Minh laughs, and it lights up her whole face. "I will, promise. If you trust me."

"Of course," Dong Nhi says, scornfully. And she's gone, slipping through the open door into sunlight.

Minh turns, again, to Hoa. "Please, teacher. Come to court with me."

She's unfit to rule, Ai Hông's voice whispers in Hoa's mind. *But she'll learn. It's old history. It happened before I was born.*

Dai Anh Sang. Hoa remembers blood and mud and the churn of magic in the air, but that time has passed into children's games—into stories told at night, myths as unreal as Uncle Toad, something toothless and faded and holding no power anymore. An era that has gone.

Things have changed.

Minh is not her mother. Ai Hông has only scorn for her; but Ai Hông's scorn comes from hurt. Hoa remembers the dragon, and their tireless chipping away at the pollutants, their ceaseless quest to cleanse the earth. She remembers the tightening in her chest when Dong Nhi showed her the magic—the incisive sharpness of Minh's words to her, and the easy, careless way Minh knelt before Dong Nhi. She's still flush with the elation of fixing the machine, standing grounded in her own house with the thrill of water in her whole body.

Small things. Small details, so easily dismissed, so easily insignificant— except that they're the foundation of how the machine works or breaks.

The Empire is people.

"You were right," Hoa says.

Minh stares at her. "I don't understand—"

"It's no longer time for ruthlessness or cruelty," Hoa says. "But you don't need me to tell you this." Or that the small things—keeping a compound alive, raising children, cleansing the water—matter as much as the larger ones.

"Teacher . . ."

It's Hoa, now, who pulls herself to her full height, feeling the thrum of the machine echo in her muscles and into her bones, the song of the river filling her to bursting. "Your mother is dead, and she has no hold over you anymore."

Minh starts to speak, stops. Instead she bows, very low—always with that same careless ease—not displaying weakness, but simply choosing the most appropriate behaviour. "Teacher. Dragon-born."

Hoa shakes her head. She's old and weary—and if she pauses to consider what she's doing, she'll stop, aghast at her own audacity. "Go home. Apologise to Ai Hông, and go home."

Minh opens her mouth.

"Yes, I know. She hurt you," Hoa says. "But it's not messengers who apologise to empresses-in-waiting, child. That's too easy."

A silence.

"You say you're not like your mother. That you want love and loyalty to hold up your empire. Loyalty starts with the smallest things. With one person."

"Teacher . . ."

"Go."

This is the woman who saw the dragon's shadow.

Of all the Empress's daughters, she's the one who looks most like her—the one the court clings to as her mother's heir, their one chance to keep the Empire whole.

When she comes back from the provinces with a messenger in tow, she's silent and grave, as if listening to something only she can hear—changed in a way the court can't quite pinpoint, the light in her eyes fey, as grey as moonlight dancing on water.

And when she speaks—when the messenger by her side looks up with an undefinable expression in her dark eyes, pride and affection and the shadow of old hurts—when she speaks, her voice echoes with the thunder of rivers and seas; and her words are weighted like pebbles.

When she speaks, they attend.

Hoa goes out, afterwards. She sits alone in the darkness by the water room, one hand on the earth. Beneath her are the pipes, and the distant sound of the river. Overhead is the moon, a ragged, grey thing with nothing of life left on it; and the heartless stars blinking in the darkness of the sky— the faint suns that might be dead or alive, separated from them by so much distance and time, their light coming from beyond the gulf of the past.

"You should have gone." Thanh Ha's voice is low, and affectionate, her spouse effortlessly slipping by her side.

Hoa says nothing.

"I don't want you to be forever unhappy, away from court."

Hoa thinks of Ai Hông, and of Minh. "I don't think I'd have been happy, at court," she says, finally. "Court was a dream. An illusion of a time I can't claim back. You can't make a kite fly back to your hand after you've cut the string."

Thanh Ha snorts. "Are you turning wise in your old age?"

"I don't know." Hoa thinks of that bright, brief moment when she told Minh to go home—she could say it all coalesced into meaning, but in the end it was exhilaration as much as anything that carried her through.

Under her hand is the steady tug of water; oily eddies and swirls, the same fragments of letters she once saw, before the dragon appeared. She thinks of them—swimming underwater in some faraway river, stubbornly cleansing the river one pollutant at a time, the light of the dying sun shimmering on their scales. She thinks of their touch on her skin; of being held with utter singularity of purpose—of Tuyêt Xam's unbending belief in herself. She thinks of the compound and the machine, and of Quynh and Dong Nhi and Mei and the other children, and what it all means to keep them all thriving.

"I don't know," she says, again—and, bending over, kisses her wife, breathing all of her in—holding that other, beloved body as tight and as close to her heart as everything she's ever built.

Story Notes for Out of a Dragon's Womb

Aliette de Bodard

The theme of how much cruelty is needed to build and hold together a society is an old one—Machiavelli's *The Prince*[1] is probably the most well-known reference in the west, advising rulers to be feared rather than be loved if they cannot balance both. This story was to a large extent inspired by a different tradition, namely the ideological differences between the Legalists, the Confucians and many of the Daoists in the Hundred Schools of Thought period of Ancient China: the Legalists believed that people were selfish, short-sighted and couldn't be trusted. The application of these principles led to the brutal and short-lived Qin dynasty, which established the first great Chinese empire but whose paranoia, cruelty and lack of care for the people led to its downfall. The others, by contrast, believed in the fundamental goodness of people and the capacity of everyone to become better people through practise, and these ideas proved much longer-lived than Legalism, which fell into disrepute following the fall of the Qin dynasty. (Note that though the inspiration is Chinese philosophy, the cultural background for this story is Vietnamese rather than Chinese.)

The other idea that led to this story was weighing small things versus the large ones, and the value of love and community building against that of larger concepts. These are concepts that I think often get ignored in genre: we like to think of large sweeping acts and not so much about the small things and the importance of small kindnesses, and how much these matter as much as the large ones. As a mother of two young children, I always get very frustrated by the idea that raising children isn't an Important Thing—as if making a Whole Human (not only a in physical but also in a moral way) was an afterthought in the grand narrative of our lives. And I've always found it much easier to envision the small things than the large ones—friendships rather than society, which can to me end up feeling rather abstract and disconnected.

Finally, this story touches on choices and free will, and how much meaning we attach to events that feel significant: in the case of Hoa, the act of her birth and whether it predestines her to be some kind of chosen one figure. I thought it would be interesting to have a story where that was very much not the case, and where something that feels like it should matter does, but not in the way that everyone thinks. Hoa's birth is taken as a sign by the Empress, but she herself remains uncertain and with no particular revelation or wisdom, even at the end. Despite every sign surrounding her, Hoa makes her own path and her own choices, and what she builds in the end has very little to do with what the dragon gave her. It's also deliberate that both the Empress and her daughter are the ones seeing signs, which are grandiloquent signs of larger purposes, whereas Hoa's own search only leads her back to what she already has built.

Notes

1   Machiavelli, N., *The Prince*, Quentin Skinner and Russell Price (eds.), (Cambridge Texts in the History of Political Thought), Cambridge: Cambridge University Press, 1988/1513.

6

Whale Fall

Wendy Nikel

You hurled me into the deep, into the very heart of the seas. (Jonah 2:3)

Jemina ought to have turned around at the first sign of the great beast's anguish. Its moan surrounded her tiny pod, rumbling like the thunder of a dying storm through the thin metallic layers that protected her from the acid of his second stomach. On the dashboard before her, lights blinked yellow, orange, then red—a cacophony of color whose meanings shone dimly on her contorted face.

Yellow: Pale. Sick. Dying.

Orange: Fear. Panic. Stress.

Red: Anger. Blood. Death.

"Oh, Odonto," Jemina clicked on their communication device, which would convert her spoken word to the rolling whale-song he could understand and, in turn, translate his tones back to her. She closed her eyes and pictured his enormous, trusting face. He wasn't even thirty years old; far too young to be dying of natural causes. She shouldn't have encouraged him to swim so fast, so far into unfamiliar waters. She should have freed him long ago. "Odonto, what have they done to you?"

The whale didn't answer.

Jemina's finger hovered over the ejection button. Two pounds of pressure on the tiny red circle is all it would take to unclamp the metal appendages that held her pod against the stomach wall and release a fast-acting laxative that would cause him to expel her. She needed to press it now, before Odonto lost consciousness. Before he gave up on them both. She touched its edges, felt its smooth surface on the tip of her finger, but couldn't bring herself to press down.

What good would it do to send her pod floating upward as he sank below the waves? Both sides of this ghastly war would be scanning the surface for anything out of place, and she wouldn't find sanctuary with either—up or down. Not after what she'd done.

Besides, she thought as she felt Odonto's massive bulk shudder around her and rumble with the final beats of his 25-ton heart, *no one wants to die alone.*

During the first stage of the whale fall, soft tissue is consumed at a rate of about a hundred pounds per day by sleeper sharks, amphipods, hagfish, and crabs. With claws and teeth designed for efficiency, these mobile scavengers tear at the whale's soft tissue and blubbery outer layers, feasting on its carapace for up to two years after the carcass has fallen to the ocean floor.

Jemina's mother had been a ruthless scavenger in a hopeless world, who'd learned early on that she could get more for the wares she'd found throughout the cities' broken-down and abandoned buildings if she had the tear-streaked face of a hungry child at her side. But like ovoviviparous sharks, who know that a larger litter means more competition for food, she'd never kept more than one at a time.

The day her sister was born was the last day Jemina laid eyes on either of them. Her mother's latest beau, an out-of-work miner named Darren, walked twelve-year-old Jemina to the docks. There, the Federation's smoke-belching warships lined the coast like massive beached whales. She'd never seen the sea before, but she'd heard of its power and terror and strength, so her first glimpse of it was oddly disappointing, for on that day it was so glassy and smooth that it looked like a vast mirror laid out beneath the sky.

She'd heard also of the wealthy men and women who, when conditions on the surface grew too dire, had escaped to begin life anew in their hideaways far beneath the surface. For generations, they'd dwelt there, sipping on wine pressed from now-extinct grapes and nibbling strange ocean delicacies. But there was no sign of them that day, either, in that smooth and watery glass. Jemina wondered if those stories, too, had been lies.

Darren bought her a lollipop from a street vendor with discolored nails and, in retrospect, Jemina ought to have known then that whatever he had to say was nothing good. She ought to have been wise enough to know that he'd walk away, leaving her with nothing but the clothes on her back and the gnawed-on paper stick. But she knew better than to turn down a gift, even if it was too sweet, too sticky, its taste tainted by the stench of industrial waste.

"You know I think you're a fine kid, Jemma," Darren said, and she'd nodded amiably, though he never seemed able to get her name right. The wooden railing of the pier creaked as he leaned his weight against it, and an ugly part deep down in Jemina's heart imagined pressing her own foot against it and applying just enough pressure to make the splintered wood crack, just to see what would happen when it snapped.

"It's not that your Mama don't care for you," he continued. "It's just, sometimes, life doesn't give you any good options. Sometimes, it surrounds you on all sides and any way you choose, it'll tear you up and spit you out like a great old wad of tobacco. Sometimes, no matter what you do, you lose out."

Jemina ground the lollipop between her teeth. She refused to be the one to lose out.

When the candy was gone, and Darren told her to stay right there and be a good girl now, that he'd be right back in a jiff with another, she'd known from the sweat on his lip that it was a lie and decided then and there, she didn't even care that it was.

She stayed there just long enough to catch him glancing back one last time and meet his eyes with a hard gaze of her own, one that would assure him she'd known all along; that he'd never fooled her. That no one would.

Then she marched up to the nearest Federation ship and enlisted in a war she neither knew nor cared a thing about. It only mattered that she'd be away from the city and that she'd be fed.

The officer in charge, Captain Monston, had known with one glance that the scrawny girl was nowhere near the eighteen years old that she claimed but, fortunately for her, he'd just lost an entire squadron and had been just desperate enough for new recruits to ignore that detail.

Now, so many years later, a sleeper shark silently glided past the cameras, barely moving its body as it circled, and Jemina recognized the look on its face. She knew the hunger in its eyes and understood both its daring and its hesitation.

A scavenger trusts no one, save for itself.

The second phase of a whale fall is the enrichment opportunist phase. Over the course of the next two years, invertebrates such as mollusks, worms, and crustaceans create colonies within the carcass and feed on the scraps of meat and blubber left over from the scavengers and the nutrient-rich sediment around it. Though these creatures are not so aggressive as the scavengers, they are more thorough, and when they are done, all that's left of the great beast is bare bones, picked clean.

When it came to natural resources, the Terra Federation was not one to leave those opportunities unexploited. They had eleven other whales besides Odonto—massive sperm whales bred in captivity, with brain implants and stretched-out stomachs that allowed them to be controlled by the Digestible Oceanic Vessel Experiment (or DOVE) pods. They were trained to swallow these one-man vehicles at the beginning of each mission and, when man and beast had safely returned to the Federation facility, the pods were released and passed out with their waste. Remote-operated cameras imbedded in the giants' 14-inch-thick skin gave the operator inside a high-definition view of the oceanic world outside—including the submerged cities and bases of the Nautical Alliance.

So long as the Nauts didn't know that the Federation were using the whales, they were the perfect vehicles for Jemina and the other pilots to bypass their blockades and gather reconnaissance information. The sperm whale's only natural predators were orcas (which were nearly extinct), and the Nauts were, by necessity, far more concerned with the welfare of undersea life than those who lived on land cared to be. The sea was the Nauts' home, and the creatures within it their neighbors. They would never harm one of these gentle giants, even if they knew what was concealed inside.

Or so the theory went.

"Easy for those fish-loving elitists to wax poetic about protecting the precious environment now." Captain Monston had often grumbled such sentiments when he'd had too many drinks or lost too many men in a battle—or both. "They're just as guilty as the rest of us for our ruined soil and bombed-out cities; they're just the hypocrites with the means to run off and leave it all behind. Now they're down there snug in their metal nirvanas while we're left with nothing but scraps of the world left behind."

"And now us scraps are taking the fight to them." Jemina had raised her glass heartily in agreement. She'd heard their self-righteous speeches on the vid feeds, full of vitriol for those surface-dwellers who continued to pollute the air and land. Never mind that most people up here were just trying to get by, that the upgrades to the clean energy solutions the Nauts extolled were too costly for most surface-dwellers. It simply wasn't fair.

But now, as the dash before her blinked with the pod's increasing depth readings and she felt the strange, sudden stillness around her that told her Odonto was truly dead, Jemina bitterly considered whether she'd been wrong all along. Despite her promise to herself, she'd been too trusting of the Federation. Which was costlier: a never-ending war, or giving their people a better life?

Nevertheless, she didn't panic.

Her years in the Federation's ships and subs and pods had trained her to remain calm and controlled in any situation, and that included being trapped in the second stomach of a dead sperm whale, slowly sinking to the bottom of the sea. It was too late now to eject from Odonto's body, but that didn't mean all was lost. She ran diagnostics, scanned the area for anything—organic or otherwise—that might prove useful, and redirected power from the maneuverability controls and communication relay to the O2 recycler to maximize the amount of time before she'd run out of breathable air in her DOVE pod. A sperm whale can dive for up to ninety minutes before resurfacing to breathe, but since her pod's systems relied on his respiratory functions to replenish those resources, she wouldn't last much longer than that without him.

The pod finished its testing; the readout was splattered with red. It flashed her options in bright letters: "Send Distress Call: Y/N?"

One push of the green button, and the Federation would be sent her coordinates. A team of rescuers would scramble into one of their heavily armed submersible tanks, outfitted with rockets and missiles to defend against any ambush. They'd scoop her up mid-fall, tear open the whale's insides with their powerful blades in a burst of blubber and flesh, and she would be back in her bunk before dawn.

And then?

Then there'd be an interrogation. An investigation into her actions. She'd have to lie. She'd have to bribe the security department, destroy the video evidence, *anything* so they wouldn't know that she'd discovered the truth: The whales were dying. Exhausted. Depleted. They were dying faster than anyone had expected, too soon to justify their expense, and the experiment with the DOVE pods had failed.

She checked the clock on the dash. Had it only been six hours ago that she'd been fixing a faulty incinerator and had stumbled across an inadequately-singed copy of the official orders stuck inside? Orders that laid out the plan to send Odonto and his dying siblings on a one-way trip to the Nauts' nearest base, their bellies filled not with DOVE pods, but with bombs?

For the Federation—always the opportunists—it'd be making the most of a costly mistake.

For the whales, a suicide mission.

For her, nothing less than betrayal, further proof that no one could be trusted—that they only cared about their own bottom line.

She'd flown from the incinerator room, not even bothering to stop in her bunk for a shower or change of clothing and raced down to the giant tanks where they held the whales. Odonto had stared at her with his wide, questioning eyes, but it wasn't until she was strapped into her DOVE pod, with the base a mere dot on the horizon behind her, that she dared open the communication lines and spell out the end they'd planned for him. That she dared to let him take the lead, to go—for the first time in his life—where *he* wanted.

Now, she stared at those two blinking lights: Y/N? and the question wasn't whether to send a distress call, but *can you live with that knowledge?*

Fist clenched, she punched down on the "N."

The final stage of a whale fall is the longest, lasting up to fifty years or longer. During this stage, mussels, tube worms, and other organisms derive energy from the sulfophilic bacteria, breaking down the fats and oils in the bones. These creatures in turn serve as food for other animals, creating a deep-sea community with as many as 30,000 organisms inhabiting a single skeleton—one of the most richly diverse ecosystems in the world.

Odonto had been a 50-ton ten-year-old when Jemina had first met him. Soon, he'd be nothing but bone.

She felt like she was falling apart with him.

With every bit of flesh that was torn from him, her confidence waned. What had she hoped to accomplish anyway, in stealing him away in the dead of night? Had she really thought she could save him? And now what? He was dead, in the middle of nowhere, and as soon as her air ran out, she would be, too. The realization came with an edge of spite; it would serve them right to lose a top pilot along with their whale. She'd thought she was using the Federation—for stability, for survival, for life—but really, she'd been the one picked clean. The arrangement she'd thought was symbiotic was cruelly parasitic.

She was angry enough to die.

The oxygen levels dipped, and the needle shuddered downward. There was nothing to do but watch the sea around them—particles floating about like thousands of stars, and shadows passing back and forth through the gloom—and wait for the end.

Except it wasn't just dancing starlight and the slow-moving forms of wise and ancient sea life. There was something out there, just beyond that, something barely visible, but too rigid and symmetrical to be organic. Jemina stared at the screen, adjusting the dials until its form became clearer: a shadowy outline of a dome. She pulled up her map and checked her coordinates, already knowing what she'd find. There was nothing here, or at least there wasn't meant to be, and the dome was far too small to be a military outpost.

"Odonto," she said with a chuckle, recalling how hard he'd pushed, how determined he'd seemed to reach this place. How long had he known what was out here?

The Federation would have been thrilled with their discovery—almost as thrilled as she was to now withhold it from them. Let the Nauts keep their little settlement, for at least they saw the whales as creatures worthy of respect, of life. As Captain Monston had always said, they'd never harm a creature of the sea.

Jemina watched the hagfish and sleeper sharks circle, watched as a crab skittered over Odonto's skin.

Yes, the Nauts may be pompous and condescending, but at least they were trying to make things better somehow. At least they weren't careless with the lives in their hands.

"Your siblings deserve better," Jemina said aloud to Odonto, and with that it was settled, her mind set. She knew why he had brought her out here. Her hand flicked the controls, sending a spark of power to the short-range communication relay. The needle on the O2 sensor wavered and fluxed. She'd lose air faster the longer she kept the relay open, but all that was behind her now.

She clicked "record" and pleaded from the belly of the whale.

In the control center of the Nautical Alliance settlement, operators picked up a strange, short-range message, though there were no vessels in sight.

"My name is Jemina, pilot and defector of the Terra Federation. I am sending you this message of warning . . ."

Within the subaquatic city, people rushed around in their crisp suits through glass-paneled corridors, putting plans into place, organizing teams, finding solutions. They'd put the whales down as humanely as possible and allow their bodies to drift to the ocean floor. There, they could carefully extract and diffuse the bombs, leaving the carcasses where they lay, scattered about—each one a rich ecosystem for years to come, contributing to the bounty of the sea—rather than blasted bits of meat contaminated with chemical explosives.

The message looped again and again, long after the oxygen in the concealed DOVE pod was gone. Long after its pilot took her final breath and relinquished her body to the sea. It played on, slower and more drawn out, as the Nauts in the nearby settlement scrambled to pinpoint the source, to aid this unexpected messenger. It echoed on until the power waned, until the sound became so long and drawn-out that it morphed into something else: something strange and low, that reverberated through the sea.

Something akin to a whale-song.

Story Notes for Whale Fall

Wendy Nikel

I first learned about the process of a whale carcass's decomposition through a video entitled "Whale Fall (After Life of a Whale)" by Sweet Fern Productions, which is currently available on Vimeo and YouTube[1]. This beautiful four-and-a-half-minute animation fascinated me, and I've watched it again and again since first discovering it. With soothing music playing in the background, the construction paper-cutout whale dies and its carcass settles to its final resting place on the ocean floor. But as it does so, we see the myriad of undersea creatures that benefit from the bounteous feast provided by the massive creature's remains so that, even as it's a picture of decay and destruction of one creature, it's also an image of growth and renewal of others.

As I researched more about this amazing process, I found myself drawing connections to the science fiction subgenre of dystopia, which is often in itself a picture of the growth and renewal of humanity that can come from the carcass of a broken, dead, or dying world. In *The Hunger Games*[2], Katniss uses the very competition that destroyed so many lives to incite a rebellion. In *The Lorax*[3], the Once-ler encourages the boy to grow a new forest from the last Trufflula seed after the others have been destroyed. Through the titular *Giver*'s own death and his protégé Jonas's escape, the Community is forever changed. Through these deaths, the characters find opportunities for widespread change and growth.

In my story, renewal also takes place at the individual level, with a single character—Jemina—who, despite her own personal struggles and hardships in her broken world, chooses to make something important and meaningful come from her death, in order to benefit others. She realizes that the role she plays can have far-reaching consequences, even after she's gone, just as the carcass of the whale continues to support a thriving ecosystem for decades after its death.

Jemina's story also plays upon another classic dystopian-world theme: the struggle between the wealthy, who can afford to live apart from the consequences of humanity's mistakes, and the poor, for whom these consequences are a constant, daily struggle.

Many dystopians have clearly defined "good guys" and "bad guys," but in the real world, the lines aren't usually drawn so clearly. Even the most corrupt, self-serving groups may provide positive, worthwhile services, and even the most altruistic groups can have dark secrets and skeletons in their closets, so that's what I depicted here. Each group in this story sees themselves as the heroes: the wealthy because they are striving to avoid the mistakes of the past and make responsible choices to preserve their new ecosystem; and the poor because they are underdogs, struggling for survival and resources in an unjust world that has left them no other options.

Just as Jemina didn't see the Nauts' positive attributes until she'd befriended Odonto and began looking out for his well-being as well as her own, oftentimes in the real world, it's difficult to see the positive qualities of opposing groups until we view things from the perspective of people who are not like us or whose needs differ from our own. Only then do those with opposing views cease to be "enemies" and become, instead, people with whom we can empathize and relate.

Not everyone would have made the same choice Jemina did—switching sides at the last minute to aid a group that's just as flawed as the one she was defecting from—but sometimes we don't get to choose between good and evil. Sometimes, we can only ask ourselves which option will allow the greatest opportunities for renewal and growth within our own broken world.

Notes

1   "Whale Fall (After Life of a Whale)." directed by S. Shattuck and F. Lichtman. YouTube Video, 4:28. Posted by "Sweet Fern Productions," Dec 4, 2013. https://www.youtube.com/watch?v=BppKscns1Rk.
2   Collins, S. (2008). *The Hunger Games*. New York: Scholastic Press.
3   Seuss, Dr. (1971). *The Lorax*. New York: Random House.

7

Monsters and Soldiers

Mark Silcox

The pot-bellied Oliofrissan waddled down the beach past a tumbledown sandcastle and a picnic basket, then glided out into the bright blue water. A slick wake of chemical effluence spread out on the surface behind the alien's back. A little boy and a girl playing catch with a beach ball stopped their game to watch as the greasy trail expanded, while an old woman in a purple bikini crinkled her nose at the unpleasant odor.

Loder glanced up and down along the rows of holidaymakers sitting on their spread-out towels. Most of the people there were clearly at least as repulsed as he was. A woman who looked to be the kids' mother leaned forward, watching the green-skinned monster's progress intently, chewing on her bottom lip, Loder figured she was deliberating over whether to summon her children away from the ominously roiling water. He grabbed his rucksack and walked toward her.

"Morning!" he said, flashing a blandly amiable smile. "Mind if I park my stuff right here?" He nudged the sand a few feet away from her towel with his toe.

"No problem!" She looked up at him, shielding her eyes with one hand against the brilliant, honey-colored light of the morning sun.

"Thanks." He dropped his towel next to hers and sat down.

The Oliofrissan had begun stroking back and forth lazily in waist-deep water, gurgling to itself as its shiny chemical leavings blossomed outward. Loder opened a cool globe of citrus nectar and drank deeply before speaking to the woman again.

"Those kids yours?"

"The two with the beach ball?" The slime was starting to gather around the little girl's upper thighs. "They're my children, yes—Ganon and Angelika." She shuffled a little closer and offered her hand. "My name's Laura."

Approaching unfamiliar women in this way had at one time made Loder uncomfortable. But Commander Blythe had explained how he could use his natural good looks and easy charm to help the cause. "My name's Christoph," he said, and gave her a warm, lingering handshake.

With a muted splash, the alien submerged itself entirely. The little girl was visibly shuddering now as the thing wriggled close to her beneath the surface. Loder had to repress a powerful urge to rush into the dark water and drag her out. But that wasn't what he was here for today.

"Angie!" the woman called out. "It's okay, baby. Come and sit with me for a while. Ganon, you too."

"I'm all right, Mom!" the boy called back. "This is sort of cool." He was holding his nose tightly and peering deep into the swirling darkness of the alien's slippery trail.

Loder leaned close enough to the woman to whisper. "I'd recommend that you have your little guy come in too, Laura. You never know what sort of toxins those critters might leave behind."

"Really?" Her eyes got wide. "But they told us at the Acclimation Center that it was harmless. They said it's just like vegetable oil."

"Mm hm," said Loder. "They'll tell you lots of things, at the Acclimation Center."

"Oh!" She stared keenly at her son now, while trying to look like she wasn't. "But surely they wouldn't—"

"Brinker's World is a beautiful planet," said Loder, quickly. "It's one of the few really magical places still left in the galaxy since the wars ended."

"We absolutely love it here. It seems like the beaches go on for hundreds of miles. And the glorious sunsets—I've never seen anything like them, that color. . ."

"Mm hm," said Loder. "It's no wonder that the aliens—sorry, pardon me, the *exotics*—no wonder that they insist on coming here. But their presence forces the authorities to cover over certain *truths*, about how. . ."

"Oh, look at you, honey," Laura cried out, "you're all sticky!" The girl had walked back up the beach to where they were sitting. A shiny film of the alien's excreta covered the tops of her legs. Laura began frantically wiping her clean.

A few of the other vacationers who looked over at them now wore pious, judgmental expressions, as though the young mother's concern in some way offended them. *Probably not much more progress to be made amongst these hypocrites,* Loder thought to himself. Before he left he tucked a couple of Commander Blythe's pamphlets under the corner of Laura's towel—*Our Common Enemies* and *To Be Fully Human.*

It was still early in the morning, but the planks of the boardwalk that led back to his hotel were steaming in the unremitting sunlight. They were hot enough to make Loder's bare feet sting. He was glad there was only a week left in this assignment. Most of his associates in The Corps had been jealous when they'd heard about his posting at the most popular resort world this side of the galaxy. But Loder had been born and raised on Plettix, an austere, ice-covered research world with a population of less than fifty thousand. The blazing sunlight, the festive music, and the endless cheerfulness of the people here had all begun to wear on his nerves. It sometimes seemed to him as though they were all in some sort of trance—couldn't they even see the hideous monsters that surrounded them?

As he strolled through the hotel's courtyard he caught the unmistakable whiff of a female Borborough. Sure enough, a couple of the quivering, shapeless abominations sat by the edge of the swimming pool, their fragrant nether ends raised high above their heads. Some of the other human bathers nearby were packing up their things, their faces twisted into expressions of disgust. But most just rested in deckchairs, dabbing at their noses with the perfumed towelettes that hotel employees were passing around. Loder knew that if he crept up behind these two repulsive specimens and tipped them forward into the chlorinated pool, they'd both be laid up for a week or more with painful sores on their faces. But once again, he managed not to give in to temptation.

At the far end of the yard a girl stood at the top of a ladder hanging up a bright canvas banner over the front edge of a second-floor balcony. Trying not to breathe too deeply through his nose, Loder walked closer to take a look. The banner said

WELCOME BACK, SIR!

in bright green capital letters.

He stepped through an open doorway into the front lobby. "So who's the welcome for?" he asked the teenager at the check-in desk.

"The what? Oh, the banner? Didn't you see the announcement on ResortNet this morning?" the kid said through a wad of gum.

Supercilious little punk. "I came to this planet to get away from the newsnet," said Loder, "not to stare at it all day."

"It's real exciting! The Founder's visiting Brinker's World for the weekend. He's gonna be giving a speech at the Acclimation Center tomorrow, ten AM. We all got the morning off so we can go see him in person!"

"Your 'founder?' What, you mean the guy who built this hotel?"

"Nooooo!" The kid shook his head. "Who would care about that? The founder of the whole resort, after the war. Colonel Aendros! You've, uh, heard of him, right?"

The mechanical clock on the desk quietly chimed. Two girls in wet towels wandered in from the pool deck, laughing. Loder could feel his fingernails digging hard into the palms of his hands.

"Hey, sir, is there anything wrong?" the kid asked after a long moment of silence.

Loder had to open and close his mouth a couple of times before he was able to speak. "No," he said, "nothing really wrong." He took a deep breath. "Tell me, would you happen to know what time the Colonel's shuttle will be landing?"

The kid shrugged. "Guess all that sort of stuff's pretty secret. You don't need a ticket for the speech tomorrow, though. Just gotta show up!"

A few minutes later, Loder was gripping the balcony rail outside his hotel room, swaying back and forth on his feet while a warm breeze blew from across the mainland. Past the intervening rooftops, he could see the peaked gables of the Acclimation Center and the high docking bays of the shuttle port where the famous Colonel's orbital ship would be landing later that evening. Loder knew there was bound to be a big crowd at the speech tomorrow. Probably all but the very laziest holidaymakers, human and otherwise, would want to get a glimpse of the great "war hero."

He and his comrades in The Corps had learned all about Aendros. The Colonel's fame had blossomed spontaneously after the war out of a thin subsoil of exaggerations, outright falsehoods, and sentimental gossip. He had supposedly almost died in at least a dozen interstellar battles, rescued several planets from destruction, and killed his fair share of the enemy while serving in the Galactic militia. But he was also one of the few post-war political figures who had managed to stay popular after all the ugly wrangling and unsavory compromises of the New Accord, and during the fragile peace that followed. He had burned through his family's ancient wealth setting up a broad array of schools, companies, and other enterprises—including the resort on Brinker's World itself—all established with the aim of encouraging inter-species co-operation. Nobody had spoken more consistently than the Colonel about the need for humanity to be friendly and tolerant of its "exotic" former foes.

Now that the Galactic Militia had been dissolved, there were only a few scattered paramilitary organizations like The Corps left to stand guard against the monsters. It was because of this that Loder and his brothers-in-arms prayed fervently to the gods of his homeworld that the Colonel would one day meet an ugly and painful death.

Loder walked back into his room and dug his tachphone out from a drawer in the nightstand. He dialed the number for The Corps' dispatch office.

The voice of Grecco Blaine, his immediate supervisor, sounded even more abrasive than usual through a layer of interstellar static. "Hello, Brother Pinske! I'm surprised you found the time to call. All those sugary drinks and midnight swimming parties must keep a man busy."

Loder sighed. "This assignment is as risky as anyone else's, Grecco. Just because it's a resort world..."

"Oh yeah, I can totally imagine. Passing out copies of *Our Ancient Enemies* and *Your Child's Dark Future* to a bunch of middle-aged wives and sun-tanning civil servants. You must be in agony, brother."

"Look," said Loder. "I don't have time for this. Something has come up here—I need to speak to the Chief of Oversight."

"That's what I've been *trying* to *tell* you, Pinske. Oversight has been busy calling and re-calling you all morning. What, d'you leave your tachphone in the sauna or something?"

Loder cursed under his breath. He was supposed to keep the phone with him at all times, but the heavy, ludicrously expensive piece of equipment made him nervous. Tachphones were rare enough to be a distraction to potential recruits, and nobody important had ever tried to contact him before in mid-mission. Still, orders were orders.

"Aw, crud," said Grecco. A low buzzing sound came down the line underneath his voice. "That's them again, actually. No idea what they might want with you, Loder. Patching you through now."

A violent crackle of static was followed by the sound of a much clearer signal. Loder heard low steady breathing at the other end of the line. Nobody said anything to him for almost a minute of costly airtime. Then he heard a soft, but unmistakable voice murmur "Is this thing working? Am I speaking to Brother Pinske?"

It was Commander Blythe!

In his four and a half years as a member of The Corps, Loder had only ever had two conversations with the Commander. The first was at the start of his first trip to the secret training camp on Grewall's World, just after they'd removed his blindfold. The other had amounted to little more than a handshake and a few encouraging words when he was sent on his first recruitment mission. But now, he had their mysterious and brilliant leader's undivided attention.

"Commander Blythe! I . . . um . . . I . . . um . . ."

"At ease, Loder, son. At ease. I'm sure relieved we finally got hold of you."

"I'm sorry, sir! The phone . . . sir . . ."

"So how's recruitment been going over there on Brinker's World, Loder?"

"Very promising, sir! Maybe half a dozen interested parties. I've been . . ."

"That's good, that's very good. Now, we wanted to get into touch with you, Loder, because we've intercepted a message from the local Peace Guard. There's a ship called the Torn Banner that's passing through your system over the next few days. I don't know whether the name is familiar to you, but the vessel is usually used by a person of considerable interest to The Corps."

"I'm aware of the situation, sir. The ship must belong to Colonel Aendros. He's going to be visiting tomorrow – right here on the planet, just a few miles from my hotel. Giving a speech."

Loder heard a ghostly whisper of sound, like a wave crossing dry sand. It might have been the Commander licking his lips. Then there was another long, expensive silence.

"Um, sir?"

"What is it, Loder?"

"Is there anything you want me to do, Commander?"

A low chuckle. "Ohh, Loder. There are so many things that I'd like to see done to that arrogant, monster-appeasing piece of human garbage. So he's coming to put on a show on that pretty beach world of yours tomorrow? Remind me how long you've been in The Corps, please, Loder."

"Five years, Sir! Almost. Just under. Sir, if there's any way at all . . ."

"Five years. Gods! You've barely walked through the door. No offense, son – I have your personnel file right here in front of me, and I can see you've done some useful work. Brought in a number of very solid recruits. But you're really not supposed to be involved with operations at this high a level."

A tremulous sensation of nausea had begun to creep upward from the pit of Loder's stomach. "Sir," he said, "When I was eleven years old, back on Plettix, my father . . ."

"Listen, son. I'm going to say goodbye to you for now. I have to confirm a few facts about the scope of our operations up in that corner of the galaxy. Keep your phone close by for the rest of the day. Try to maintain a low profile. I should be in touch again within a couple of hours. You got that?"

Loder could barely move for the seventy-nine minutes that he had to wait before the Commander called him back. He stared out the window toward the placid ocean, trying not to think about what he already more or less knew he was going to be asked to do.

Their second conversation took a lot longer. Commander Blythe asked him about his early life on Plettix. Loder described the endless snowstorms, the isolation, the glorious churches carved out of the ice. He told his superior about the dire battles with the Q'inx and the Borborough, and what had happened to the rest of his family. They discussed the anti-government protests he had attended as a teenager when the terms of the peace were declared, and the Commander seemed to get quite wistful while they chatted about his early days in The Corps. He even told Loder a very funny Borborough joke that Loder had never heard before.

By the time Loder had been given his assignment, he was smiling to himself, buoyed up on a wave of heady nostalgia and species pride. He set off down the beach toward the little tourist gift shop he had been told to visit.

A pair of Dactylons were gliding through the air above the water. The creatures were performing their disgusting mating ritual in full public view beneath a radiant sky. This spectacle weighed a little on Loder's mood as he crossed the hot sand, but he cheered up when he reminded himself that the Commander had called him "son." Under his breath, he recited the words of a long prayer to the Old Gods they had spoken together at the end of the phonecall. By the time he was finished with the last verse, his hands had stopped shaking.

The shop sold snacks, sunscreen, plastic toy souvenirs, and cold drinks. Loder waited for a pair of customers standing by the fridge to clear off, then approached the checkout counter. "I'm looking for something ..." he started to say.

"Yeah, what's that?" The cashier was standing on a plastic crate restocking a high shelf with bodily unguents.

"...something that Joshua left for me."

The guy turned around sharply to look back over his shoulder and almost fell. "Really?" He was a pale, damp-eyed adolescent, surely no older than eighteen. "Joshua?"

"That's right. I'm sure you recognize the name."

"Okay. Wait a minute." The kid dropped to his knees and pulled a loose tile up from the floor, then lifted a metal box out of a compartment. Loder reached across the counter and took it from him.

"Don't open it in here!" The kid's voice was suddenly panicky.

Loder lifted the lid just a crack and peeked inside. "Take it easy, brother," he said. "Just need to be sure about what you've given me."

"The four extra rounds at the bottom of the box are incendiaries. Supposedly, they make a really big mess. Only use them if you're in a tight spot."

Loder nodded. "You've fired one of these before?"

"Nuh-uh," said the kid. "I start first-tier training on Grewall's World in three weeks."

"This'll send the monster-lovers a message, won't it?"

The kid's expression was difficult to read. "So, you're actually going to do it, huh?"

"Of course I'm going to do it," said Loder. "I'm a soldier." He slid the box into the bag over his shoulder and walked back to his room.

That night, while a moist breeze blew through the screen window on his balcony, Loder dreamt about the ice mountains of Plettix. He and Commander Blythe were hiking through a valley together, searching for a hidden underground cave. They had to hide behind a snowdrift while a patrol of male Borborough slid by, the cold air thick with the aliens' pungent herbal stench. He woke up stiff and headachy.

The gun had been packed with a plastic holster that strapped onto the upper thigh. Loder slid it on underneath a pair of baggy shorts. The short thick-barreled weapon was well-concealed.

He arrived at the Acclimation Center half an hour early. Three rows of bleachers had been put up along the edges of the building's front lawn. A plastic lectern was mounted on a stage at the far end of the grass. A squat purple beachcar sat closeby, probably waiting to whisk Aendros away to his next performance.

The crowd that had already arrived was about sixty per cent human. Other species had their own heroes of the peace to revere, though few had the fame and political clout that Aendros continued to wield. As Loder walked toward the stage, he saw a repulsively geriatric six-legged Sziltbagger flicker its moist wings and spritz a family of six sitting in the front row of the bleachers. The father pulled an angry face. Loder made a mental note to try to track him down later for possible recruitment, if chance allowed.

Eventually, the front door of the Acclimation Center opened and three figures walked out across the bright grass toward the stage. Loder's skin prickled as they passed by a few feet away from where he was standing. He became aware of a thin layer of sweat forming on his thigh underneath the holster. He had just looked directly into the eyes of the man he was supposed to kill.

The Colonel left his two minders and ascended the stage without fanfare or introduction. The audience barely had time to offer up some scattered applause before he started to speak.

"Thank you, my friends, thank you all," said Aendros, lifting up his hands, palms outward. "I'm touched that so many of you would want to come hear me ramble, on such a beautiful day on this radiant world. I vividly remember the weeks I spent here when we first opened up the resort, and made it a haven of pleasure and relaxation for all of the galaxy's diverse array of sentient, water-based species."

Loder was paralyzed with fascination. The Colonel was an unexpectedly small man—surely no more than five and a half feet. He had a thick pink scar near the corner of his left eye, which had been edited out of all the video footage Loder had seen. Aendros spoke in a clipped, competent tone that was somehow out of sync with the dreary platitudes he was reeling off about inter-species fellowship and the stability of the peace.

It occurred to Loder that he had no idea whatsoever how long the speech was going to last. To be sure of completing his assignment he would have to move fast. He started to nudge his way through the crowd. His elbow banged into one elderly lady, and he stepped on an enraptured Grendrish's scaly big toe, but nobody else ahead of him showed much resistance. He was sweating heavily now, tasting salt on his upper lip and wiping away the moisture from his eyes.

Within a couple of minutes he could see the individual buttons on Aendros' shirtfront. Loder knew that he was in range to get off a killing shot.

There was no sign yet of the speedboat that the Commander had told him would enable his getaway. But he remembered Blythe's warning that it would have to come by at the very last minute, so as not to arouse undue suspicion.

Loder flexed and unflexed the fingers of his right hand and closed his eyes. He took a moment to visualize in advance the smoke from the weapon, the sudden backward jerk of the Colonel's head, the spray of bright blood in the morning air. The corners of his mouth quirked upward. He slipped his hand into the cut-out pocket of his shorts, toward the holster.

Immediately, he felt a huge, firm hand close around his upper arm. "That's not going to happen today, Mr. Pinske," said a voice from behind his left shoulder. "Or any day in the foreseeable future. You'll need to come with us now, please."

Loder turned his head and saw one of Aendros' burly guards, who had apparently been following him through the crowd. Immediately behind him was the silently hovering purple beachcar, which also seemed to have appeared out of nowhere. As the passenger door slid silently open, Loder tugged against the hand that was holding him. The bodyguard squeezed back just hard enough to make it clear that there would be no contest. From inside the car another heavyset man grinned up at him with perfect teeth, then patted the passenger seat.

"How did you know I'd be . . .?" said Loder.

"Shh," whispered his escort, squeezing once again. "All will be revealed, Mr. Pinske. Now get in."

Aendros continued waving his arms and speechifying. Apart from perhaps a couple of dozen people who had noticed the guards' intrusion into the crowd, Loder's removal didn't seem to be disturbing the event at all. The beachcar swerved behind one of the rows of bleachers, then took off further into the mainland along a gravel road.

"Gonna hand me over to the authorities, guys?" Loder asked his two minders. "The weapon I've got strapped onto me must be pretty illegal on this world."

Neither of the pair seemed to register his remarks at all. Loder allowed himself a quick, only partly forced chuckle. He had been briefed by Commander Blythe about what would happen if he fell into the hands of Aendros' private militia. There would be no torture, no sleep deprivation, and no threats of violence from these pacifist weaklings. Just a long series of interrogations, aided by the latest in biometric mindreading devices. They would also make some feeble attempts at indoctrination, *via* a lot of sentimental movies and earnest rap sessions about Our Exotic Brethren. It would probably be at least a week or two before they finally passed him off to the local cops.

Loder found that the failure of his mission weighed curiously little upon his spirits. The whole thing had happened so fast. And nobody who had been born and raised on Plettix was going to be daunted by the prospect of even permanent exile to one of the galaxy's so-called "rehab" worlds.

The car pulled up next to a small windowless outbuilding next to somebody's private shuttle bay.

"Loder Pinske," said the woman who came to the door. She had long red hair and tired eyes, and looked to be maybe twenty. "Born at Research Station Vespucci on Plettix, Year 238 of the Galactic Era. Recruiting officer, second class in the Humanistic Interplanetary Corps. Please step inside, and sit over there in the chair with the restraints on the arms."

Loder was astonished. "How did you know . . .?"

Inside the building, two others sat at desks staring at a pair of glittering Newsnet interfaces. "Our man did OK at first- and second-tier training on Grewall's World," said one of them, a scrawny, sunburned kid who didn't seem to notice Loder entering the room. "Good with guns, mediocre at cryptography. Some temper issues that came out when they asked him to . . ." Then he glanced up at Loder, and his voice trailed off.

The last of the three, who looked at least a little bit older, stood up quickly. "Please sit down, Mr. Pinske," he said, in a weirdly amiable tone of voice. "You'll need to slip your hands and feet through those four cloth bands. They only become uncomfortable if you strain against them."

Both of the guards walking with him wore sidearms. They had the over-muscled, vacant appearance of rented security grunts: not *real* soldiers. A vision flashed through Loder's mind of a quick struggle and a firefight. But the Commander had told him not to engage in any heroics if he got caught. He sighed and sat down. "All that information," he said, "how long have you been . . .?"

"We've been collecting data about you ever since you first joined The Corps," said the girl, sitting down at her own table. "We have biosamples from your hotel room and tachphone recordings from the day you arrived on Brinker's World."

"No!" Loder pushed forward in his chair. The smooth woven armbands instantly tightened and became hard as steel. "No way—you're lying to me! The guys at dispatch always make sure our tach lines are totally secure."

"*You're really not supposed to be involved with operations at such a high level,*" said the older guy, in a nearly perfect imitation of Commander Blythe's voice.

The stagnant air inside the room suddenly seemed to thicken in Loder's throat. He choked back a mouthful of phlegm and his head tilted forward.

"Easy there, comrade," said the older guy, holding a bottle of cool water to Loder's mouth.

Loder snarled and turned his face sharply to the side. It took him another minute or so before he was able to speak. "So, you have a few spies in The Corps. Hooray for you."

"Spies?" said the woman. "Oh—sure, yeah, we have some spies. Pretty rare that we have any use for them, though." She glanced up from her work and her eyes met Loder's.

Something that she saw there made her pause, lean back in her chair, and draw her hands back from her interface. "You guys!" she said. "You always seem so surprised when you find out how much we already know about you. Do you really think your silly little political cults are so terrible and mysterious?"

"Don't condescend to me, monster-lover," growled Loder. "Why don't you go make it with a Dactylon? Your face looks like you could use it."

The girl just sighed. "You know," she continued, "there have been men like you around ever since our ancestors first got up onto two legs."

"Like me, hm?"

"That's right. The first ape-man who ever wanted to kill those monkeys over the hill, 'cause he thought they looked funny. The slave owner who'd cheerfully have sex with the dark people from overseas, but wouldn't let them own land."

"Okay," said Loder. "I get the . . ."

"The pre-war diplomat who thought the Borborough must have wanted to kill us, 'cause they smell so nasty."

Loder rolled his eyes. "Get to the point already. If I'd wanted a sermon I would have tried to shoot a priest." He thought he heard a brief chuckle from the older guy.

The girl smiled too, surprisingly. "I bet you would have, too, Mr. Pinske." She leaned toward him with her hands pressed flat on the table. "The point is just this: as I'm sure you know, we come from a very old species. And in spite of our celebrated shortcomings, we've managed to learn a fair bit about ourselves over the ages. Or some of us have, anyway. While guys like you were busy throwing rocks through windows, or blowing up temples, or doing pushups at some training camp, a few of the rest of us were busy drawing up extremely precise maps of our own interior workings. It's a project that was started up by poets and musicians and painters, a long time before we could read the syntax of brain states or fly between the stars. And yet, you seriously believe that the rest of us haven't figured out how people of your type think and act by now?"

Loder tried to think of something to say back to her. But the odd way she looked at him—with a sort of attentive indifference, as though she was trying to catch a glimpse of something directly behind his left shoulder—left him tongue-tied. The other two were fiddling away at their virtual machines. They both seemed a little embarrassed by the woman's diatribe.

For a while the room was completely silent apart from the sound of Loder's ragged breathing. Then the door swung open and Aendros walked in. He was still dressed in the antique military uniform he had been wearing onstage, and he was sipping some sort of fruit drink from a frosty plastic globe.

None of the others saluted or even got up from their chairs. "How'd the speech go, sir?" asked the older militiaman.

Aendros shrugged. "Tried my best not to bore 'em. I stopped when I could see a few of the little kids getting antsy. So this is our would-be assassin?"

The woman nodded.

"Aha." The Colonel glanced at him briefly, then did a double-take. "Hey," he said, "am I wrong, or does our friend here still have a firearm strapped to his thigh?"

"Oh!" The older man jumped out of his seat. "Sorry, Colonel, that's my bad. Doug and Ephraim did a facial scan and skin galvanics profile in the car while they were driving here. Ninety-seven per cent probability that he wouldn't try to go down fighting."

The Colonel put his drink aside. "Well, there's always that extra three per cent, though, isn't there? Plus, it's bad form to put temptation in a fellow's way."

"Yes, sir."

Aendros pulled up a spare chair directly across from Loder and sat down so that their faces were less than two feet apart. Then he rummaged in his pocket, eventually drawing out a palm-sized folding knife. Loder could smell the sugary fruit juice on his breath.

The Colonel leaned forward to take a handful of Loder's pant-leg into his scarred fist, then pulled the material taut and cut a neat slit with his knife. He reached in and drew out Loder's gun as though he was removing a painful sting. "How's that analysis coming, by the way?" he asked the others over his shoulder.

"I should have some pretty solid projections in a couple more minutes," said the sunburned kid.

"Sooner the better." Aendros patted Loder on the knee. "Don't worry, son," he said. "We'll get you all fixed up sooner than you think."

"*Don't* call me *son*!"

"As you wish, Mr. Pinske." The Colonel stood up slowly, wincing, as though some of his joints or an old wound might have been giving him pain. "I have to hand it to you—not many aspiring terrorists I've met would have taken such a crappy mission on such short notice. Of course, that pipsqueak Blythe has filled your head with a lot of speciesist nonsense. But we'll clear that up in no time. We'll get you a clean bed and some decent food, and introduce you to some other guys and girls who've managed to escape from just the kind of life you've been trying to lead."

Aendros walked around behind the redhead's desk and rested a hand on her shoulder. She looked up to him with a mixture of indulgence and reverence, as though she had heard the speech he was making at least a dozen times before, but didn't mind.

"These kids," he continued, "with their history books, and their psych degrees, and their biostatistical modeling algorithms—they're the real soldiers, now. We've come so far beyond the days of drugs, and surgery, and coercive behavioral therapy. We've even learned a neat trick or two from our alien friends."

"Don't you mean 'exotic?'" said Loder.

"Oh. Ha ha! Yeah, I guess I do," the Colonel replied, winking at him. "Some old habits die hard."

The kid with the red face had been clearing his throat and gesturing for a while; now he interrupted the conversation. "Um, sir," he said, "I think you might want to come and look at these numbers."

"What is it, Jorn?" said the woman.

"I'll show you." He did a bit of fiddling with his interface, then leaned forward to look at it very closely. The others walked over to see what he'd figured out. After a few seconds, the redhead inhaled sharply, then clapped a hand over her mouth. The older guy moaned to himself. It was like a frigid wind had suddenly blown through the tiny building.

"*What*?" said Aendros. "What is it? You guys know I can't understand all of your fancy charts and models on the fly."

The one named Jorn pointed into the data field with a shaking finger.

Loder glanced back and forth between their two faces. "What the hell's going on?" he shouted.

"Wow," said Aendros eventually. "I've never seen projections like that before. Are you sure the figures for galvanic skin response . . ."

"Uh huh," the kid said, sounding miserable. "We took them from his hotel bed, the car, and the chair he's sitting in right now. Just those stats all by themselves would be enough to get him institutionalized, but we . . ."

"We try to be more liberal, yes." Aendros' tone had changed completely.

"What the hell are you all messing around with?" said Loder after another long stretch of silent calculations, sighing, and head-shaking.

"All right, enough," said Aendros. He walked back over and sat down again on the chair in front of Loder.

"Tell me something, Mr. Pinske," he said. "Do you consider yourself to be a soldier?"

"Why don't you tell me?" said Loder. "You seem to know everything else about me."

The Colonel just waited.

"Of course I do. I'm more of a warrior than you ever were, monster-lover!"

"Who knows," said Aendros. "Maybe you are. You're certainly a rare specimen, at any rate. My young friends here are true believers, Loder, like you. They believe in the almost infinite human capacity for change. But they just showed me some information that picks you out as a statistical anomaly."

"Sir?" said the girl, standing up from behind her glowing device. "Colonel . . . may I ask just what you're doing sir?"

Aendros glanced back at her. "You three have done the job we brought you here for. There's no reason you need to be around for what comes next. We've got another forty-eight hours before we leave Brinker's World—go on out and run around on the beach, relax for a while."

The two men started toward the door. But the woman stood her ground. "No, sir," she said in a quiet voice, "I don't think so. We're staying."

The Colonel looked for a moment as though he wanted to press the issue, but then he shook his head and clicked his tongue. "According to their calculations, Mr. Pinske, it's really just a long procession of improbabilities that brought someone with your genes, your history, your biochemistry, your cognitive architecture, to where you're sitting right now."

Loder shrugged. "People are people."

"They can be," said Aendros. "If things were a little different, I'd ask Jorn or Angela to try to explain some of their methods to you. It's fascinating stuff, I have to admit. You might eventually even learn a little about what the word 'monster' really means."

"I know what the word means," said Loder. "I . . ."

"But in your case, ultimately, all of the calculations really don't tell the important part of the story. In my opinion, anyway. There's only one fact about you that really matters, in the end."

"What's that?" Loder meant to come across as defiant, but the words sounded petulant and childish in his own ears.

"Captain," said the older guy. "Surely you don't intend . . ."

"How did your father die, Mr. Pinske?" asked the Colonel. "Aliens did it, didn't they?"

Loder bit his lip, then nodded. "Our house was bombed by a Q'inx recon patrol. I was eight. I was in the next valley over, playing in the snow."

"And ever since then ..." said Aendros. The Colonel's expression was steady and purposeful now. He sighed, then stood up very slowly and picked up Loder's gun.

The others in the room were all wide-eyed and shouting at once. The boy named Jorn gave out a ragged gasp. Loder caught a flicker of movement from his left as Angela pushed a chair aside and threw herself forward. But then, as the old man lifted the weapon and aimed it directly at his forehead, their eyes met. And Loder was amazed to see that, contrary to what he had been told throughout all of his training, his enemy really was a soldier, too.

Story Notes for Monsters and Soldiers

Mark Silcox

In *The Open Society and Its Enemies*, Karl Popper describes the *paradox of tolerance* in the following way:

> Unlimited tolerance must lead to the disappearance of tolerance. If we extend unlimited tolerance even to those who are intolerant, if we are not prepared to defend a tolerant society against the onslaught of the intolerant, then the tolerant will be destroyed, and tolerance with them.[1]

Philosophers of the analytic tradition have in general tried to restrict the application of the term "paradox" to puzzles in logic and semantics. So it's a little odd when Popper goes on to suggest that the "solution" to his own paradox can be attained *via* the medium of public policy. A properly "open" society, may, he contends, "claim in the name of tolerance, the right not to tolerate the intolerant."[2] This very suggestion itself seems a bit paradoxical, though – surely as soon as one exercises the "right" to be not-P, one ceases to be P.

If we're safe in assuming that there have, as a matter of fact, been at least some genuinely "open" societies during the course of human history, then we know perfectly well how they have dealt with the type of practical problem Popper is gesturing at. What has usually happened is that, at some point in their histories, ruling elites have initiated a scrupulous and carefully maintained division of labor. While encouraging ordinary citizens to experiment with a wide range of "tolerable" opinions and affiliations, such elites have also retained the services of a corps of loyalists ready to enforce exceptions to this policy of permissiveness – often *via* overt harassment or violent coercion – whenever they become sufficiently concerned that the society's very identity is under threat.

One of the deepest challenges facing liberal political philosophy is to describe practically implementable standards for determining what it takes for particular types of ideas and opinions to fall outside the scope of a general rule of tolerance. The philosopher who attempts to articulate such standards surely cannot expect to receive much guidance from folklore, conventional wisdom, or explicit public policy. Public opinion about when the intolerant become intolerable seems to be fairly chaotic these days in liberal democratic societies – witness the apparently interminable squabbles that have arisen over the past few years about de-platforming, trigger warnings, and "punching Nazis." And those who are actually *paid* to defend a society from the intolerably intolerant tend not to be inclined to discuss such matters in public – or, at least, not with full frankness and transparency.

Part of the fun of science fiction is the way it allows us to entertain the possibility that solutions to such apparently thorny, abstract problems might somehow arise spontaneously, as a cheerful side effect of the more general growth of human knowledge. The society I have depicted in *Monsters and Soldiers* is one in which detailed information about stochastic patterns in human character make it possible to predict and prevent "intolerable" political action, as well as to exert the kind of corrective influence upon its perpetrators that might eventually eradicate the beliefs and attitudes that lead to such behavior.

Inhabitants of contemporary societies that are equipped with the capacity to engage in this sort of potentially intrusive surveillance are deeply divided about the ethics of subjecting supposedly free citizens to such relentless scrutiny. My story leaves this issue mostly unaddressed. One could reasonably infer from what I have written either that I regard the predictive capabilities exhibited by Aendros' colleagues as an inevitable side-effect of more widespread technological progress, or that a society still recovering from a bitter, catastrophic interstellar war might be not quite so haunted as our own is by the image of the Panopticon.[3]

But Popper's paradox also has ramifications for how individuals should organize their inner lives and private conduct independently of the political sphere. In periods of history such as our own, when public discourse is heavily factionalized – along lines of taste, cultural allegiance, and social etiquette, as well as those of political ideology – the question of precisely how much an active citizen who aspires to tolerance should be willing to tolerate becomes especially difficult, and especially urgent. The decision that Colonel Aendros takes at the very end of the story signals my own skepticism about the possibility of those with any genuine political power finding a way to *internalize* the norms of tolerance that could preserve a liberal society. It seems to me that the best we can reasonably hope for as political agents is to merely *embody* Popper's paradox – to understand of ourselves that we are both tolerant and intolerant, without qualification and even occasionally at the same time. Perhaps there are ways that we can still manage to keep ourselves out of ethical trouble in spite of being thus internally divided. But if so, when it comes to figuring out how, it seems unlikely to me that we can expect to get much help from the logician or the semanticist, let alone from the legislators of an "open" society.

Notes

1   Karl Popper, *The Open Society and Its Enemies*, London: Routledge, 2002, p. 668.
2   *Ibid.,* p. 668.
3   This is the name for a type of prison first envisaged by the philosopher Jeremy Bentham in 1788 – a circular building whose inmates in their cells around its circumference would be perpetually under observation by their warders at the center. In *Discipline and Punish: The Birth of the Prison* by Michel Foucault (New York: Vintage Books, 1995), and many subsequent works of social philosophy, it is often invoked as a metaphor for the intrusive surveillance of private citizens, usually by the government.

Part Three

Gods and Families

Introduction to Part Three: Gods and Families

Helen De Cruz

Consider these central questions in philosophy of religion: "Why do we suffer?", "What happens after death?", "Is there a god?" How do religious traditions tackle such questions? By and large, not through abstract reasoning, but through stories. Take the *Bhagavad Gītā*[1], part of the larger epic narrative *Mahābhārata*. This dialogue opens on the battlefield with Arjuna, a warrior steeped in an existential crisis. He is confused and afraid as he faces the prospect of fighting against members of his own extended family. His charioteer (the god Kṛṣṇa in disguise) provides him with reasons to fight. Along the way, Kṛṣṇa reveals important religious insights, such as that action can be a spiritual practice, where you work without being invested in its fruits. Done in this way, action is a form of liberation. By contrast, action that depends on success or recognition creates bondage because you are beholden to its fruits. Arjuna—and the reader vicariously with him—experiences a range of emotions, including doubt, despair, hope, and, toward the end of the dialogue, also awe for Kṛṣṇa when he reveals himself.

Religious traditions teem with stories, and that is no coincidence—some philosophical ideas are best explored in the context of narrative.[2] It is possible to treat suffering as an abstract problem, but it becomes more vivid, and our emotions are more invested, if we imagine one person's suffering in detail. Philosophy professors often assign stories as readings for their philosophy of religion courses. One example is a dialogue from Dostoyevsky's *Brothers Karamazov*, during which Ivan describes in vivid detail concrete instances of the murder and torture of children, after which he declares that he cannot accept a world in which God's justice is compatible with this suffering of innocent children.[3]

Fiction engages the emotions. Given that religion responds to emotional and existential demands (grief, suffering, longing, the duties toward family versus the wider world), fiction is particularly suited to explore themes in the philosophy of religion. Indeed, most philosophical exposition does not adequately engage the emotions, and as a result, fails to deal with the weight of philosophical questions. For example, philosophers of religion who try to come up with reasons for why an all-good, all-powerful, and all-knowing God would allow evil to occur, often come across as callous because they do not consider the standpoint of those who suffer, but rather look at the problem of evil from a detached (God's eye) point of view.[4]

Next to engaging the emotions, speculative fiction genres, including science fiction, fantasy, and magical realism, can help us engage in what-if thinking, which is also eminently suitable for philosophy of religion. What if, for example, technology would allow us to reincarnate into different bodies after we die? In an unequal society like our own, this would undoubtedly give rise to differentiated access to this technology. In *Lord of Light*[5] Roger Zelazny explores this idea and introduces the concept of a Buddha who can free people from the cycles of existence and suffering. For Zelazny, Buddhism allows one to step out of reincarnating in an unequal society, where gods and priests exert too much power over a population they deliberately keep at a low technological level, and where dissidents are reincarnated in disabled bodies. By engaging in fiction as a long form of thought experiment, we are better able to draw non-obvious conclusions, such as the potentially transformative egalitarianism of the Buddhist conception of nirvana.

The philosophy of religion stories in this volume deal with two perennial questions. One is the problem of evil, which asks how one can reconcile the existence of a perfect God with the existence of evil. For example, if an all-perfect God exists, would God allow creatures to suffer? One might appeal to freedom to explain suffering caused by human agents. But that does not explain illness, earthquakes, and other forms of evil not caused by us. A traditional response is to invoke supernatural free agents, such as demons. Demons choose to do evil things and to rebel against God, thus causing us harm. The story "I, player in a demon's tale" takes this demonic solution as a starting point, and asks further questions. If demons exist, then we might be able to detect their presence. But how do we do that? Perhaps, as the story suggests, we have a special sense of the demonic to recognize the presence of such evil agents.

Two other stories in part III do not explicitly endorse demons as a solution to the problem of evil. "God on a bad night" invites us to reconsider the idea that God is all-perfect. If it is possible for anyone with the right equipment and knowledge to bring about a new universe, how can we know that its creator would have the features theologians commonly attribute to God, such as being all-good, almighty and all-knowing? By contrast, in "Hell is the absence of God," we do have some knowledge about what God is like. God has the attributes of divine perfection, yet evil exists, and the reader is left in no doubt that God is the cause of it. This story challenges a common response to the problem of evil, namely that God's conception of the good is different from ours. Even if that is true, the protagonists' suffering and eternal separation from God seem unjust.

The second perennial question these stories address is how to balance ethical duties to family against those of strangers. Many religions have radical, universalist ethical commandments that exhort their adherents to take care of people who are not related to them. For example, a central Christian ethical rule says that one should love one's neighbor as oneself. "The eye of the needle" explores a conflict between this ethical demand and the demands imposed on us by those close to us, in particular, our children. To be able to fulfill this demand, the protagonist chooses to change her psychological outlook. While this makes the commandment psychologically more attainable for her, it still results in deep conflicts between herself and her family. In "God on a bad night," we see how the protagonist is unable to cope with the loss of custody for his child, leading him to engage in a reckless decision. This action makes us wonder: what sorts of duties does a creator have toward his creation? In "Hell is the absence of God," we see a conflict between love for oneself and the ability to love a god. If God is the originator of bad things that happen to people we love, should we still love God? In other words, if the first and second commandments of Christianity (love God, and love your neighbor as yourself) are in tension, how should this tension be resolved?

Obviously, stories will not replace philosophical argumentation in the philosophy of religion. But philosophy needs stories for their vividness and emotional engagement, without which we might not fully appreciate the weight of the questions. Particularly, philosophy of religion needs speculative stories that invite us to imagine scenarios outside of the normal run of mundane, secular experience.

Recommended Reading/Viewing

Fiction:

- *Battlestar Galactica* (TV series, 2004–2009, developed by Ronald D. Moore), starts from the premise that humanity is all but destroyed by its former android slaves; it explores multiple ideas in the philosophy of religion, such as monotheism, polytheism, prophecy, and providence.
- *The Witness* (computer game, 2016, Thekla), a puzzler that embodies religious ideas in the puzzle solutions such as *wu-wei*, as well as featuring audio-recordings scattered across the landscape with quotes by scientists, theologians, and philosophers.

- *The Sparrow* (novel, 1997, Mary Doria Russell), features an expedition led by Jesuits who discover extraterrestrial life and the protagonist's crisis of faith encountering a world for which his religion does not seem well designed.
- *Small Gods* (novel, 1992, Terry Pratchett), set in the Discworld universe, this comic fantasy story about a novice monk explores the relationship between faith and metaphysics.
- *Three Versions of Judas* (short story, 1944, Jorge Luis Borges), a short story in the form of a scholarly article, reflecting on Christian ideas of incarnation, redemption, and atonement.

Non-fiction:

- Augustine (5th century/1961). *Confessions* (trans. R.S. Pine-Coffin). London: Penguin. A highly influential spiritual autobiography, where Augustine of Hippo, a 5th century African theologian, discusses his spiritual journey, struggles, and doubts, as he converts from Manicheism to Christianity.
- Hudson, H. (2020). *A grotesque in the garden*. Grand Rapids: Eerdmans, a philosophical essay and a work of fiction about the angel Tesque who was left to guard the Garden of Eden after it was abandoned, and who contemplates leaving his mission.
- Ibn Tufayl (12th century/2009). *Ibn Tufayl's Hayy Ibn Yaqzan, a philosophical tale* (edited and translated by L.E. Goodman). Chicago: The University of Chicago Press, a 12th-century treatise that tells of a boy growing up on a desert island, who learns about the world around him and God's existence and attributes.
- Stump, E. (2010). *Wandering in darkness: Narrative and the problem of suffering. Oxford: Oxford University Press*, explores the specific knowledge we can acquire through narratives, focusing on Bible stories and how a benevolent God could allow so much suffering in the world.
- Tsai, C.C. (2019). *Zhuangzi: The Way of Nature* (trans. B. Bruya). Princeton, NJ: Princeton University Press, a classic Chinese Daoist text that conveys its philosophy through many short stories, skillfully put into a comic book format by C.C. Tsai.

Notes

1   Lombard, S. (trans). (2019) *Bhagavad Gita, a new verse translation*. Indianapolis, IN: Hackett.
2   Stump, E. (2010). *Wandering in darkness: Narrative and the problem of suffering*. Oxford: Oxford University Press.

3 Dostoyevsky, F. (1880/1912). *The brothers Karamazov*. trans. C. Garnett. New York, NY: MacMillan, chapter 4.
4 Griffioen, A. (2018). Therapeutic theodicy? Suffering, struggle, and the shift from the God's-eye view. *Religions*, 9(4), 99. https://doi.org/10.3390/rel904009
5 Zelazny, R. (1967). *Lord of light*. New York, NY: Doubleday.

8

I, Player in a Demon Tale

Hud Hudson

Remembrance softly hummed a hymn while sucking on the end of the glass shard with which yesterday he had hurt the calf. The humming was a ritual. What better accompaniment to torment the innocent than the music of God?

He slouched in the corner of a spacious living room, bored with himself and his activities, but never allowed his indifferent and colorless eyes to glance away from the frightened eyes of a shivering terrier who was pressing its body against the far wall in order to achieve as much distance as possible between the intruder and itself. Remembrance quietly evaded the preoccupied couple, who were rushing through a meal whisked from room to room as they prepared for an evening out, and fed off the anxiety of the terrified dog as he patiently waited for their opportunity to be alone.

Remembrance was a coward and a demon, and for years now his target of choice had been domestic animals. He had perfected a long game with his victims: first alarming them (by abruptly appearing in their homes), then confusing them (with a presence radiating a hatred always puzzlingly and entirely ignored by the people in whom the animal put its trust and to whom it turned for its cues), and finally pointlessly hurting them (not severely, but deliberately, slowly, and repeatedly). Inflicting pain was not as delightful as eliciting its anticipation, and in this Remembrance was expert.

Chance intervened, and Remembrance's attention was caught by a passing exchange:

"We're sure to be chatting about demons at the bar again. I'll bet Darius brings it up before we've been there five minutes. It's like all he can talk about these days—his latest bizarre fascination."

"I know, he even worked it into our faculty meeting this morning. Said something about preparing to teach us all a thing or two about 'those confused and benighted, misguided beings'. Doesn't that sound just like him? Arrogant as fuck."

"Still, I don't really mind the posturing all that much. I mean, he *does* know a lot, and he's entertaining enough to make it worth letting him hold court for a while."

The speaker paused to put on gloves and a scarf and absentmindedly patted the air in the direction of the now openly shivering little dog, telling her to be a good girl and to watch the house, oblivious to the fact that he was not being heard.

Remembrance hesitated. In another two minutes the couple would be gone and the terrier alone and his to play with, unmolested. But intelligent people discussing demons? *Confused, misguided beings?* Surely there was action here worth exploring. Remembrance dipped the glass shard in what remained of the discarded beef-stew supper and placed it on the carpet as a gift for the dog whose company he would have to forgo this evening. He then slipped out the front door as it closed, danced vacantly in the snowprints carved by the heavy boots of the pair trudging in front of him, and passed through the exterior of the car to sprawl out in the back, still invisible to its occupants, a stowaway awaiting transport. He amused himself on the way by steaming up the rear windshield and spilling the remainder of a coffee on the beige fabric of the backseat, but mostly he just picked at the loose material on the side panels and watched the drab town slowly slide by through the window.

The bar was old and cheap and in disrepair as were all of its customers. Walking though the ill-fitting front door behind his unwitting chauffeurs, Remembrance was violently struck by a wave of longing. Not his own. Another's. A thick and putrefying fog of dissatisfaction and disappointment in oneself. We are all of us disappointed in ourselves at times, but this was the squalid and long-standing dissatisfaction of a genius who had let himself go, who had not measured up to his vast potential and was at fault for the fact, who had squandered his recent years on tepid pleasures and trivialities, who was desperately trying to regain some sense of self-worth by lording his considerable gifts over those willing to spend an evening with him, who was present tonight to drink and to show off his thoughts about demons to a handful of unexceptional minds from whom he hoped to earn applause and admiration and in whom he intended to instill a vague sense of fear, awe, and inferiority. This was Darius. Remembrance was transfixed. *What luck.* The combination of transparent vulnerability, self-importance, wasted talent, and willingness to participate in his own demise (although not self-consciously or under that description) was an aphrodisiac, indeed. Remembrance, pleased, maintained the mask of shadows that prevented him from being seen, took a seat on the bar above the table of a half-dozen people who would have incorrectly referred to themselves as friends, turned a bottle of vodka on its side allowing the contents to run onto a stack of paperwork behind the counter, and listened.

The conversation limped along for three hours. The sagging bar lights flickered, providing (as did Darius) just barely enough illumination to continue the discussion. Occasionally, Darius pretended to be interested in someone other than himself and suffered his conversational partners to talk until one of them happened to voice a question to the company that he would then take upon himself to answer masterfully—whether it had been directed his way or no. Sometimes, Remembrance had to admit, the answers were somewhat sophisticated (if somewhat overbearing), but even when they fell short of sophistication, the conversational smoke blown by Darius was so opaque no one would throw a challenge against him for fear of looking laughable.

Remembrance's chauffeur had predicted correctly. Darius was obsessed with talking about his favorite current fascination and found ways to redirect every hopeful attempt toward a new topic back to a discussion of demons. The chauffeur had not, however, correctly ascertained why. Darius certainly had no desire to teach his companions anything, nor could he be said to have learned anything recently worth teaching (despite his apparent boasting excuse for arranging the evening's get together). Learning something would have required effort, and Darius had long since been content to avoid real effort, finding it relatively easy to get by on past achievement and present cleverness. Moreover, a desire to teach would have intimated more good will towards his tablemates and their well-being than he really could have generated. No—Darius was simply passing yet another evening in a mixture of scotch (to help hide his choices from himself) and a word-stew of impromptu lecturing (to generate enough social supremacy over his fellows to fuel another day's worth of avoiding feeling miserable by feeling superior).

And—Remembrance noted with a spontaneous smile, a smile that hadn't been flashed to the world in weeks—this exceedingly gifted but now pathetic man, this creature that could have been a pillar of his community, a balm to his neighbor, and a good to himself, this failed prodigy who had traded such substantial promise for a slow slide into mediocrity, this fool—*this fool*— thought himself equal to the task of engaging in *a priori* demonology. *What low-hanging fruit.* Domestic animals can wait, thought Remembrance, helping this dumb brute to his ruin is worth a share of my time.

One by one the little band of tavern-theologians left the awkward table of faux-fellowship. The terrier's owners disappeared back into the winter night, no better for the company they had kept, and Remembrance never thought of them again. In the end, Darius sat alone. Remembrance had occupied the final few moments of mutual-goodbying debating the merits of different shapes with which to approach the table and its amateur demonologist.

What gets this creature's attention? What form to assume? Shall I arrive a cartoon devil, pitchfork and sulfur, hooved and tailed, demanding satisfaction? Remembrance laughed, his first noise of the night. No—for all his brave and fine words about our kind, Darius doesn't yet fully believe in us, and wresting from him his indecision on the matter with supernatural spectacle will only frustrate my aim. *A woman?* A woman too tipsy to assess the unappealing shape across from her but not too tipsy to be manipulated? No—lust perhaps lives in Darius still, but almost certainly it is now directed at images on a screen, images of bodies that belong to no one and to everyone at the same time. A fussing matron to dote on his ego? A wispy, runaway girl to elicit a sense of magnanimity and pride at the depths of his own generosity when he graciously stoops to help her? No and no, again. *A man?* Someone handsomer, healthier, fitter, better dressed, more at ease in the room and with himself ... someone alert, quick-witted, well-read, widely-traveled, ambitious, and confident ... someone who adopts the same affectations of speech but with more flair ... someone just ever so slightly superior in all the externally visible ways that might be taken in over the course of a evening in conversation? Ah, yes, *that*. Most of all, the apparition must present himself as a cut above Darius intellectually. The enticement of a mental competition should be temptation enough, Remembrance decided, for he had noted that Darius had repeatedly displayed a weakness throughout the evening—a willingness to easily and casually forgive any faults in himself which might be exposed by such a foil, provided that he could surprise and best the better man in argument, humiliate and humble him, transform competence and self-respect into confusion and embarrassment, *dominate* him in thought.

Thus committed, Remembrance quietly assumed the form of his preferred strategy and stood erect, without affect, beside Darius's table and waited to be noticed. It didn't take long; Darius looked up.

"I really couldn't help overhearing. Fascinating stuff you were on about all evening. Fascinating but, in the main, wrong. Still, I don't imagine any of us should think ourselves very likely to have reliable insights on such outlandish matters." Remembrance shot forth his hand, perhaps smiling; it was dark and hard to tell. "My name is Brance. I'm just now heading out and thought a 'thank you' was in order for providing a diverting evening of eavesdropping."

"In the main, *wrong*?" echoed Darius, his pitch rising with the last word. "Really? How intriguing." His open-mouthed, skeletal smile, lips momentarily pulled back in an involuntary sneer, might have seemed welcoming at a glance, but anyone listening carefully to his tone of voice would have heard notes of unmistakable contempt. And Remembrance was listening carefully.

"Yes, wrong." The words were separated by a full two seconds. Just enough. "In what particular?"

Remembrance selected a seat opposite Darius. "I suppose you had their origins right. Demons would certainly have been created by God, as you correctly noted. But then I'd have to say you lost your way and wandered from your theme into wishful thinking."

"A *believer*. How refreshing in this day and age."

"A believer in *God*?—Oh yes," said Remembrance quietly and with a scarcely noticeable shudder, "but definitely not a believer in the malformed demons you conjured in your conversation this evening: domesticated, delicate, perplexed little things, shamefully crouching in their shadowy doorways, ready to do a little mischief here and there to be sure, but mostly pouting and yearning to be welcomed back into the arms of the Creator."

"I do suspect," began Darius gleefully, prepared to rehearse a speech he had given twice earlier this very week, "you'll discover it more difficult than you might imagine to believe in God but not also in demons."

"No, you've misunderstood. I don't disbelieve in demons. I simply remarked that you mischaracterized them."

"You'll have to forgive me. Not everyone in my audiences is so readily willing to concede that particular controversy at the outset of our conversations. Or even ready to concede the mere existence of God, for that matter. In my Spring course in philosophy of religion, for example, I'm *forever* combatting childish objections freshly harvested after a first season at university and then doing my best to redirect those little freshman recruits to atheism with (if I do say so myself) rather *excellent* reasons which (bless their hearts) they often can't appreciate, until once flummoxed enough to listen and learn they—"

"Reasons?" echoed Remembrance. Darius started. He was unused to having odes to himself interrupted. "I'm not surprised you can upend unstable arguments for atheism spouted by your inexperienced students—pardon me, your *audiences*—and I'm not surprised you can stun the same crowd into silence by spinning theistic arguments they can't follow or evaluate, but you think these reasons of yours compelling?"

"But, of course. I would have expected the same of you—*a believer*—as you just now confessed."

"I'm not much in need of reasons," said Remembrance. "Perhaps you've confused having reasonable belief with producing good reasons for belief? It's a common error. One I'm sure you could transmit to your audiences on the first try."

"And you can explain this putative error?" asked Darius, half annoyed by the insult, half enticed by the promise of a distinction, and wholly convinced he might be able to pick up something he could exploit in later conversations without paying any real price for it in this one.

"If you like—a simple difference, really. Some beliefs you hold on the basis of other beliefs, and some you don't. Among the latter, you'll find some beliefs that are rational to maintain even in the absence of arguments. Beliefs about the existence of God can be like that. We are all equipped with an (unfortunate and) inescapable sense of the divine, a capacity to recognize the presence and signs of God, a *sensus divinitatis* as it has been called. Once triggered by an environment, it works much like memory or sense perception in yielding reasonable beliefs independently of argument, but where, say, vision takes shape and color as its proper objects, the *sensus divinitatis* registers divinity instead."

"And it is your considered opinion that this amounts to some sort of demonstration—a proof—that you prefer to the classical arguments for God? I must say, it's not much to my ear."

"I didn't say it was a proof," corrected Remembrance. "It's an explanation of the presence of reasonable belief in the absence of arguments. Creatures both great"—and for a slight moment he paused to look closely at Darius— "and small have experiences, reflect on them, and acquire beliefs using memory, sensation, introspection, reasoning, any number of cognitive faculties with which they've been endowed. If those faculties were designed to produce true beliefs in those circumstances, and they do so as a result of the creature functioning properly, that's all it takes for them to be rational. But as for what I *prefer*—I would prefer to be rid of this particular awareness and never think on God again."

Unsure of what to make of this last remark, Darius ignored it. "If I understand you, then, you haven't shown that God exists at all, you've just hinted at how belief in God might be justified apart from arguments, *provided* you can find someone willing to grant your assumptions that God designed your faculties and invested you with that deity-divining-rod of yours."

"Well, then I was successful. You'll recall that's what I set out to do."

"Oh. So it was. But let us not forget, you also said you believe in *demons*." Darius sang the last word, and let it hang ridiculously in the air. He was quite accomplished at combining an open acknowledgement of his own belief in some unpopular thesis with barely concealed ridicule once he detected the same belief in others. It came from learning that he could nearly always bluff his way through a defense if challenged and that his conversational partners, as a rule, could not. Soberly maintaining a position while simultaneously belittling it in another was a fine rhetorical advantage in debate, and Darius meant to secure it now. "So, do you have a similar magical shortcut to explain how you are justified in believing in your demons, or must you now appeal to arguments, after all? Are you really so prepared to stand with me against our enlightened community with your medieval commitment to supernatural evil spirits? Weather the scientific storm they will undoubtedly visit upon you? Have you faithfully memorized your Aquinas as I have? I should think—"

"Let's just say I have an unshakeable conviction on the matter," interjected Remembrance, as flat in his tone as Darius was animated in his. "But, as you've asked—yes—in fact, it is precisely the same magic, as you put it. There is a second sense, a *sensus daemoniaci*, with which all creatures are involuntarily fortified. It almost compensates for its sister sense."

"What?" Darius struggled to disguise his intrigue with a scoff. "A basic, God-given sense whose object is the demonic?" Remembrance made no reply. "You mean an ability to simply *perceive* that there's a demon in your midst? What an outrageous, delicious idea! But surely, it can't be as easy as all that." Darius forced a laugh, which despite its origins became oddly genuine, momentarily disorienting its host. "I mean, why isn't this sense of yours going off all the time? Just look at the miserable state of the world; surely there are enough demons mucking about to continually ring those internal bells you've just posited."

"Ah yes, I suppose there are. And the mechanism works perfectly. Undoubtedly, its bells are sounding their alarms for you even as we speak."

Darius struck what he took to be a comic pose of deep concentration. "But I don't detect them, dear boy."

"No, you do detect them. But you haven't recognized them for what they are. It's a burden people like you are often spared. You are so busy scanning your surroundings, surveying your options, estimating your position, weighing what you'll say next, deceiving and flattering yourself—so committed to cognitive engagement with your world (to the extent that you're capable of it)—that your fallen and overworked intellect competes with the purity of the experiences furnished by the senses with which you were created and successfully cloaks them for you."

"My fallen intellect," Darius began and then stopped, realizing he had no idea how he intended to complete his sentence. Perhaps he had slightly underestimated his companion. His mind darted through strategies for the next move in the exchange. He wasn't sure how they had reached this point, he didn't have a sense of control, and he wasn't at all accustomed to his position. Remembrance patiently watched and waited.

"I see. I see. But I shan't let you continue to go off on this tangent of yours. I'll just take your demonstration of the existence of demons as read and won't put you through any more paces in defending yourself. We really must get back to your earlier accusation of my alleged mischaracterization of them."

Darius drew himself up in his chair and looked stern. "In particular, I recall your frankly puzzling failure to recognize that the demons wish—in their heart of hearts—reconciliation with God. I can assure you, young man, every creature, from tyrant to slave, sage to fool, virtuous or vicious, you yourself—"

"No. They don't wish it," interrupted Remembrance, successfully lying to himself and speaking in pain. "They don't daily crave it. They don't nightly dream of it. They don't secretly ache for it. Be welcomed into His arms? They would annihilate Him if given the chance. You innocently paint demons as ever-hopeful sufferers who don't really know their own minds, who simply need to be afforded a chance to come home and be forgiven. You underestimate their choice and their will and their hatred."

Darius's eyes involuntarily opened slightly wider at the crispness and unqualified confidence of the speech. Usually those cloudy and silent judges spent their days half-closed, unfavorably evaluating all that swam before them, but Darius once again had been taken slightly off guard and efforts to regain his balance were visible only in the slight movement of his lashes.

"I'm afraid, my friend, that your suggestion doesn't make much sense of their interactions with human beings," Darius objected. "I mean all that desire to be free of God and God's creation you're so ready to impute to them could hardly motivate a demon to come sniffing around to catch the attention of those like me who bear the divine image in a rather less sullied way."

At the phrase 'divine image' Remembrance imperceptibly flinched, and then, with just a hint of anger, pressed, "Why do you suppose a demon would deign to interact with a human being? Why would a being of such magnificence bother to disturb a séance conducted by bored housewives equally incapacitated by chardonnay and leisure, or commune with whispering teenagers exposing their insecurities to an Ouija board in a damp basement, or slave for some would-be Faustette who fancies herself armed with an incantation empowering her to satisfy her darkest (yet utterly pedestrian) desires by command? Take yourself, for example. Consult your vast repository of information on demons; think. Why would any demon sit at table with you?"

Missing the point of the examples and interpreting the invitation to answer this question as evidence of his first score in their conversational game, Darius lowered his voice: "*Me?* Well, who knows if I'll ever have the honor?" Darius briefly looked downward, humbly doing his best to blush. "But I suppose I'd have to say that if a demon were ever to come my way surely it would be to gain a kind of power, a kind of access to the world, you see. I—well, I don't mean to boast—but I've enjoyed some measure of success in my career, lots of influence in the journals, a monograph or three, too many gifted students to count, really. I should think I'm just the sort of man a demon might like to befriend, to influence and manipulate, a tool to help him leave a hoof-print (so to speak) on the world of man." Darius smiled modestly at his own witticism.

"Yes, I can see a demon viewing you as a tool," Remembrance replied. "Perhaps, though, such an interaction would have little to do with your great potential to affect the world around you. Maybe he wouldn't want to make demonic use of your power or your position or your prestige or your horde of student-disciples. Maybe he would be content just to hurt you. Yes, I think he will be content just to hurt you. No other motives. No power grubbing. No over-reaching plans with you at their center. Just the theater of an evening's worth of pain and humiliation."

Darius shifted in his chair. He had been better pleased with his depiction in his own example than in Remembrance's. "But then why someone like me? If agony were really the only thing these poor, despairing beings sought after, why not mindless animals? Why bother with the intellectually elite?"

Remembrance stifled a sharp and unkind laugh at the mention of animals. "I'm sure the (not quite) mindless animals get their ample share of attention," he said. Darius furrowed his brow. "But I see you aren't persuaded. Permit me a further word on the animals," continued Remembrance. "For all your pride in your intellectual capacity, their cognitive simplicity affords them something I earlier noted was unavailable to you. Their minds are not so disordered and deformed by the noetic effects of sin that the fallen world inhibits their receptivity to the *sensus divinitatis*. Their access to God far outstrips your own."

"Doubtful," snorted Darius, offended to be named runner-up to a housecat in anything. "And where, I wonder, in your supposed zoo of believers, are we to find their prayer shawls? Their mosques? Their defrocked priests?"

"I didn't say they were believers," explained Remembrance, amused at the indignation on display. "I said their access to God far outstrips your own. They fully experience a divine presence which, to be sure, would eventually lead to belief in someone with your slightly increased capacities (were you able to share that experience unclouded by the other things you routinely do with those very capacities). Not that I think this access improves them. Significantly unfree and barely remedial agents, they're unable to reject His offer of debasement in the invitation to worship, and thus repeatedly do so in their laughable and imperfect ways largely as a consequence of their natural inclinations. Scarcely more than automatons, they sing to Him, and He is in turn present to them with an immediacy and intimacy that your saints shamelessly begged for and could never achieve. But this same simplicity of mind is what makes them so vulnerable to the *sensus daemoniaci*. The stupid brutes never fail to respond to a demon walking amongst them, whereas an intellect like your own would prevent you from discerning the situation you were in even if it were prolonged and dangerous and right in front of you. The animals have no illusions, no pretentions or pride to comfort them and are always attentive, for they never second guess what they sense. There is pleasure to be had in those disconcerting moments. But those who take themselves to be intellectually superior and who rejoice in that fact are capable of a qualitatively different kind of pain. Less satisfying in the end, but one suspects variety occasionally entices."

'So'—thought Darius nodding politely, not fully taking in the details and impatient for his own turn to resume—'this adversary of mine is a pinch more clever than he seemed at first glance and is willing to drone on and on with a degree of confidence wholly mismatched to anything he could possibly know about the topic.' Irritated and reaching into his thirty-year career of tricks he tried another angle. "OK, OK, Brent," Darius tried to sound charming while scrambling for redirection, "I see you've got some interesting ideas there. But if we're going to do this right, we should start again and from the beginning. Can't be too casual with serious stuff like this. Tell you what. Let me buy you a drink. I'll state my position, and then you state yours. All I ask is that you'll state it with the same level of *precision* you'll hear from me." Darius interrupted his amiable offer long enough to ascertain whether he had hit a nerve with his back-door accusation of carelessness in speech. No sign.

"*Brance.*"

"Pardon?"

"Brance, not Brent."

"Apologies. Brance is it? What do you say, then? A drink?"

"Yes, I accept. State your position with precision. I'll drink."

Darius reached behind him and took a bottle off the bar, winked at the bartender who suppressed his annoyance, and poured a drink in one of the unused glasses left over from the religious conclave that had worried the table earlier in the evening. "*Demons, demons, demons,*" he chanted with a world-weary shake of his head, "where to begin? The greatest creaturely puzzle and God's sorest disappointment. Individuals made so very perfect, wanting for nothing, fully aware of the presence and majesty of their Maker, and yet pointlessly rebellious. They simply and inexplicably said 'No.'"

"Inexplicably?" asked Remembrance. "Maybe they didn't like the terms of their good fortune—servile and humiliating subjection."

"Yes—quite so. That's it exactly. They weren't willing to submit." Darius gave a conspiratorial nod to his new prize student and continued. "God then granted them lives on their own terms, and, my word, what a mess they've made of themselves." He made a soft sound of compassion. "Poor things."

"A mess," repeated Remembrance. "And now?"

"Well, their natures haven't changed, have they? They were still made to love and to serve and to delight in God. They can't find satisfaction independently of that end. They must somehow be reunited with the true source of their happiness. That's why God favors their continued existence over a brief and merciful obliteration. He has a plan of reconciliation. A glorious plan, I can tell you."

"Can you? Are you party to this plan?"

"Well," Darius quickly located the most unassuming look he could master, "not in so many words." Then leaning across the table he confided in a whisper, "I wouldn't presume to know the mechanics, of course, but rest assured, God will find a safe path for their return, and I, for one, would do my small part to help."

"Yes, yes," chanted Remembrance. "That was the theme from earlier in the evening in which I was most intrigued. An hour ago, however, it took the form of your strategy for fighting a demon should you happen to encounter one, but I see now that your thought was to advise your friends how properly to wrestle with demons so that you can best position yourself to advance God's plan of rescuing them from themselves."

"Oh, you heard that? Quite right. It is a two-step procedure. Your average demon will approach a man like me with antagonism, spying in me a relation with God he secretly covets. Finding himself unable to secure the goods he desires for himself on his own power, as I explained earlier, he will try to increase his influence by manipulating me. I must first fight him to refuse him that power. And then—and this is the difficult part—I must love him as my neighbor, extend my finest self to him, provide an example of the kind of character he can regain in himself. Show him the way back to God."

"Fascinating," hissed Remembrance. "The fight—that's not the hard part then?"

"Oh no. Confidence, you see, confidence. Upon recognizing my demon brother, I would begin by denouncing him in his present state. Letting him know where we stand."

"Courageous. But will he stand and listen to your admonishments? Will he not simply strike or crush or tear you for your impudence as you are lovingly denouncing him as a prelude to your demonstration of good will? Presumably God will have the same mysterious reasons to observe without interfering in any such treatment of man by demon that He has for permitting man's own inhumanities to man."

"Yes. Quite right. He will have weapons, but I would avail myself of a quick experiment."

"An experiment?"

"Yes, a quick but crucial test, a way of discovering what capacities I face. Now I doubt the poor wretch can really do much to me without my consent. Between you and me, I wouldn't be at all surprised if he would be altogether incapable of affecting me physically. I've thought long and hard about this you understand, and it is my theory that demonic powers are exhausted by suggestion and persuasion. He would be wholly dependent upon frightening me into a state of panic, bringing me to believe that I was in this or that precarious situation through the power of mere suggestion. Impotent soul that he is, he would channel all his efforts in an attempt to maneuver me into hurting myself."

"But you would resist him?"

"I would successfully resist him. I would slip to the ground, close my eyes, stop my ears, block all the usual channels of sensation connecting me to my environment. That way if I should experience the hallucination of continued sensory interaction, I would then know it to be illusory and avoid being deceived into danger by what only seems to be real." Darius leaned back and smiled broadly.

"I see. And no prayers?"

"Oh yes," he added hurriedly, "and pray."

"And you wouldn't worry that the demon would sit with you on the ground, quietly wait you out, his face inches from yours when you finally decide it's safe to reopen your eyes?"

Darius pressed on as if he hadn't heard this last remark. "Then I would softly speak to my fellow creature in distress, reach out to him in his misery." Darius paused as if to catch and suppress a rising feeling of sympathy that threatened to make impossible continuing his narrative without an emotional betrayal of the depths of his inward conviction to help such beings in need.

"All right," said Remembrance, "that's enough. Here's my theory."

"Oh, I'm not finished."

"You are for now. We'll take turns. I think at best a demon would find you by chance. Would be more likely to be interested in some peculiarity of the twists and turns of your name than he is of any intelligence, art, skill, or character you could bring to the table yourself. Would take no interest in you or your purported profound affection for your neighbor whatsoever. Would certainly not see you as a conduit to accessing and shaping the world. Would hold your words of brotherly love against you in the one long and intimate night you spend together. Would hurt you and forget you. What do you think? That seems precise to me."

Remembrance had spoken slowly and the room had chilled. As the demon's voice filled the empty spaces around them, Darius faintly heard the melody of a hymn while the other patrons in the bar dropped out of focus and seemed to fall silent, diminishing into the shadows. As Remembrance reached the word 'precise' Darius sat immobilized as if frozen under the gaze of Remembrance's indifferent and colorless eyes, only a cluttered table between them, the light continuing to dim.

Minutes crept by wordlessly as Darius experienced the first full and unadulterated deliverance of the *sensus daemoniaci* of his lifetime, an experience every bit as pure and terrifying as the confused terrier's from several hours earlier. And to compound this simple horror (usually reserved for the brutes alone), Darius exhibited the first evidence of the night of the qualitatively different sort of pain earlier alluded to by Remembrance, a pain reserved for those who identify themselves with their intellectual superiority and who make mistakes about its significance and scope.

Darius moved only to swallow and to search for a path, any path, of retreat. Finally overpowered by the gravity of his situation yet pretending still to be in charge of himself, he demanded in a voice whose claim to authority was betrayed by its pitch, "What do you want from me?"

"*Want* from you? Nothing."

"What do you intend to do?"

The game now concluded, Remembrance shrugged as he extracted a curved, glass shard from his vest pocket, once again bored with himself and his activities.

"What do you expect me to do?"

"Perhaps you could consult your list of strategies. Remember, I'm confused and misguided, a benighted and disappointing wretch, impotent . . . a mess. Oh. I know. Why don't you try closing your eyes?"

Story Notes for I, Player in a Demon Tale

Hud Hudson

Widespread belief in supernatural agents including demons is not just a historical curiosity confined to our credulous ancestors who were infected with base superstition and overactive agency detectors, and who were all too inclined to imagine intention and design behind every rustling leaf where there were only natural phenomena awaiting observation, proper unveiling, and scientific description. On the contrary, belief in demons continues to coexist uneasily and in tension with *our modern worldview*, that ever-changing-yet-ever-confident blend of the current deliverances of astronomy, physics, geology, paleoanthropology, genetics, evolutionary biology, and all their scientific brethren.

Advocates of the supernatural (whose demon-beliefs often strike them as non-negotiable features of the authoritative texts and traditions of their religious institutions—including, of course, strands of Judaism, Christianity, and Islam) clash with various champions of science (whose rejection of supernatural agents seems a clear and certain consequence of scientific progress under a research program of naturalism, a consequence in no danger of being overturned by any further developments arising from serious inquiry into the world and its structure).

I believe this apparently irreconcilable opposition can be overcome. As in similar standoffs, the two views can be rendered compatible with one another by way of some attention to the background metaphysics and epistemology. Such reconciliation involves deferring to the authority of the scientists in those areas where their expertise has been established and well-earned. At the same time, however, it involves exposing those other areas in which naïve metaphysics and epistemology are masquerading as genuine science, and it does not permit gratuitous philosophical additions to scientific theories merely on the grounds that the philosophical views are highly popular among the scientists of the day.

Consider one standard complaint that initially appears to involve something of a concession to the believers: *Perhaps* demons exist—but even if they do, we do not have any compelling arguments for their existence and consequently do not have rational belief in their existence.

Of course, a set of story notes and the short story they precede cannot hope to establish a full-scale reconciliation. Yet a philosophical story can do something. A philosophical story can furnish a hint of one of the early moves in an attempted reconciliation. With respect to the complaint above, it can illustrate how belief in the existence of demons might very well be rational in the absence of compelling arguments by introducing the existence and function of a *sensus daemoniaci*, modeled on the more widely discussed *sensus divinitatis*.

The foregoing story touches on five philosophical themes:

(i)   What is a *sensus divinitatis*, and how have philosophers (following suggestions made by the theologian, John Calvin) argued that it can render belief in God rational, on the assumption that God exists?

(ii)   Given this model, what is a *sensus daemoniaci*, and how might it likewise render belief in demons rational, on the assumption that they exist?

(iii)   In addition to human beings, could non-human, non-persons (e.g., shih tzus, water buffalo, hippopotami) be equipped with a *sensus divinitatis* and a *sensus daemoniaci,* and might there be significant differences in the respective manifestation of these capacities in persons and non-persons?

(iv)   Would demons, if they exist, be our neighbors—i.e., does the Christian commandment to love your neighbor as yourself extend to love for the demons?

(v)   If demons exist, what dangers might threaten those curious or rash or arrogant individuals who (armed with a little intelligence and a measure of neighborly love and a fascination with the demonic) wade into the uncertain waters of philosophical demonology in the hopes of indulging their fascination and experimenting with their pet theories concerning interpersonal human/demon interaction?

9

The Eye of the Needle

Frances Howard-Snyder

Arriving home after the rest of the family had gone to bed, Imogene took in the living room, the watercolors from a market in Tuscany, the masks from Venice, photographs of the three of them in Siena, and the tiny statue of Romulus and Remus with their she-wolf. But the gorgeous Italian feel of the room was spoilt by the dirty dishes on the coffee table, the used napkins, the coats and computers littering the sofa. The house would be neater after Caleb left for college, but also emptier. It had been a rough day. Imogene found a bottle of Merlot and a glass and headed to her computer.

First, she checked her email. Nothing beyond the word of the day (*Schadenfreude*) and the Literacy Site. She clicked *donate*. Caleb had been rejected from his first and second choice universities. Imogene herself had had a paper rejected. She reached for the bottle and poured a glass. On to Facebook. A friend was celebrating losing another seven pounds. *Yay,* Imogene thought weakly. *I wonder what her secret is.* Another friend, Vicki, was mourning her husband who'd died a year ago today. Now that was really sad. They were a lovely couple. He was a great guy. Imogene heard the toilet flush and wondered what she'd do without Philip. She didn't like to think about it. She clicked the crying emoji and considered writing a message of support. But if she did that she'd get a never-ending stream of people also commenting on Vicki's sad post.

Moving on. She shared some funny political posts, and then skimmed through other academics' complaints about grading. Another glass of Merlot seemed in order.

Then her gaze landed on a teenager in a black and orange sweatshirt adorned with a tiger. Seriously! Sylvia got into Princeton! Sylvia's mother thought it was cool to brag about it on Facebook. Look at all the "congratulations," all the likes and loves, all the tender jokes. Should Imogene add her congratulations? Would her failure to comment be noticed? Were they really all so happy about this? Was it possible that none of them hated the mother who'd put this up? Were they all so much better than Imogene?

Then there was a video from *The New York Times.* A Yemeni girl staggering on a grotesquely twisted spine and then clambering into a wheelchair. "I used to go to school and run around like other children," she said. "Then the Saudis bombed my village." Her next words were inaudible, although Imogene knew—somehow—that they were important. "Please stop the war in Yemen," the child concluded. Imogene hit the crying emoji and the angry emoji and vowed to send a check.

Scrolling on. Another post from a friend who was so happy, her book had just been bought by HarperCollins. So proud. The culmination of so many dreams. *Damn her!* Imogene hurried on. Why couldn't she share her friend's joy? Why did her friends have to brag? Why did she drench herself in this daily round of misery and self-loathing?

The Yemeni girl came to her in the night. The child's suffering could not be ignored or discounted. It could not *be*. Imogene had sometimes imagined her son being grievously hurt or dying. She'd always known that this news would be unbearable. She would fight it with everything she had, every minute, every ounce of strength, every cent she could get by emptying accounts or selling her possessions. She would give her blood, her organs, her very life, to save him. Existence without him would be intolerable. Giving her life to save him would be a small price. The Yemeni girl in the wheelchair was no different from her own child, she saw in a flash. She struggled to get to a place where she could act and struggled against the inexplicable weight that held her down.

"Honey, Honey," her husband whispered. "Wake up. You're having a nightmare." He held her while she cried into his shoulder and described her dream between choking sobs. "Hey, it was just a dream," he murmured.

But the child was real. Her agony was real. Imogene was drenched in the reality of that pain. The pulse in her ears continued to thunder, but slowly, more softly, more distant, while Philip held and rocked her.

He had to go, he said after a while. Would she be all right? She assured him that she was fine. She turned on the shower and washed most of the dream residue away in hot water and lavender soap. She would send a check. It was the least (and probably the most) she could do.

She had a breakfast date with Maggie. Walking from the parking place half a mile from the café, she pulled her coat tight around her against the chilly wind and cursed the car that sent up a spray of icy mud that drenched her pants.

Inside the café, Imogene's hand relaxed and let her coat fall open. Kitschy primary-colored art decorated the yellow walls. The open plan kitchen was loud with the clang of frying pans and the sizzle of bacon. Her friend waved from a small table in the corner. Imogene grinned back and pushed through the tightly packed crowd. Maggie was a good-looking woman in her late sixties, who somehow always managed to look elegant. She was a member of Imogene's church, universally well-liked, a painter who taught art to homeless teenagers. Imogene felt grateful that this wonderful woman made time for her.

They embraced quickly. A heavily tattooed waitress brought black coffee and took their order.

"So, how've you been?" Maggie asked. "You look a little under the weather."

"Terrible." Imogene sighed.

"Tell me." Maggie's smile was so warm that Imogene was pretty sure she could confide all her troubles without being judged. She told Maggie that her article had been rejected. Maggie listened with her whole body, her head cocked, leaning forward, eyes on Imogene's face. She didn't say that it wasn't a big deal, that Imogene should just keep trying, or that maybe this was a sign that Imogene's work was no good; she just sat and shared the pain. Imogene added the second item. "And Caleb got rejected by Cornell and Princeton."

"Bummer. I know what that feels like." Maggie touched her hand. "He's a brilliant boy. He'll get in somewhere good. He'll be successful. You know he's got the grit and the natural smarts to make it anywhere."

"And then my friend posted about her kid getting into Princeton on Facebook, and I felt like she was rubbing it in and I—I know it's wrong—but I just hated her."

Maggie shook her head and touched Imogene's arm. "Don't beat yourself up. Envy is part of human nature." She leaned back while the waitress topped up their coffee mugs. "And I suppose it's also human nature to want to celebrate your kid's achievement. Don't be too hard on your friend either."

Imogene nodded glumly and sipped the too-strong coffee. "I suppose you're right. I would have been posting photos of Caleb in sweatshirts if the situation had been reversed. I suppose I shouldn't blame Barbara."

Imogene felt warmer as she returned to her car. The protein and grease had fortified her against the cold and Maggie's kindness had fortified her against the cruel world. Maggie was so very nice. No wonder everyone loved her. What did Maggie have that she lacked? Empathy, she realized. Maggie was empathetic. She listened, she understood, and she cared.

Imogene was conscious of her own empathy deficit. This was not a new thought. You don't get to live 47 years and become a full professor of philosophy without some dim awareness of your own moral failings. Mostly this knowledge had bobbed in the back of her mind without bothering her much, but last night and this morning had shone a light on it.

After work, Imogene googled, "How to be more empathetic." Brené Brown had a TED talk on the topic that involved cartoon animals. Empathy is different from sympathy, she said. The bear who exemplified empathy got down in the hole with the sufferer, whereas the sympathetic antelope called down from above. Empathy involved knowledge—listening, imagining, trying to find something in your own experience to connect to the sufferer's experience. That made sense. When she'd read about Vicki's grief at her husband's death, Imogene had imagined losing Philip and shared a little of Vicki's pain. But then again. Her friend Barbara was happy about her daughter getting into Princeton. Imogene knew what that would be like; she wanted the same thing for Caleb. Did that make her more empathetic? If Princeton had rejected Sylvia, would Imogene have shared Barbara's disappointment? Especially given her own so very similar disappointment? No. To be brutally honest, Imogene would have been *pleased* if Sylvia had been rejected. This of course was a sign of Imogene's awfulness, but it was also a sign that knowledge wasn't the whole answer. Same thing with the friend whose book got accepted the day Imogene's paper was rejected. Imogene wanted something very similar, but that shared desire didn't mean she shared that woman's feelings. These women were her competitors. She hated their success and would prefer them to fail. That meant—probably—that they felt the same way, that when *she* boasted of some success of her own, they would be secretly hating her. The realization tasted like gingivitis. How monumentally depressing! You either had to suffer disappointment or you had to make people hate you. Or maybe other people were not like her in this respect. Maybe other people were like Maggie and Brené Brown, genuinely empathetic. Imogene wondered what it would be like to see the inside of others' minds. She'd seen an exhibit at a museum in Canada called *Bodies*, which showed the inside of dead bodies, all the tobacco-tainted lungs and fat-larded guts exposed to the public's gaze. Imagine an exhibit called *Minds*, that somehow showed the inside of human minds. Would they be tainted with envy and jealousy like her own or would they be pure and wholly empathetic? Maggie's would be totally untainted, Imogene guessed. She really hoped Maggie never saw her, Imogene's, worst inner thoughts. But then again, wasn't that what she wanted: to be open and guileless and loved by her closest friends? This would be possible only if her insides could be pure.

Other advice included reading more literary fiction. Imogene already read more than her share of literary fiction, reading about African slaves and Burmese beauty queens and refugees, and seeing a slice of the world through their eyes. She recognized that some of these characters were truly loveable and wanted to be like them.

One site suggested prayer as the answer. Imogene bent her head and closed her eyes and prayed for more compassion and more empathy. She felt vaguely pious for making the request but didn't feel much nicer. Maybe the prayer would take time.

How about something more scientific? She tried googling, "medical treatments for lack of empathy." On page three she found, "Experimental treatment activates mirror neurons." Could this be an answer to her prayer? It couldn't hurt to call the 1–800 number. The deep, lilting Scottish accent of the woman on the other end of the line was reassuring. She explained the treatment in broad outline and suggested that Imogene come in and speak with Dr. Williams if she wanted more details. The first consultation was free. She had nothing to lose except a couple of hours, it seemed.

She found the office in a strip mall, nestled between a Vietnamese restaurant and a tanning salon. The gold copperplate lettering somehow made the place look better than the surrounding establishments. The receptionist had Imogene fill out a long questionnaire, and then called her into the doctor's office. Aside from the white coat, Dr. Williams looked like a television news anchor, tall, clean-shaven with a high hair-line touched with grey. A man you could trust. With some embarrassment she explained her problems. He nodded, assured her that hers was a common issue, nothing to be ashamed of, but surely something many people desired to remedy. She was normal, slightly below average but certainly not an outlier, not the monster she imagined herself to be. Moreover, she was quite reasonable, admirable even, in desiring a change.

That was a relief but it could be an advertising ploy. She asked him to explain how the device worked. He told her that if she decided to participate, she would take a pill in which the microscopic device was inserted. The device would migrate through her system and attach itself into the right hemisphere supramarginal gyrus which is a part of the cerebral cortex and is approximately located at the junction of the parietal, temporal and frontal lobe. The procedure would activate her own neural pathways, particularly her mirror neurons. He continued in this vein, uttering soothingly incomprehensible terminology. "Totally natural," he said in a silky tone, "not unlike taking melatonin for sleep." And the procedure was reversible. The initial installation would cost two hundred and fifty dollars but the first month's trial would be free. If she did nothing, it would continue (and she wouldn't need to return.) She'd be charged a monthly fee of $39.99 for wireless maintenance of the device.

"Any side-effects?" she asked.

"Headaches, a little dizziness, weight loss, nothing too serious."

Imogene raised an eyebrow at the mention of weight loss. "How will it work?"

When you meet another person and talk to her about what she wants, you will experience her desire as she experiences it. That is, you will want what she wants, be pleased when she gets it, disappointed when she doesn't. You will literally feel *with her*—which, I take it, is what you came here seeking."

"That sounds potentially dangerous."

"It could set you up for a lot of sadness, sure, but also for a lot of joy. If your own level of desire satisfaction is more or less average, at least within your community, then the ratio of good feelings to bad feelings will stay more or less the same. They'll just be realigned, so that you are more in tune with your neighbors. You'll be like a choir member singing the same notes as the rest of the choir, which will of course, make them like you more and make you like yourself more and the end result—perhaps paradoxically—will be more happiness."

His account sounded a little slick, Imogene thought, but then again, she only needed to sign up for a month. If the device didn't suit her, she could stop using it. "Does this mean I'll want what everyone I encounter wants—the woman who wants the Cartier watch, or the teenager who wants to get into his girlfriend's pants, or the guy who wants the Seahawks to win?"

"And the other guy who wants the 49ers to win." Dr. Williams laughed at their shared joke. "That could make one a little seasick, I admit. But no, you have to have eye contact and really to be listening to their desires. The desires of people on the bus or on the other side of the room won't light up the device. That's not how mirror neurons work."

"I'm part of a prayer team at my church," she said. "People come forward with prayer requests. They're usually pretty heartfelt. I've never heard anyone ask for prayers for a watch or for their football team. That would be a good place to see how it works. Will I be able to turn it off?"

"Well." He paused. "Actually, we've found that this mechanism works only if you don't have moment by moment control over it. That turns out to be counterproductive, like the device we developed to control people's addictions to tobacco, alcohol, and sugar. When we gave the test subjects the opportunity to turn it off at will, it didn't do its job."

"I see," Imogene said. Her lack of compassion was like an addiction. "Do you think I'll need this device for the rest of my life?"

"Not sure. We're hoping that your brain will develop new pathways so that the device will become redundant after a year or two. If you're sure you'd like to try our treatment, we have a cancellation in the next hour. I could install it for you today. Save you an extra trip."

She agreed. After the installation was complete, the doctor informed her that the mechanism would start slow and reach its full effectiveness within a couple of weeks.

On Monday, Caleb was accepted into one of the colleges he applied to, the flagship state school with in-state tuition. On Tuesday, he was accepted into a small, somewhat exclusive private college in the Rocky Mountains. All the other places he'd applied to had said no. He said he preferred the private college. She wanted that too—because he wanted it and because the tiny campus, with its high faculty-to-student ratio, and administrators who prided themselves on a nearly 100% retention rate was what her sensitive, talented child needed. The college savings account that she and Philip had contributed to monthly for eighteen years wouldn't cover the entire cost, but perhaps some tuition assistance, loans, and refinancing would make it possible. She needed to convince Phillip. Getting Caleb off on the right foot was the most important thing. If he could earn a good degree, make it into graduate school (which would hopefully pay for itself) find a career where he could contribute to the world and earn a decent living, then she and Philip could relax. When they talked, Philip expressed some qualms about the plan. Wouldn't it be nice to have the boy close by? Did they really want to spend that much money on his education? Imogene heard his worries and knew she shared them to some degree.

She wondered whether the device was influencing her interactions with Caleb and Philip, or whether these were just natural maternal and wifely responses. When she found herself responding more generously to her students' requests for extensions and extra office hours, she decided the device must have started working. She was becoming nicer. She was getting her money's worth.

Next Sunday, Pastor Jeff stood in front of the church, blessing the congregation, inviting anyone who needed prayer to come forward. Imogene stood waiting, dressed in a black velvet dress with nylons, next to a large vase of pale lilies. The organ started playing Handel's *Messiah*, one of the upbeat parts. Imogene supplied the words in her mind, "Lift up your heads . . . Oh ye gates, . . . and the King of Glory will come in. Who is the King of Glory?" She felt her own spirits rise.

The church had a high ceiling soaring above the two stories of seating. She watched dust motes fall through the light that passed through the faded stain glass. She glanced at the simple cross above the altar and tried to be worthy of her task.

A man she recognized slightly from a Bible study a few years ago approached her. Nice looking, slight, dressed in slacks and a sports jacket, he had a daughter in Caleb's class and a younger son, she vaguely recalled, wishing she could remember his name. He shifted from foot to foot, his fingers moving agitatedly. Imogene wanted to help him. She wanted to really want to help him. She felt a little electric current zigzagging across her right temple. Could she be imagining it? She felt excited and terrified.

She smiled. "I'm sorry. Can you remind me of your name? I should know it, but my memory for names has been slipping recently."

"Adam," he said, smiled and swallowed. "You're Imogene, right? That's a nice name. Unusual. Sounds like *imagine*."

"Thank you. What would you like me to pray for?"

"My son."

"What's his name?"

He hesitated. "That's part of the problem. He wants to change his name. We call him Ethan. But ..."

Imogene waited. This wasn't about a name change. Not primarily.

Adam glanced around and then moved a couple of feet further away from the elderly couple who were the other members of the prayer team.

He trusts me, Imogene realized. "Tell me about Ethan," she said in the gentlest voice she could manage.

"He says ... he says he's really a girl. He wants to wear dresses and heels and jewelry and makeup. He wants everyone to call him Elsie and use female pronouns for him."

Adam's hands were gripped tight in front of him, so tight Imogene worried that he might break his own fingers. She felt the pain in her own hands but knew the physical pain was just a distraction from the mental pain. He was terrified, worried, afraid of humiliation for himself but more concerned about his child's welfare. Imogene's thoughts moved to Ethan or Elsie. How hard it must be to defy her father like this. Imogene wanted Elsie to be a girl and to be recognized as a girl. Imogene wanted Ethan to stay a boy and get over all this nonsense. She felt the desires of father and daughter pulling her in different directions.

"Let's sit down," she said to Adam and led him to the first pew where she put a hand on the back of the seat and held tight to keep herself from flying apart.

"Will you pray for us?" he asked.

She took his left hand in both of hers. "Dear Lord, please bless Adam and his family, especially his child, Ethan. Please comfort them all. Please help Ethan find his way. Please help Adam listen to his child and help them through this difficult time."

Adam yanked his hand away. "Hey, what are you doing? You're using your prayer to lecture me? That's not what I asked for. You think this is about me being selfish. It's not. It's about me loving my son and not wanting him to ruin his life."

"I didn't mean ..." Imogene stumbled.

He turned away and stalked fast up the aisle.

The woman behind Adam stepped forward, 50ish, bird skinny, with sharp cheekbones and jaw, a dark bob, a smock dress, and something girlish about her demeanor. Imogene registered these details although Adam and Ethan/Elsie still occupied the front of her mind.

"It's been on my heart for a while now to pray for the world," the woman was saying. "Will you help me?"

Imogene took the woman's hands, inhaling her delicate, orange blossom scent. She absorbed the woman's desires: desires for peace in Yemen, desire for Ebola to be cured in Africa, desire for a solution to climate change, desire for the safety of immigrant children on the border, vague waxwork desires with none of the living urgency of Adam's desires, not so very different from desires Imogene herself had had a week ago. Imogene kept skidding back towards Adam and Elsie and fought the impulse to dislike this woman for her mild, generic prayers.

The woman, perhaps sensing Imogene's disapproval, added. "I do care about these things. But I don't care enough."

Imogene nodded.

The following Sunday, the organist was playing *Amazing Grace* as the congregation shuffled out. The front of the church was brightly lit by sun through the stained glass and heavy with the scent of lilies. Imogene had volunteered to serve on the prayer team again. The first person to approach her was a woman around her own age, a little plump with chaotic blonde hair. Imogene recalled her face as usually lit up with a bright smile, but today there were dark smudges under her eyes.

"I'm Lori. I want you to pray for my son, Jason." A sob caught in her throat.

Imogene took her hands. "Tell me about Jason."

"He's twenty years old. He's a handsome boy, very smart. And not just a nerd. He ran varsity cross country four years in a row. He was very popular."

Jason sounded a bit like Caleb, Imogene thought. She waited for the bad news.

"But it's all destroyed." Lori paused to wipe her face with a handkerchief and had difficulty continuing. "It started almost two years ago when he had his wisdom teeth removed in July after he graduated, and the dentist prescribed Percocet. There were some warning signs. He seemed depressed, but we thought that was due to breaking up with his girlfriend. Then he started gaining weight—and I figured that was the depression or the lack of daily exercise. Anyway, we sent him off to college in the fall. And the next thing we knew he'd failed three of his first quarter classes."

She put her hand to her mouth and seemed to bite the side of her palm. "Jason never got less than a B in his life! We freaked out. He got angry. He tried going back to school but pretty soon he dropped out. He came home in late January. I confronted him. He got so mad I thought he was going to hit me, then he left the house and stayed away for a week. I called the police, but they couldn't do anything since he was over 18. He came back eventually, said he was sorry, and asked for money. I gave him some. I can't ever say no to my son."

Imogene listened intently. She found it easy to put herself in Lori's place. Jason's situation could happen to anyone. It could happen to Caleb.

Lori kept talking—about the apathy, the strange irrational behavior, speeding, drunk driving, the night in the county jail, the bone pain when he tried to go cold turkey. Imogene imagined the despair of knowing her child was addicted, that he wanted to poison himself just to feel normal, that he'd lost any sense of priorities and was willing to burn bridges, drop out of college, destroy relationships, break the law, risk his life, give up his dignity, all for a fix. "Can you get him into rehab?"

"We've tried three different places but none of them have worked. There's a facility in Utah that's had really good results . . . but it costs thousands a day and he needs at least 45 days." She was crying. When she caught her breath, she said, "Pray with me."

Imogene had almost forgotten her role, so focused was she on thinking about Jason's plight. She prayed, "Please help Jason come to his senses, please help him find the power to control his addiction. Please help his family find a cure." It wasn't enough. Imogene felt the inadequacy of prayer. It wasn't OK that she would pray, pat this mother on the back and then walk out of the church unscathed.

"Thank you," Lori said with a smile that briefly curved her lips but didn't reach her eyes. "I can tell you really care. It means a lot."

Imogene wrapped her arms around the woman, feeling the wet face against her cheek. She drew back. "Let me know what happens. I will be . . ." she was going to say *worrying* but that seemed inappropriate and somehow impious. "Thinking and praying for you and Jason," she added instead.

The woman nodded. A couple of people were waiting but Imogene shook her head and pointed to her prayer partner and then stumbled down the aisle.

At home she googled *opioid addiction symptoms, side effects, withdrawal, treatments*. Over and over the stories ended badly. A young woman in rehab for the twentieth time. A young man dead of an overdose. A child born addicted. Most of these people started out normal—smart, kind, athletic. It could happen to anyone. It could happen to Caleb, she noted again but did not dwell on that fact. Caleb was in no immediate danger. Her mind was full of Jason's plight. *I wonder*, she thought, *perhaps I could contribute something to help defray the costs of the treatment. Perhaps if I cut back on my daily latte, if I went to a cheaper hairdresser, maybe if I shopped at Costco rather than my local grocery store.* She started doing calculations. Yes, she could come up with a few hundred dollars that wouldn't be missed out of the family's budget.

She withdrew the money and found the address in the church directory. The house had porch of greying wood and an untended lawn with feral tulips. She used the heavy knocker shaped like an owl, imagining Lori finding it in an antique shop and attaching it to her door and feeling a sort of delight in it every time she opened the door. Before everything changed.

No answer.

She tried again. Eventually, she heard heavy steps. A man answered—presumably Lori's husband. He would be nice looking if he exercised and slept more and maybe smiled a little.

"Yes?" he said with narrowed eyes.

Imogene introduced herself and said she was from the church. He shook his head and, saying he'd fetch his wife, left her on the doorstep.

Lori appeared with her husband and invited her inside and into the kitchen. Imogene glanced around, noting the cobwebs in the corners of the sage green walls, the copper pots hanging over the stove, the little pots filled with dead herbs above the sink. The kitchen table felt a little sticky.

"Any news?"

"Nothing's changed. We just keep plodding along."

"I have some money." Imogene held out the envelope, suddenly feeling awkward.

"How much," the husband asked. "Because we need about $60,000 and anything less—not to be churlish—is more for your good than ours." His eyes met Imogene's and she felt the third degree burn of his pain.

"Oh, David," Lori murmured. "Imogene is trying to help. We can use the money she's brought. Patch it together with other money. Maybe we can do a GoFundMe appeal. Everything helps."

"Sure," he muttered and left the room.

"I'm sorry." Lori said. "Can I get you a cup of tea?" She used a moldy-smelling sponge to wipe the table. "I used to be very house proud. But nowadays, I'm just too tired. Housework and gardening don't seem to matter. I am sorry about David too. He is usually such a charming man. He hasn't been sleeping recently. He's often late for work. I'm afraid he will lose his job at the refinery."

"Is Jason here?"

"Yes. But he keeps to his room most days. He's probably asleep."

Meeting him would be out of the question, Imogene realized. "Could I see a photograph?"

"Sure." Lori's smile bloomed momentarily on her tired face. She left the room and returned with an album, then pulled a chair around and sat beside Imogene. "Here he is as a baby. Here he is as a toddler. Look at that—riding a little bike with training wheels. Look here he is on the monkey bars.

You can see how happy he was. And here … and here … and this is his graduation photo."

Wide-spaced, green eyes, under tumbling blond curls like his mother's, gazed frankly into the camera, no guile, no misery, no evil. Imogene touched the photograph under its plastic cover. "Handsome boy." Imogene could see that there were no more photos.

Lori closed the book and pressed it against her chest, sobbing uncontrollably. Imogene found herself crying too but tried to suppress the sound. She turned and embraced the woman, and then stood up. "David's right," she said. "It's not enough. I'll see what else I can do."

Imogene made an appointment to talk with Pastor Jeff, who seemed very concerned about Jason, said he would pray for him, and call at the house, but he said the church was on a tight budget and couldn't contribute a significant amount towards his treatment. Their church was not one of those megachurches that dealt in millions and paid its clergy big salaries, Imogene knew.

She racked her brains to think of someone else who might help. She asked to meet Maggie for breakfast again. Maggie ordered oatmeal instead of eggs and hash browns. She was trying to lose a few pounds before her big trip, she said. Imogene launched into the story of Jason. Maggie inclined her head, listening with palms up on the table. She grieved for Lori and Jason, Imogene sensed. She wanted him to be free of his addiction. In spite of her overriding gloom, Imogene felt a burst of joy in her chest. Now *we're alike; now I'm as empathetic as Maggie.*

But then Imogene sensed a hint of discomfort in her friend. "Well, I guess I could come up with a couple of hundred but … ." She didn't want to have to cancel the trip she was planning, the grand tour of Europe, visiting the Uffizi, the Louvre, the Van Gogh museum in Amsterdam, the chance to see the greatest works of art that had so inspired her, the chance to stand within a few feet of canvases touched by the hands of Van Gogh, Rembrandt, Breughel. She wasn't about to give that up, Imogene realized, not even to save a young man's life.

"Sorry," Maggie said with an awkward laugh, and fumbled in her purse for her checkbook.

Imogene walked away with a curiously muddled feeling. She was disappointed, but she couldn't condemn Maggie. It *would* be hard to sacrifice the trip of a life time. Still, Imogene had to find a solution to the problem. Jason was a clever, creative, imaginative boy. He wasn't a drug addict. He was just a kid with a toothache. The only thing was to get him to the best possible care. Although the place in Utah cost a fortune, it was better to treat him once and be done with it than to do the cheap version twenty times. If they didn't sort this out, he would die. That would be intolerable. Nothing mattered more than that.

Imogene found herself thinking about the problem all the time, even when she was supposed to be preparing lectures or grading papers. It kept her awake at night. She talked to Philip who was sympathetic but fairly quickly moved on to other topics. She found herself out of sync with him. *What would we do if Caleb were in this situation?* she asked herself. *How would we manage? Could we keep working? We'd have to, to pay the bills and because we'd need more money, but how would we keep our minds focused on our jobs? What would we do?*

And then it hit her. *We'd remortgage the house, sell the house even, use the college fund. What good was a college fund if your son died before he could use it? We would empty our retirement accounts.* She and Philip were not wealthy exactly, certainly not in the one percent, but they were comfortable, and they had saved in the past and made wise investments.

Imogene called the college fund company, made up a story about her son's tuition, and they agreed to send her a check without too many questions. She dropped the check off at Lori's place, listened to Lori's immense gratitude and left with a light heart. The place in Utah promised a 95 % recovery rate. The testimonials were excellent. This place would save Jason. Everything would be all right if Jason could be saved. Nothing else mattered.

Lori called again the next week. Her voice sounded sticky, as if her mouth were dry. The center was asking for more money, she said. There was a long pause. Imogene knew what she wanted, what she was afraid to ask. *Can you give or lend us more money?* Imogene wanted what Lori wanted. She wanted to give whatever it would take to save Jason. So, she called the college fund again. She felt a little nervous doing this. Would it hurt Caleb? No, he could go to the state school and do fine. Maybe if he got a job or a loan, they could cover the costs. That would build character.

Philip had tidied up, straightened the gold cushions on the bronze tapestry sofa, cleared off the pine coffee table, adjusted the photos and the paintings so that they looked sober instead of rakish. He was seated in the corner of the sofa next to the lamp, a book on his lap, lean, fit, with a small dark beard.

"Hello, darling," Imogene said landing a small peck on the top of his close-cropped head.

"Hello, Imogene. Why don't you sit? There's something we need to discuss."

She sat in the other corner of the sofa. Something about his tone suggested that distance might be required. "What is it?"

"I've been looking at Caleb's college account. I've noticed that there have been several large withdrawals recently, really large. $10,000 and $5,000 and another $8,000. I'm afraid we might have been hacked. You don't know anything about that, do you?"

She could pretend to be ignorant, but of course, the truth would soon come to light. Why hadn't she anticipated this? Because she'd been so preoccupied with the crisis, because, essentially, she'd been frantic.

"Well . . ."

Her pause had been too long. "I took some money out."

"Oh, for what?"

"You remember that boy I told you about, the one with the opioid addiction, Jason?"

"Right. I think you mentioned something about it a couple of weeks ago when we were at the Indian restaurant. Sure. Very sad. But, Imogene, can we focus on this issue of Caleb's account. Please. What the hell is going on with it?"

"Well, Jason . . ."

"Stop changing the subject."

"I'm not. Jason's situation is precisely the reason I took the money out. All indications are that he will die if he doesn't get proper treatment. The best place for treatment is the . . . Pinewoods Institute in Provo."

"Hold on!" Philip was shaking his head vigorously. "Hold on a second. I'm having a hard time getting my mind around what you're saying. Are you telling me that you used Caleb's college fund for this stranger?" His blue eyes had darkened in a frightening way. All his muscles tensed. Imogene felt his anger, hot, so hot it hurt, and righteous. She felt his terror too, terror at being yoked to a crazy person, his life and the fate of his family inextricably tied up with someone whose values he couldn't understand. His terror was streaked through with her own. She wanted to escape. She sat breathing hard, unspeaking.

"Please explain it to me because I'm afraid I'm having a difficult time understanding."

"Yes," she whispered.

"You gave this money to a stranger? Why? Are you having an affair with Jason's father? Is Jason now something like a stepson to you? Are *you* on drugs yourself? What possessed you?"

His rage made her inarticulate. "I don't know. I can't explain it. I care about him."

"More than you care about your own son?" He stood up.

"No, not more, but about the same." She wanted to make him understand. She wanted him to see what she saw. "If Caleb was in this kind of trouble I would use this money for *his* treatment."

"But Caleb is *your son*. How can you care about some other kid *the same?*"

Imogene briefly considered mentioning the device and Dr. Williams, but she knew that Philip would assume that she was part of a cult or had been the victim of medical malpractice, perhaps have her committed and sue the doctor. The device was beside the point anyway. It had helped her to see something, something that was true and needed seeing. The device itself wasn't the issue.

"You're a Christian," she tried. "You know how we're supposed to love our neighbors as ourselves."

Philip puffed out a sigh. "Really, Imogene, really? You think we're supposed to take that literally?"

"Well, other moral theories tend to agree. Utilitarianism . . ."

"Spare me the intro philosophy lecture, darling. You're the philosopher and I'm just a mere economist, but I can tell you that that is not how human beings work. Look, I'm not going to have a theoretical discussion with you. The bottom line is this: This is my money—half of it at least—that you persuaded me to save for our son. Christ! When I think of all the sacrifices I made to make those savings. Either you stick with the plan, stick with your beloved son, or you go off and save the world. If you don't choose us, I'll divorce you and sue to get as much of that money out of your flakey new-age, mixed-up hands as I can." He moved towards the door. "I'll be staying at my brother's place for a few days. Let me know what you decide." And then he was gone.

Imogene moved through her house. Caleb was away for the weekend. She emptied his waste basket and stripped his bed, threw clothes in his hamper and folded and put away clean ones. She usually left these chores for him, but she needed to keep her hands busy while her mind raced. Dusting his desk, her hand paused on the photograph from the local newspaper taken of Caleb playing chess in the second grade. His head was in his hands, knowing that he was losing the game and desperate to figure out an escape. An odd picture to take, but one that had always moved her. If she continued on her current course, she would lose Philip and probably Caleb too. A prospect she simply could not bear.

The simplest solution was to call Dr. Williams and have the device removed or turned off. He'd said this would be a straightforward matter. She would then return to her old life of loving wife and devoted mother, fighting tooth and claw for her darling bear cub.

Her old life as a selfish bitch. She couldn't go back to that. Her mind and heart had been changed forever. She now saw the randomness of her attachments to one or two people. Easily and chemically shifted to one or more other people. If there was anything intrinsically "worthy" in Caleb that made her fierce love of him right, then the same was true of Jason. And presumably of that Yemeni girl she'd met on Facebook a few weeks before and then again in her dream. She couldn't return to her old self. Could there possibly be a middle way, some sort of third option between these intolerable alternatives?

She would return to Dr. Williams and discuss the matter with him. Perhaps he could turn down the intensity of the device so that she would be compassionate, but not so compassionate that she destroyed her own family. He seemed like a wise man. At the very least, he would be able to advise her on the next step.

The next day, after a fitful sleep, she returned to the strip mall. She didn't remember the doctor's office being so difficult to locate. Perhaps she had the address wrong. All strip malls looked alike. But no. The address was correct. There was the Vietnamese restaurant; there was the tanning salon; but between them was a nail salon. She tried the doctor's number, but it was out of service. She questioned the owners of the restaurant, but they just shook their heads. She sensed their fear. Maybe they were illegal immigrants who didn't want to get mixed about in anything that could involve the authorities. She talked to the couple who ran the nail salon but they had no knowledge of the previous occupants of the office. They were terribly busy, struggling to keep their financial heads above water. They didn't have time to watch over their neighbors. Imogene felt bad for them. She asked for the number of the property manager who had rented them the office. The property manager said she'd rented to a Mr. Williams but had no current contact information. She was in a difficult position, Imogene recognized. There was so much pain—everywhere—and no escaping it. Still, Imogene needed to find the doctor. The more she searched, the more dead-ends she hit.

Dr. Williams wasn't available to save her. Imogene would have to save herself.

Story Notes for "The Eye of the Needle"

Frances Howard-Snyder

"The Eye of the Needle" explores the way we fall short of the demands of morality. Moral theories disagree on exactly what these demands consist in, but almost all agree that we should care about the suffering of others. For example, utilitarianism, a view defended by J.S. Mill[1], Jeremy Bentham[2] and Peter Singer[3], holds that we ought to maximize utility across all people and all sentient beings. An ethics of love[4], a moral view that derives from the Christian commandment to love our neighbors as ourselves[5], where "neighbor" essentially means anyone we encounter[6], implies that we should have the same concern for others that we have for ourselves and our nearest and dearest. Insofar as this idea is close to the Golden Rule, it is also present in many other religious traditions, including Islam, Judaism, Hinduism, and Confucianism. Even Kant[7], who is often considered the antithesis of utilitarianism, argues that we ought to act only on that maxim that we can at the same time will that it become a universal law. This Categorical Imperative is often understood to imply that we should consider the interests of others as counting for as much morally as our own.

If any of these theories is true, Imogene's life prior to the introduction of the device is seriously immoral. The story also explores the way our desires (typically) are out of sync with those of our fellow human beings, and how this leads to the pain of competition, where my success is your failure and vice versa. The way Imogene ends up behaving after she has acquired the device, however, is not really compatible with family life or with any other ordinary personal commitments, at least as she, her husband, and most of us understand these.

What Imogene lacks at the beginning and acquires after the insertion of the device is empathy. The story explores the nature of empathy. Is it simply a matter of understanding at a deep level, how others feel? Imogene's intense feelings of envy suggest otherwise. She knows what her rivals feel and does not share their feelings. She needs not only to *understand* what others want, but to *want* what they want.

Finally, the change Imogene undergoes is a *transformative experience*, an experience where a person's desires are reordered in a way that changes her outlook in a totally unpredictable way, and so which cannot be rationally chosen or rejected, a concept ably explored by the philosopher, L.A. Paul[8], in *Transformative Experience*. Paul discusses real and fanciful examples to illustrate this: choosing to become a parent or choosing to become a vampire, and argues that choices regarding transformative experiences present difficulties for rational choice theory.

Notes

1   Mill, J. S. ([1861] 1998), *Utilitarianism*, ed. R. Crisp, Oxford: Oxford University Press.

2   Bentham, J. ([1789] 1907), *An Introduction to the Principles of Morals and Legislation*, Oxford: Clarendon Press.

3   Singer, P., "The Why and How of Effective Altruism", YouTube video, 17:19, posted by "TED", May 20, 2013, https://www.effectivealtruism.org/peter-singer-ted/

4   Soble, A., ed. (1989), *Eros, Agape, and Philia: Readings in the Philosophy of Love*, New York, NY: Paragon House.

5   Nygren, A. (1953), *Agape and Eros*, Philadelphia, PA: Westminster Press.

6   Evans, C. S. (2004). *Kierkegaard's ethic of love: Divine commands and moral obligations*. Oxford: Oxford University Press.

7   Kant, I. ([1785] 1964), *Groundwork of the Metaphysic of Morals*, trans. H.J. Paton, New York: Harper and Row.

8   Paul, L.A. (2014), *Transformative Experience*, Oxford: Oxford University Press.

10

God on a Bad Night

Christopher Mark Rose

Arlo finds her in the arrival wing, among a clutter of overlapping greetings and nudged luggage. There she is, pulling her little suitcase behind her, a nannybot hovering over her shoulder. She's six.

"Hi Pumpkin! I'm so glad to see you!" he says, squatting down to hug her. He smells her hair, feels her smooth cheek on his stubbly one. Kirtana is her name, her mother's decision, but over time she'd become just Tana.

"Daddy," she breathes, and gives him a squeeze.

He glances up, out the huge spaceport window. The big wheel looms, its caption word-bubbling in his eyeglasses: Extreme Particle Accelerator for Cosmological Experiments (EPACE). Beyond, the asteroid belt stretches away, its archipelago of human settlements glimmering. He tries to imagine what he should say next.

"How are you? Did you have fun?" he asks.

"I had a super lot of fun. It was dot-jamma fun!" He doesn't know what this means, but it sounds convincing.

"Oh, really? Well, tell me." He stands up, makes as if to move away from the crowd.

"I'm going back right away."

"What?"

"We have to get all my clothes and things and pack them into three big suitcases, and then I can get on this shuttle before it leaves, and I can go back to Mommy and Roger right away."

"That's not what we'd planned."

"Mommy said you might be upset." She looks at him solemnly.

Arlo doesn't know what to think of this, if it could be serious. He wonders about the legal aspects, thinks of calling the mediator appointed by the divorce court.

"But why, Pumpkin? Why would you want to go back right away?"

"They have horses now. Roger has horses." Roger is Zeeya's new husband.

Arlo asks, "How could they have horses, on Ceres? Horses come from Earth."

"They're specially made horses. Horses just for Ceres. Roger owns them."

"But isn't it all just dust and rocks there? And no air? Where would you ride with a horse?"

"No, Daddy, they made air. They made air everywhere there, with special plants. It took them a long time, Roger said, but they did it, and not in as long as you'd think, because dandelion drones helped."

How had he not known any of this? Was he so self-absorbed?

"Isn't the gravity too low?"

"That's why they can jump so high on Ceres. So, so high! You should see them!"

"But, isn't it dark on Ceres? Dark because the sun is so far away?"

"It is dark. That is true. But everything glows and shines there! They make the grass special, and the trees special, and the birds special, and the horses special, and they all shine in the dark. They shine different blues and greens and pinks and purples and it's dot-jamma beautiful! You should see that! I wish you could see it."

"I wish I could see it too, Tana. Someday." Arlo says this, or thinks he says it. He feels his throat go dry, and tries to swallow.

Had Zeeya done this? Was this something she had planned, or just what Tana wanted?

There's a pain in his stomach, or in the bottom of his lungs. Something heavy like uranium has appeared there and he can't breathe. His chest is sagging and crushing in on him. Had Zeeya done this? Or Roger?

"But Daddy, I need some big suitcases! We need to pack me up right away, so that I can get on the spaceship, before it leaves to go back to Ceres! Can we go and get suitcases? Mommy told me I need three suitcases."

Arlo looks up at the list of Departures. The ship was due to head back forty-eight hours from now.

"Are you sure, Tana? Are you sure Mommy and Roger want you to come live with them forever? And not come live with me, sometimes, again?"

The flow of disembarking passengers has stopped, and a cold silence solidifies around them.

"Yes."

"But I am still your Daddy. I'll always be your Daddy, and I should get some visits too."

"But Roger is a kind of a Daddy too. He can help. He knows how to pour cereal and tie shoes and kiss boo-boos."

"I'm sure. I'm sure he can do all those things."

"And they have a place for me, a purple room with pink rainbows and round-the-clock 3-vid and a big bed with a big window above it, so you can look at stars."

But Daddy will be lonely without you, he almost says. "But you have a room here, with Cherrybop and Mr. Twoggle and all your friends here," he does say. Cherrybop and Mr. Twoggle are zebrafish, the kind engineered to live long lives—longer than your kid will be a kid, anyway.

"But I can have my own horse there," says Tana. "They bought her just for me. Her name is Chlöe. She has curly hair you can brush."

"That's kind of a fancy name for a horse," he says.

"And you can feed her carrots! Oh, she loves carrots!"

To this Arlo says nothing at all.

"Why do you have to live here in a big wheel?" she asks. "Roger doesn't live in a wheel."

It's quiet for a long time as he considers how to answer this. The other people in the arrivals wing have all left. He's not sure if it's music he's hearing, or the sound of many quiet machines.

He might say the station revolves in the asteroid belt, because material from the asteroid belt was used to build it.

He might say he's here to investigate a new physics, to finally prove or disprove ideas about superstrings and monopoles and inflation, to understand the Big Bang and what must have happened right after. That all the theories have no value, he believes, if they can't predict. He might say this is the only place humans have ever made where he could test the predictions.

He might say *I'm only really good at things that take a lot of math to understand.*

Or he might say he's hiding from confrontation, from the kind of encounters that make his stomach churn like this.

"I live in the small wheel," he says. "I only work in the big wheel."

"I'm going to go live with Mommy and Roger," she says.

"I'll call her," he says, though he doesn't want to.

"Arlo, you've done nothing to accommodate a six-year-old girl into your life. I feel the same way for Tana that I felt for myself," the face of his former wife says, blinking at him from a vidmessage. The tidal pull of attraction he used to feel for her is a hollow absence now. "She would be better off free. She deserves to be in a place where she can have friends her own age, run around, just be a kid."

He wants to respond to this, to say that the zebrafish and the bedroom with the tiny furniture and exterior windows and cable 3-vid are all accommodations. The expensive nannybot, the remote classes, the careful saving up of leave time, the initial trips to Ceres; all of these things were accommodations.

But it's a one-way message.

"Roger and I think it would be best for her, for Kirtana, if she came to live here on Ceres, with us. We all have to do what's best for her. Don't put yourself first."

It's true that there aren't many other kids here at EPACE, that it's a serious, unbeautiful place—assembled piecemeal from asteroids, processed and extruded, an accidental brutalism filled with unengaging bots and scientists. But still.

He wants to curl up on the couch and cover himself with the quilt, the quilt his mother had sewn for him. His stomach feels like a crumpled sack. He wants to just stay there for days, under the quilt, and try to breathe.

Instead, they go climbing up the scaffold in the zero-G spindle of the small wheel. Tana is expert at this, at letting go and spinning, at giving up to forces larger, and laughing as she tumbles. Her voice echoes over asteralloy and glass, with the wind soughing through spaceframes as if through trees.

Arlo tries to feel it, to let go, let the spiraling forces take him. He feels awkward in his kite-suit, like a wayward thought. Once, he does a little loop, laughs out loud as the spirals line up, and he joins hands with Tana in mid-glide. For just a moment, awash in starlight, they might be flying together.

He'd tried to get some of the apples she likes, the small tart ones from the zero-G greenhouse, as a surprise, but they're out of season. So instead they go out for ice cream after the spindle, even before dinner.

He tries not to ask, but it's as compelling as picking a scab.

"What are your days like, at Roger and Zeeya's house?"

"You mean home?"

"Uh, yeah, your home."

"We have a lot of friends, and rainbow-dot food, and parties sometimes. Roger always comes home in time for dinner."

"I see." This was something Zeeya and he had argued about. Arlo would lose track of time, among a big bang of gabbling physicists, and come home late. He had tried to be better at this, but only after several big arguments. Eventually, he'd gotten worse again; it was easier, late in the day, to sketch Feynman diagrams of singularities, to spin simulations out into new oblivions, than to come home and face her disappointment. Their disappointment, truth be told, that there was so little drawing them together at the end of the day. 'Day' felt like such a tentative and theoretical concept, on the little wheel.

"Do Zeeya and Roger ever argue?"

"Yes. Sometimes."

"What do they argue about?"

"Ice cream."

"OK. What's the argument?"

"Mommy likes lupus-lilly best, but Roger likes 'good old chocolate.'"

"I don't think 'lupus-lilly' is an actual flavor. I think that's something they just made up."

"It is a flavor. It's a flavor of ice cream!"

"Ice cream?"

"Ice cream."

"Ok," said Arlo.

"Yay! We said ice cream three times!" She bounces up and down.

"Why is that a big deal?"

"If you say the same thing three times in a row, and one person doesn't know about it, then it means the thing you said will follow you wherever you go!"

"Who taught you that?"

"Friends, on Ceres."

"So now ice cream will follow you everywhere?"

"Yeah, isn't that dot-baba great?"

"I suppose so. Remember to brush your teeth though."

He stands, jangling keys in his pocket, as she looks over luggage for sale, in a grubby stall over the top of the docking bay. There are suitcases in anachronistic brown leather, and a small herd of wooly herringbones. Some, blunt plastic in primary colors. Backpacks bigger than her. The kinds of things academics might see themselves using. All uninteresting and inappropriate for kids.

He needs to message the lab, tell them he'll be taking another day off.

"Daddy, I don't like these. Don't they have some pretty ones?"

The legal documents from Roger had arrived overnight. They referenced obscure provisions of small-body law, children's innate right to self-determination after divorce, appropriate living conditions for children in space. Roger is a principal in a law firm in the archipelago, specializing in property rights; he'd have a lot of eager young lawyers who would be glad to contribute plenty of hours to his case.

Arlo had wanted to fight, to call his lawyer Lenny on Mars and yell at him, to start a whole further round of legal skirmishing, but now he is exhausted, emotionally and financially, and when she talks about horses, what can he offer to compete with that?

He sighs. He'll call down to the model shop, ask if they can print something special for her, suitcases with 3-vid characters drawn on it in saccharine colors.

Why should it be this way? Tana is his own blood, after all. Not Roger's. He's ashamed to have this thought, but there it is.

"I'll get you something pretty."

At the terminal the next day, she gives him a little hug, a kiss on his cheek, and a fistful of wildflowers. Where she got these flowers, he can't imagine.

"These will help you feel better," she says.

No amount of flowers will ever make him feel better.

He holds her for a long time, until she squirms to be free; then he lets her go. It feels like someone has stabbed his heart with an icicle. He stands up and waves.

"Bye Pumpkin."

"Bye Daddy."

"See you."

She walks up the ramp, the nannybot gliding behind. She doesn't look back.

When she is out of sight, he sits down on a little ledge. His breathing becomes jagged, as if a strong wide band is tightening across his chest. He closes his eyes, tries to empty his thoughts, to not prod the open wound she has left him with.

Finally his breathing is normal again. A wheel of pain turns in his chest, and will for days. He stands up, wanting to leave before the rocket launches. Later, hearing the thud of launch, he vomits in an empty corridor.

At home, he curls up on top of Tana's little bed, and stays there for a day and a half. Finally he gets up, squeezes a bulb of water from the water tree in his little kitchen. He can't eat anything.

He feeds Cherrybop and Mr. Twoggle. They seem disinterested, as happy without Tana as with her.

A day later he notices the wildflowers, dried up and falling apart, a little archipelago of ruin scattered across his kitchen counter. He regrets not having put them in water. It's too late now.

For a while, nothing about his research matters to him. He only sees the bleak years piled up ahead. How long could he live here? He sleeps every night in Tana's bed, gets up to use the bathroom, walks through the clouds of new results from the supercollider that are accumulating in the 3-vid field of his living area. He ignores them all. Messages from colleagues blink, unanswered.

Tana had taken almost nothing from her room, leaving behind the narwhal dolls and their tea set, the origami zoo, the Strumbles family who won't play their music without her.

He feeds the fish again. How long has it been? He needs to do something about their water and the green gunk accumulating on the sides of their tank. He fiddles with the filter.

Going from one room to the other, he clips his forehead on the shelf protruding by the doorframe. He's blinking, a huge pain over his eye, and he realizes he's on the floor. He sits up, and his head fills with swoop and throb and vertigo.

What if he'd really hurt himself, he wonders irrationally? Would anybody notice? How long before someone found him there, on the floor of his kitchen? A discolored goose egg begins to grow over his eye.

Finally, one night, Arlo looks up from Tana's bed, through the exterior skylight, and sees the long superconducting spokes of the big wheel turning there, and the gleaming beads of fusion reactors strung along the rim. It's more than a century old. It's still beautiful, he thinks. It's why he came here to begin with.

He starts to work again, goes up into the big wheel, stands over a 3-vid "ideation floor" sketching dataflows, comparing probability fluxes against the endless river of data pouring from the collider. What would a Big Bang "look" like, from an adjacent universe? How fragile would a "new" universe be? The questions are endless. The experiments to answer them definitively are controversial, are considered immensely dangerous.

It's hard to keep metaphysical questions from intruding into the science. Must creation be an "act"? If so, who was the actor, for the universe he lives in and ruminates over, while picking at a twice-warmed frozen dinner? Is there necessarily some "root" universe from which the others were "inflated"? Would it be, somehow, different? Do other universes, if they cannot be sensed or accessed from our own, even continue to exist?

Couldn't Zeeya and Tana see how important this is? That we are standing on the rim of something profound? A new understanding of the moment of creation, how it happened, what it needed?

No. No was the answer to that question. They never saw.

A text message comes to him from Tana. It's as if the moment of their flight in the spindle and the moment of her leaving are superimposed in his heart. He reads: "Daddy, I wanted to show you what it's like on Ceres! I made a video so you can see. I hope you enjoy it!"

It's a four-hour video. His head races, trying to imagine what's in it. He gets a beer, sits down in the living area, and cues it up.

Her friends in the 3-vid are an odd mixture. Kid-shaped creatures with big, plasticky faces, expressive like puppets. Noodle-limbed friendly spiders. A girl with another doll exactly like herself, and that girl with her doll, down some uncertain staircase of scale.

Is he wrong to be disapproving of this? Of some kind of intentional smudging of the line between human and manufactured? Is he a bigot, for not wanting her to be normalized to this?

"Let's go to the jump pool!" says one of them, a pink Playmobil dinosaur head on a boy's body. They whisk her away, through a doorway the camera doesn't follow through.

He waits, uncertain what will happen next. Probably the scene will cut abruptly, he thinks, to some other event, some more rambunctious action.

Maybe the horses he's been imagining since the day she described them. He waits.

He takes a sip of his beer, and then a longer swallow.

How long, he wonders, before the cut to whatever's next?

He doesn't want to miss anything, even if it's only voices from another room. He turns the sound up.

He watches and watches. Nothing ever changes; it's always just the same scene. Eventually he tries to do some work while keeping an eye on the video. He finds that hard to do, while worrying that he's missing something.

He's startled when the lights dim in the room being filmed. Probably an automatic circuit.

He gets a second beer, peers harder at the over-gaudy furniture, the eye-teasing rugs, the bulbous chandeliers. Is there something he could learn from this? None of it would be bought for sane adults. Really it could only have been chosen for a kid. Is this really Tana's room?

He wakes, the beer bottle empty and resting against his thigh. He's slept through the end of the vid. He'll have to watch the whole thing again, to be sure he hasn't missed anything.

He gets up, goes back to the girl's room, lays down on the bed. The sound of machines again, the shushing of air handlers and the tick of heaters. Something's not right. His glance hunts in widening circles.

Cherrybop and Mr. Twoggle are gone. How can that be? He gets up, goes over and looks straight down into their tank. Sees nothing but colored gravel.

He'd been fiddling with the water filter, a cheap plastic widget upon which the fishes' lives depend. He'd removed the intake nozzle because it kept getting clogged with algae. Now, with growing dismay, he pries the lid off the device. The desiccated bodies of the little fish lay there, compacted against one another. They'd been sucked into the filter, and died.

He puts the lid back onto the device, climbs back into Tana's bed, and pulls the quilt over his head.

It's New Year's Eve. Arlo's been trying to get a direct temporovideo connection to Ceres so that he can wish Tana Happy New Year's. Direct two-ways are expensive, the first use of a seemingly impossible new technology, something akin to an ansible. But he's paid the fee in advance. He's done this twice before: on her birthday, and on his, so she wouldn't miss the chance to wish him happiness. This time though, the connection isn't working.

"I'm trying to call this number on Ceres," he explains patiently to the service chatbot, for what feels like the fourth time. In a chipper voice, she advises him again to try the same list of oblique tasks. He's done all these things before, in varying order, to no effect. Tana and her family have already left, probably, for whatever event they're going to on Ceres, to celebrate the turning of the Earth calendar.

He cuts the connection in disgust. He'd bought Tana a set of animatronic horses, little tabletop ones that can gallop and canter, that you can pet and groom and pretend to feed. It's the best he could do, over the distance and without help from his ex-wife and Roger. He'd wanted to know that she'd received them, that she knew they were from him.

He's had an old picture of her, an actual photograph from soon after her birth, on his nightstand. He turns it down now.

He's late for a co-worker's dinner party he'd accepted an invitation to, then immediately regretted. He fiddles with a necktie, then walks out of his apartment.

At the commissary, he buys a gift, a little bottle of peppermint schnapps wrapped in foil and ribbon. At Anna and Sebastian's house, he knocks on the door, then rings the bell. Someone he doesn't know lets him in.

Eventually he finds his way to the hosts.

"Arlo, great to see you!" Sebastian slaps Arlo on the back. "Where's Zeeya?" Sebastian looks across the crowd in his living room.

"Seb!" says Anna. She pinches her husband's forearm.

"I . . . just . . ." begins Arlo.

"They divorced. Zeeya's left the Archipelago."

"Oh, I'm sorry. How did I not know that?"

"Because you're ignorant and self-absorbed. I keep telling you," Anna shakes her head, curls fluttering. "Arlo, ignore him. How are you?"

"I'm OK. I'm fine."

"Good. Good! I'm glad you came. Have you tried the punch?"

"No, I—"

"Well come on then!" Anna grabs Arlo's arm, drags him into the kitchen.

"What's all this?" Arlo asks, eyeing the glowing contraption at the center of the punchbowl.

"It's 'retrocausal punch.' You drink it before you're thirsty, or it makes you drunk before you drink it. Or something."

"I don't understand."

"No one does. It's a Seb thing."

"I see."

"Arlo, have you met Marlene?" A tall woman stands close, mixing seltzer into the bowl.

"No," Arlo says, suddenly noticing her. She smiles for half an instant.

Anna makes quick introductions, then conjures up an excuse and careens away. Arlo feels trapped, but grins gamely.

Some encouraging bits of conversation occur. He asks about Marlene's holidays, her life before the supercollider. She tells him that she'd studied ballet before learning she was just too tall; then she'd reinvented herself as a cosmologist.

"So," she says, "you're married? Is your spouse here?" Marlene looks around.

"What? No. Why . . . ?"

"I just thought . . ." Marlene points to the ring on Arlo's finger.

"I'm. I'm divorced." He sounds perplexed by the word. Arlo pulls his wedding ring off, holds it up solemnly, and drops it into the punch bowl.

"Gee. Wow. Sorry, I guess." She laughs nervously, stirs the punch.

"Should have done that a while ago," he says.

There's a pause. "I don't know why I came here tonight," he says.

"Well, maybe we could just—"

"No, I should . . ." Arlo's voice drifts away.

"What? What should you do?"

"I should taste what I eat. I should see what I look at. But I'm afraid. I don't want to let go of the thing inside myself, the painful thing in my chest."

"Why is that?"

"I'm afraid if I open my chest up, even just for a moment, that pain will escape, all of it. The pain is all I have now. The pain is memory."

"I'm really sorry, I didn't mean t—"

"I want to find some way to keep all of it, and be free of it; both of those things, but separated somehow, you know?"

"I suppose so."

Marlene puts a cup of punch in his hands. Arlo drinks. His face takes on color. Marlene smiles a tight-lipped smile.

"So. Any kids?"

"Just one. A daughter."

"A daughter?"

"A dau—" Arlo gasps, his eyes going far away.

"Are you alright?"

"She's with her mother tonight."

"I see."

"She's with her mother now, maybe for always."

"I'm sorry. I shouldn't—"

"No, you're fine." Arlo's face twitches, then he shakes his head.

He turns, chin to chest, and heads for the door, not quite running. Other guests look up, seeing him zip through, Marlene following at the same pace.

"Arlo, wait—!" she says.

He's out of the kitchen, then out of the apartment. In the corridor beyond, she calls "Arlo!" And follows. He doesn't slow.

Finding herself alone in the hall, she slows, stops, raises her arms, then spins a defiant pirouette.

At the end of a long corridor, Arlo lopes through a crossroads. He hesitates. Finally, he backs up and takes a turn instead.

Eventually he arrives at the OPS center for the supercollider. He thumbs the security service, and enters. He knows this place will be empty tonight, everyone off at parties. OPS is just cycling through a series of automated experiments. He interrupts those.

He sits for a moment at the control console, his fingers resting on the keys. He tries to be empty, to let his thoughts float; eventually he's drawn back to the moment Tana left. She leaves him again and again.

"Because I'm your Daddy, and I love you," is what he hadn't said. Why couldn't he have just said that?

He looks up at the OPS displays; he sighs. The experiment he's thinking of, his experiment, could have been done several times already. It's been held up in the ethics committee for months and months.

He looks down at the bottle of peppermint schnapps that his hands dumbly carried away from the party, instead of leaving it there. He twists the cap off, takes a swig, makes a face, takes a second swig.

For what he is about to do, the administrative penalties will be severe. But really, what more does he have to lose? This thought keeps echoing in his head, blotting out the risks to himself, to others, to the universe he occupies. Something about omelettes and eggs.

Arlo starts with a magnetic Klein Bottle, a kind of insect trap for magnetic monopoles. Several of them have been waiting here. Each contains a particle of rare and fragile power.

He fires the startup charges on the EXreLPA—the Extremely Large Proton Accelerator—and remotely moves a magnetic bottle in-line. Fearful energies begin to spin through it.

The vast architecture of the collider, equations made manifest, screams out its unnatural song. Bright and terrible the OPS shines with the data of the converging forces. The big wheel turns; the little wheel turns within it.

Somewhere, down, down in the magnetic bottle, the particle strains, verges, becoming something else: first a divot, then a cup, then a dewdrop or a tear, stretching pendulously away from our own universe. It just needs the tiniest of pushes, to become something other than anything.

At the moment of *cosmogenesis*, it separates, and becomes; becomes its own bubble of creation, and in the next, its own Big Bang; it inflates, gathering within it force and dimension. From the Higgs field, it draws the space-time it needs to exist. From the inflation field, energy rushes in.

A wormhole stretches, from here to new there, then taffies thin and separates. A flash of Hawking radiation obscures the new universe from view from this one, forevermore.

Arlo slumps in his chair. Finally, his tears have come. Working back from the separation energy, he can see the fundamental constants are all wildly different, there. "There" is the wrong word—it's not a place; it's a separate everything.

Whatever that new universe will be, Arlo knows it won't have the sighs of wind through trees; no logic of blood; no tides of desire; no photographs or rusty keys; no centuries like oak barrels full of hard tart apples; no laughter of children; no rapture of stars. There will be no wildflowers; no shining, leaping horses; no carrots to feed them ecstatically. This new universe will contain none of these things; none of them would mean anything there.

Whatever that new universe will be, it will be something new, something wholly different.

Story Notes for God on a Bad Night

Christopher Mark Rose

My story owes its conception to a gut-wrenching conversation I overheard on an airplane in flight, and equally to the wonderful book *A Big Bang In A Little Room: The Quest For New Universes* by Zeeya Merali.[1]

The former was surely an instance of my eavesdropping beyond what was good for me, and the conversation has stuck with me over many intervening years. In the conversation (and this is a spoiler for my story) a child told his father that his mother and her new beau had just gotten horses, and he wanted to live only with them in the future, so that he could have his own horse. My blood went cold listening to this, surely any divorced parent's nightmare, but I couldn't turn my attention away. The child was quite young and didn't seem to consider the impact his declaration would have on his father, who took it hard.

Questions of God, that is of a creative God, and of other universes, are implicit in *A Big Bang In A Little Room*. The author documents a field of theoretical physics and cosmology that contends that a new universe could be created from our own, and without a prohibitively large requirement for energy, or even much analytic knowledge beyond what we can now provide. She interviews several prominent members of the field, not only about the physics but also about the religious and philosophical implications of their work.

The discussions of physics are heady and wide-ranging, and make for a vibrant read. But my satisfaction with the book was marred by how little philosophical engagement the interviewees possessed, combined with their almost gleeful insistence on trying out their plans. It seemed like a prime example, to me, of an instance where careful philosophical thinking ought to be a prerequisite for the job.

Western monotheism posits a creative God who is not only omnipotent but omnipresent, omniscient, all-loving. This story's protagonist is nothing like that; rather, a fallible and limited human. He is driven by curiosity but carries no great sense of responsibility for his creation beyond it being an existence proof of novel physics. We can see, though he may not, that his creation is also an expression of his own frustration and inchoate inner state. The physics suggest that such a new, parallel creation, once formed, might be entirely inaccessible, and imperceptible, to its creator.

As a writer, I saw a parallel here, between the child's unawareness of the parent's emotions, and the cosmologist's inability to access or engage with a new universe he or she had brought about. I hope I've created a portrait of a physicist who has to some degree failed as a parent, who lacks a critical amount of self-knowledge, but who is not entirely unsympathetic.

Is Arlo, the protagonist of the story, a hero of creation or a disinterested parent? In the story, Arlo surely doesn't appear the hero, and in his pursuit of knowledge disregards a great deal of risk. The full extent of the risk is left unspecified in the story.

But, crucially, we don't have access to the perspectives of any of the putative (eventual) dwellers of the creation he has bought about, who would not exist otherwise. We might imagine that, as in our own universe, life emerges in Arlo's creation billions of years after its incipience; but, in their case, their existence would still be causally linked to Arlo's cosmogenesis. It is easy to imagine that at least some of those putative beings would be grateful for having been brought into existence.

In *A Big Bang In A Little Room*, the author suggests that even our own desire to create a universe in a laboratory may be deterministically caused by God's will, and this then could absolve us from ethical concerns in creating them. Such an argument doesn't persuade me—any number or kind of ethically transgressive acts could be rationalized with the same mechanism.

Maybe the unease I feel at reviewing my own story grows from the implication that the creator of this new universe could actually in some sense be God, as the title implies. As I wrote it, it seemed a useful muddling, of God as creator of the universe (or a universe), and God in his other aspects and roles: omnipresent, omniscient, transcendent, immutable being, source of love, and ultimately judge.

I'd hoped this story might highlight the conflation of these roles that is commonly made by Western religions. My writing experience, though, made clear that I myself haven't entirely escaped a mental tangling of these aspects, and the attendant reverence impressed on me as an altar boy, long ago now.

Some amount of evidence still lurks in the text—I believe I carried, through the subconscious portion of my writing process, a (perhaps Christian) notion that Arlo's suffering is somehow linked to, or maybe a prerequisite for, his act of creation. This notion seems absurd now to my conscious-writer self. Certainly, at a personal level, Arlo is running away from the wreck of his personal life, using his research as an escape, but this is distinct from his suffering somehow magically enabling or justifying his creative act.

The machinery Arlo uses to trigger the development of a separate universe is clearly indifferent to his personal history, intent, or internal state, and is available to anybody on the 'big wheel' who has the requisite knowledge and accesses.

Arlo's lack of self-knowledge, and his obliviousness to the risks he brings about, push him further away from any conventional expectations we have of God. But the possible existence of such a mundane mechanism for creating a new cosmos suggests that that God, their abilities, ethics, and motivations might not be knowable by us.

Notes

1   Zeeya, M. (2017). *A Big Bang In A Little Room: The Quest For New Universes.* NY: Basic Books.

11

Hell is the Absence of God

Ted Chiang

This is the story of a man named Neil Fisk, and how he came to love God. The pivotal event in Neil's life was an occurrence both terrible and ordinary: the death of his wife, Sarah. Neil was consumed with grief after she died, a grief that was excruciating not only because of its intrinsic magnitude, but because it also renewed and emphasized the previous pains of his life. Her death forced him to reexamine his relationship with God, and in doing so he began a journey that would change him forever.

Neil was born with a congenital abnormality that caused his left thigh to be externally rotated and several inches shorter than his right; the medical term for it was proximal femoral focus deficiency. Most people he met assumed God was responsible for this, but Neil's mother hadn't witnessed any visitations while carrying him; his condition was the result of improper limb development during the sixth week of gestation, nothing more. In fact, as far as Neil's mother was concerned, blame rested with his absent father, whose income might have made corrective surgery a possibility, although she never expressed this sentiment aloud.

As a child Neil had occasionally wondered if he was being punished by God, but most of the time he blamed his classmates in school for his unhappiness. Their nonchalant cruelty, their instinctive ability to locate the weaknesses in a victim's emotional armor, the way their own friendships were reinforced by their sadism: he recognized these as examples of human behavior, not divine. And although his classmates often used God's name in their taunts, Neil knew better than to blame Him for their actions.

But while Neil avoided the pitfall of blaming God, he never made the jump to loving Him; nothing in his upbringing or his personality led him to pray to God for strength or for relief. The assorted trials he faced growing up were accidental or human in origin, and he relied on strictly human resources to counter them. He became an adult who—like so many others—viewed God's actions in the abstract until they impinged upon his own life. Angelic visitations were events that befell other people, reaching him only via reports on the nightly news. His own life was entirely mundane; he worked as a superintendent for an upscale apartment building, collecting rent and performing repairs, and as far as he was concerned, circumstances were fully capable of unfolding, happily or not, without intervention from above.

This remained his experience until the death of his wife.

It was an unexceptional visitation, smaller in magnitude than most but no different in kind, bringing blessings to some and disaster to others. In this instance the angel was Nathanael, making an appearance in a downtown shopping district. Four miracle cures were effected: the elimination of carcinomas in two individuals, the regeneration of the spinal cord in a paraplegic, and the restoration of sight to a recently blinded person. There were also two miracles that were not cures: a delivery van, whose driver had fainted at the sight of the angel, was halted before it could overrun a busy sidewalk; another man was caught in a shaft of Heaven's light when the angel departed, erasing his eyes but ensuring his devotion.

Neil's wife, Sarah Fisk, had been one of the eight casualties. She was hit by flying glass when the angel's billowing curtain of flame shattered the storefront window of the café in which she was eating. She bled to death within minutes, and the other customers in the café—none of whom suffered even superficial injuries—could do nothing but listen to her cries of pain and fear, and eventually witness her soul's ascension toward Heaven.

Nathanael hadn't delivered any specific message; the angel's parting words, which had boomed out across the entire visitation site, were the typical *Behold the power of the Lord.* Of the eight casualties that day, three souls were accepted into Heaven and five were not, a closer ratio than the average for deaths by all causes. Sixty-two people received medical treatment for injuries ranging from slight concussions to ruptured eardrums to burns requiring skin grafts. Total property damage was estimated at $8.1 million, all of it excluded by private insurance companies due to the cause. Scores of people became devout worshipers in the wake of the visitation, either out of gratitude or terror.

Alas, Neil Fisk was not one of them.

After a visitation, it's common for all the witnesses to meet as a group and discuss how their common experience has affected their lives. The witnesses of Nathanael's latest visitation arranged such group meetings, and family members of those who had died were welcome, so Neil began attending. The meetings were held once a month in a basement room of a large church downtown; there were metal folding chairs arranged in rows, and in the back of the room was a table holding coffee and doughnuts. Everyone wore adhesive name tags made out in felt-tip pen.

While waiting for the meetings to start, people would stand around, drinking coffee, talking casually. Most people Neil spoke to assumed his leg was a result of the visitation, and he had to explain that he wasn't a witness, but rather the husband of one of the casualties. This didn't bother him particularly; he was used to explaining about his leg. What did bother him was the tone of the meetings themselves, when participants spoke about their reaction to the visitation: most of them talked about their newfound devotion to God, and they tried to persuade the bereaved that they should feel the same.

Neil's reaction to such attempts at persuasion depended on who was making it. When it was an ordinary witness, he found it merely irritating. When someone who'd received a miracle cure told him to love God, he had to restrain an impulse to strangle the person. But what he found most disquieting of all was hearing the same suggestion from a man named Tony Crane; Tony's wife had died in the visitation too, and he now projected an air of groveling with his every movement. In hushed, tearful tones he explained how he had accepted his role as one of God's subjects, and he advised Neil to do likewise.

Neil didn't stop attending the meetings—he felt that he somehow owed it to Sarah to stick with them—but he found another group to go to as well, one more compatible with his own feelings: a support group devoted to those who'd lost a loved one during a visitation, and were angry at God because of it. They met every other week in a room at the local community center, and talked about the grief and rage that boiled inside of them.

All the attendees were generally sympathetic to one another, despite differences in their various attitudes toward God. Of those who'd been devout before their loss, some struggled with the task of remaining so, while others gave up their devotion without a second glance. Of those who'd never been devout, some felt their position had been validated, while others were faced with the near impossible task of becoming devout now. Neil found himself, to his consternation, in this last category.

Like every other non-devout person, Neil had never expended much energy on where his soul would end up; he'd always assumed his destination was Hell, and he accepted that. That was the way of things, and Hell, after all, was not physically worse than the mortal plane.

It meant permanent exile from God, no more and no less; the truth of this was plain for anyone to see on those occasions when Hell manifested itself. These happened on a regular basis; the ground seemed to become transparent, and you could see Hell as if you were looking through a hole in the floor. The lost souls looked no different than the living, their eternal bodies resembling mortal ones. You couldn't communicate with them—their exile from God meant that they couldn't apprehend the mortal plane where His actions were still felt—but as long as the manifestation lasted you could hear them talk, laugh, or cry, just as they had when they were alive.

People varied widely in their reactions to these manifestations. Most devout people were galvanized, not by the sight of anything frightening, but at being reminded that eternity outside paradise was a possibility. Neil, by contrast, was one of those who were unmoved; as far as he could tell, the lost souls as a group were no unhappier than he was, their existence no worse than his in the mortal plane, and in some ways better: his eternal body would be unhampered by congenital abnormalities.

Of course, everyone knew that Heaven was incomparably superior, but to Neil it had always seemed too remote to consider, like wealth or fame or glamour. For people like him, Hell was where you went when you died, and he saw no point in restructuring his life in hopes of avoiding that. And since God hadn't previously played a role in Neil's life, he wasn't afraid of being exiled from God. The prospect of living without interference, living in a world where windfalls and misfortunes were never by design, held no terror for him.

Now that Sarah was in Heaven, his situation had changed. Neil wanted more than anything to be reunited with her, and the only way to get to Heaven was to love God with all his heart.

This is Neil's story, but telling it properly requires telling the stories of two other individuals whose paths became entwined with his. The first of these is Janice Reilly.

What people assumed about Neil had in fact happened to Janice. When Janice's mother was eight months pregnant with her, she lost control of the car she was driving and collided with a telephone pole during a sudden hailstorm, fists of ice dropping out of a clear blue sky and littering the road like a spill of giant ball bearings. She was sitting in her car, shaken but unhurt, when she saw a knot of silver flames—later identified as the angel Bardiel—float across the sky. The sight petrified her, but not so much that she didn't notice the peculiar settling sensation in her womb. A subsequent ultrasound revealed that the unborn Janice Reilly no longer had legs; flipper-like feet grew directly from her hip sockets.

Janice's life might have gone the way of Neil's, if not for what happened two days after the ultrasound. Janice's parents were sitting at their kitchen table, crying and asking what they had done to deserve this, when they received a vision: the saved souls of four deceased relatives appeared before them, suffusing the kitchen with a golden glow. The saved never spoke, but their beatific smiles induced a feeling of serenity in whoever saw them. From that moment on, the Reillys were certain that their daughter's condition was not a punishment.

As a result, Janice grew up thinking of her legless condition as a gift; her parents explained that God had given her a special assignment because He considered her equal to the task, and she vowed that she would not let Him down. Without pride or defiance, she saw it as her responsibility to show others that her condition did not indicate weakness, but rather strength.

As a child, she was fully accepted by her schoolmates; when you're as pretty, confident, and charismatic as she was, children don't even notice that you're in a wheelchair. It was when she was a teenager that she realized that the able-bodied people in her school were not the ones who most needed convincing. It was more important for her to set an example for other handicapped individuals, whether they had been touched by God or not, no matter where they lived. Janice began speaking before audiences, telling those with disabilities that they had the strength God required of them.

Over time she developed a reputation, and a following. She made a living writing and speaking, and established a nonprofit organization dedicated to promoting her message. People sent her letters thanking her for changing their lives, and receiving those gave her a sense of fulfillment of a sort that Neil had never experienced.

This was Janice's life up until she herself witnessed a visitation by the angel Rashiel. She was letting herself into her house when the tremors began; at first she thought they were of natural origin, although she didn't live in a geologically active area, and waited in the doorway for them to subside. Several seconds later she caught a glimpse of silver in the sky and realized it was an angel, just before she lost consciousness.

Janice awoke to the biggest surprise of her life: the sight of her two new legs, long, muscular, and fully functional.

She was startled the first time she stood up: she was taller than she expected. Balancing at such a height without the use of her arms was unnerving, and simultaneously feeling the texture of the ground through the soles of her feet made it positively bizarre. Rescue workers, finding her wandering down the street dazedly, thought she was in shock until she—marveling at her ability to face them at eye level—explained to them what had happened.

When statistics were gathered for the visitation, the restoration of Janice's legs was recorded as a blessing, and she was humbly grateful for her good fortune. It was at the first of the support group meetings that a feeling of guilt began to creep in. There Janice met two individuals with cancer who'd witnessed Rashiel's visitation, thought their cure was at hand, and been bitterly disappointed when they realized they'd been passed over. Janice found herself wondering, why had she received a blessing when they had not?

Janice's family and friends considered the restoration of her legs a reward for excelling at the task God had set for her, but for Janice, this interpretation raised another question. Did He intend for her to stop? Surely not; evangelism provided the central direction of her life, and there was no limit to the number of people who needed to hear her message. Her continuing to preach was the best action she could take, both for herself and for others.

Her reservations grew during her first speaking engagement after the visitation, before an audience of people recently paralyzed and now wheelchair-bound. Janice delivered her usual words of inspiration, assuring them that they had the strength needed for the challenges ahead; it was during the Q&A that she was asked if the restoration of her legs meant she had passed her test. Janice didn't know what to say; she could hardly promise them that one day their marks would be erased. In fact, she realized, any implication that she'd been rewarded could be interpreted as criticism of others who remained afflicted, and she didn't want that. All she could tell them was that she didn't know why she'd been cured, but it was obvious they found that an unsatisfying answer.

Janice returned home disquieted. She still believed in her message, but as far as her audiences were concerned, she'd lost her greatest source of credibility. How could she inspire others who were touched by God to see their condition as a badge of strength, when she no longer shared their condition?

She considered whether this might be a challenge, a test of her ability to spread His word. Clearly God had made her task more difficult than it was before; perhaps the restoration of her legs was an obstacle for her to overcome, just as their earlier removal had been.

This interpretation failed her at her next scheduled engagement. The audience was a group of witnesses to a visitation by Nathanael; she was often invited to speak to such groups in the hopes that those who suffered might draw encouragement from her. Rather than sidestep the issue, she began with an account of the visitation she herself had recently experienced. She explained that while it might appear she was a beneficiary, she was in fact facing her own challenge: like them, she was being forced to draw on resources previously untapped.

She realized, too late, that she had said the wrong thing. A man in the audience with a misshapen leg stood up and challenged her: was she seriously suggesting that the restoration of her legs was comparable to the loss of his wife? Could she really be equating her trials with her own?

Janice immediately assured him that she wasn't, and that she couldn't imagine the pain he was experiencing. But, she said, it wasn't God's intention that everyone be subjected to the same kind of trial, but only that each person face his or her own trial, whatever it might be. The difficulty of any trial was subjective, and there was no way to compare two individuals' experiences. And just as those whose suffering seemed greater than his should have compassion for him, so should he have compassion for those whose suffering seemed less.

The man was having none of it. She had received what anyone else would have considered a fantastic blessing, and she was complaining about it. He stormed out of the meeting while Janice was still trying to explain.

That man, of course, was Neil Fisk. Neil had had Janice Reilly's name mentioned to him for much of his life, most often by people who were convinced his misshapen leg was a sign from God. These people cited her as an example he should follow, telling him that her attitude was the proper response to a physical handicap. Neil couldn't deny that her leglessness was a far worse condition than his distorted femur. Unfortunately, he found her attitude so foreign that, even in the best of times, he'd never been able to learn anything from her. Now, in the depths of his grief and mystified as to why she had received a gift she didn't need, Neil found her words offensive.

In the days that followed, Janice found herself more and more plagued by doubts, unable to decide what the restoration of her legs meant. Was she being ungrateful for a gift she'd received? Was it both a blessing and a test? Perhaps it was a punishment, an indication that she had not performed her duty well enough. There were many possibilities, and she didn't know which one to believe.

There is one other person who played an important role in Neil's story, even though he and Neil did not meet until Neil's journey was nearly over. That person's name is Ethan Mead.

Ethan had been raised in a family that was devout, but not profoundly so. His parents credited God with their above-average health and their comfortable economic status, although they hadn't witnessed any visitations or received any visions; they simply trusted that God was, directly or indirectly, responsible for their good fortune. Their devotion had never been put to any serious test, and might not have withstood one; their love for God was based in their satisfaction with the status quo.

Ethan was not like his parents, though. Ever since childhood he'd felt certain that God had a special role for him to play, and he waited for a sign telling him what that role was. He'd liked to have become a preacher, but felt he hadn't any compelling testimony to offer; his vague feelings of expectation weren't enough. He longed for an encounter with the divine to provide him with direction.

He could have gone to one of the holy sites, those places where—for reasons unknown—angelic visitations occurred on a regular basis, but he felt that such an action would be presumptuous of him. The holy sites were usually the last resort of the desperate, those people seeking either a miracle cure to repair their bodies or a glimpse of Heaven's light to repair their souls, and Ethan was not desperate. He decided that he'd been set along his own course, and in time the reason for it would become clear. While waiting for that day, he lived his life as best he could: he worked as a librarian, married a woman named Claire, raised two children. All the while, he remained watchful for signs of a greater destiny.

Ethan was certain his time had come when he became witness to a visitation by Rashiel, the same visitation that—miles away—restored Janice Reilly's legs. Ethan was by himself when it happened; he was walking toward his car in the center of a parking lot, when the ground began to shudder. Instinctively he knew it was a visitation, and he assumed a kneeling position, feeling no fear, only exhilaration and awe at the prospect of learning his calling.

The ground became still after a minute, and Ethan looked around, but didn't otherwise move. Only after waiting for several more minutes did he rise to his feet. There was a large crack in the asphalt, beginning directly in front of him and following a meandering path down the street. The crack seemed to be pointing him in a specific direction, so he ran alongside it for several blocks until he encountered other survivors, a man and a woman climbing out of a modest fissure that had opened up directly beneath them. He waited with the two of them until rescuers arrived and brought them to a shelter.

Ethan attended the support group meetings that followed and met the other witnesses to Rashiel's visitation. Over the course of a few meetings, he became aware of certain patterns among the witnesses. Of course there were those who'd been injured and those who'd received miracle cures. But there were also those whose lives were changed in other ways: the man and woman he'd first met fell in love and were soon engaged; a woman who'd been pinned beneath a collapsed wall was inspired to become an EMT after being rescued. One business owner formed an alliance that averted her impending bankruptcy, while another whose business was destroyed saw it as a message that he change his ways. It seemed that everyone except Ethan had found a way to understand what had happened to them.

He hadn't been cursed or blessed in any obvious way, and he didn't know what message he was intended to receive. His wife, Claire, suggested that he consider the visitation a reminder that he appreciate what he had, but Ethan found that unsatisfying, reasoning that *every* visitation—no matter where it occurred—served that function, and the fact that he'd witnessed a visitation firsthand had to have greater significance. His mind was preyed upon by the idea that he'd missed an opportunity, that there was a fellow witness whom he was intended to meet but hadn't. This visitation had to be the sign he'd been waiting for; he couldn't just disregard it. But that didn't tell him what he was supposed to do.

Ethan eventually resorted to the process of elimination: he got hold of a list of all the witnesses, and crossed off those who had a clear interpretation of their experience, reasoning that one of those remaining must be the person whose fate was somehow intertwined with his. Among those who were confused or uncertain about the visitation's meaning would be the one he was intended to meet.

When he had finished crossing names off his list, there was only one left: JANICE REILLY.

In public Neil was able to mask his grief as adults are expected to, but in the privacy of his apartment, the floodgates of emotion burst open. The awareness of Sarah's absence would overwhelm him, and then he'd collapse on the floor and weep. He'd curl up into a ball, his body racked by hiccuping sobs, tears and mucus streaming down his face, the anguish coming in ever-increasing waves until it was more than he could bear, more intense than he'd have believed possible. Minutes or hours later it would leave, and he would fall asleep, exhausted. And the next morning he would wake up and face the prospect of another day without Sarah.

An elderly woman in Neil's apartment building tried to comfort him by telling him that the pain would lessen in time, and while he would never forget his wife, he would at least be able to move on. Then he would meet someone else one day and find happiness with her, and he would learn to love God and thus ascend to Heaven when his time came.

This woman's intentions were good, but Neil was in no position to find any comfort in her words. Sarah's absence felt like an open wound, and the prospect that someday he would no longer feel pain at her loss seemed not just remote, but a physical impossibility. If suicide would have ended his pain, he'd have done it without hesitation, but that would only ensure that his separation from Sarah was permanent.

The topic of suicide regularly came up at the support group meetings, and inevitably led to someone mentioning Robin Pearson, a woman who used to come to the meetings several months before Neil began attending. Robin's husband had been afflicted with stomach cancer during a visitation by the angel Makatiel. She stayed in his hospital room for days at a stretch, only for him to die unexpectedly when she was home doing laundry. A nurse who'd been present told Robin that his soul had ascended, and so Robin had begun attending the support group meetings.

Many months later, Robin came to the meeting shaking with rage. There'd been a manifestation of Hell near her house, and she'd seen her husband among the lost souls. She'd confronted the nurse, who admitted to lying in the hopes that Robin would learn to love God, so that at least she would be saved even if her husband hadn't been. Robin wasn't at the next meeting, and at the meeting after that the group learned she had committed suicide to rejoin her husband.

None of them knew the status of Robin's and her husband's relationship in the afterlife, but successes were known to happen; some couples had indeed been happily reunited through suicide. The support group had attendees whose spouses had descended to Hell, and they talked about being torn between wanting to remain alive and wanting to rejoin their spouses. Neil wasn't in their situation, but his first response when listening to them had been envy: if Sarah had gone to Hell, suicide would be the solution to all his problems.

This led to a shameful self-knowledge for Neil. He realized that if he had to choose between going to Hell while Sarah went to Heaven, or having both of them go to Hell together, he would choose the latter: he would rather she be exiled from God than separated from him. He knew it was selfish, but he couldn't change how he felt: he believed Sarah could be happy in either place, but he could only be happy with her.

Neil's previous experiences with women had never been good. All too often he'd begin flirting with a woman while sitting at a bar, only to have her remember an appointment elsewhere the moment he stood up and his shortened leg came into view. Once, a woman he'd been dating for several weeks broke off their relationship, explaining that while she herself didn't consider his leg a defect, whenever they were seen in public together other people assumed there must be something wrong with her for being with him, and surely he could understand how unfair that was to her?

Sarah had been the first woman Neil met whose demeanor hadn't changed one bit, whose expression hadn't flickered toward pity or horror or even surprise when she first saw his leg. For that reason alone it was predictable that Neil would become infatuated with her; by the time he saw all the sides of her personality, he'd completely fallen in love with her. And because his best qualities came out when he was with her, she fell in love with him too.

Neil had been surprised when Sarah told him she was devout. There weren't many signs of her devotion—she didn't go to church, sharing Neil's dislike for the attitudes of most people who attended—but in her own, quiet way she was grateful to God for her life. She never tried to convert Neil, saying that devotion would come from within or not at all. They rarely had any cause to mention God, and most of the time it would've been easy for Neil to imagine that Sarah's views on God matched his own.

This is not to say that Sarah's devotion had no effect on Neil. On the contrary, Sarah was far and away the best argument for loving God that he had ever encountered. If love of God had contributed to making her the person she was, then perhaps it did make sense. During the years that the two of them were married, his outlook on life improved, and it probably would have reached the point where he was thankful to God, if he and Sarah had grown old together.

Sarah's death removed that particular possibility, but it needn't have closed the door on Neil's loving God. Neil could have taken it as a reminder that no one can count on having decades left. He could have been moved by the realization that, had he died with her, his soul would've been lost and the two of them separated for eternity. He could have seen Sarah's death as a wake-up call, telling him to love God while he still had the chance.

Instead Neil became actively resentful of God. Sarah had been the greatest blessing of his life, and God had taken her away. Now he was expected to love Him for it? For Neil, it was like having a kidnapper demand love as ransom for his wife's return. Obedience he might have managed, but sincere, heartfelt love? That was a ransom he couldn't pay.

This paradox confronted several people in the support group. One of the attendees, a man named Phil Soames, correctly pointed out that thinking of it as a condition to be met would guarantee failure. You couldn't love God as a means to an end, you had to love Him for Himself. If your ultimate goal in loving God was a reunion with your spouse, you weren't demonstrating true devotion at all.

A woman in the support group named Valerie Tommasino said they shouldn't even try. She'd been reading a book published by the humanist movement; its members considered it wrong to love a God who inflicted such pain, and advocated that people act according to their own moral sense instead of being guided by the carrot and the stick. These were people who, when they died, descended to Hell in proud defiance of God.

Neil himself had read a pamphlet of the humanist movement; what he most remembered was that it had quoted the fallen angels. Visitations of fallen angels were infrequent, and caused neither good fortune nor bad; they weren't acting under God's direction, but just passing through the mortal plane as they went about their unimaginable business. On the occasions they appeared, people would ask them questions: Did they know God's intentions? Why had they rebelled? The fallen angels' reply was always the same: *Decide for yourselves. That is what we did. We advise you to do the same.*

Those in the humanist movement had decided, and if it weren't for Sarah, Neil would've made the identical choice. But he wanted her back, and the only way was to find a reason to love God.

Looking for any footing on which to build their devotion, some attendees of the support group took comfort in the fact that their loved ones hadn't suffered when God took them, but instead died instantly. Neil didn't even have that; Sarah had received horrific lacerations when the glass hit her. Of course, it could have been worse. One couple's teenage son had been trapped in a fire ignited by an angel's visitation, and received full-thickness burns over eighty percent of his body before rescue workers could free him; his eventual death was a mercy. Sarah had been fortunate by comparison, but not enough to make Neil love God.

Neil could think of only one thing that would make him give thanks to God, and that was if He allowed Sarah to appear before him. It would give him immeasurable comfort just to see her smile again; he'd never been visited by a saved soul before, and a vision now would have meant more to him than at any other point in his life.

But visions don't appear just because a person needs one, and none ever came to Neil. He had to find his own way toward God.

The next time he attended the support group meeting for witnesses of Nathanael's visitation, Neil sought out Benny Vasquez, the man whose eyes had been erased by Heaven's light. Benny didn't always attend because he was now being invited to speak at other meetings; few visitations resulted in an eyeless person, since Heaven's light entered the mortal plane only in the brief moments that an angel emerged from or reentered Heaven, so the eyeless were minor celebrities, and in demand as speakers to church groups.

Benny was now as sightless as any burrowing worm: not only were his eyes and sockets missing, his skull lacked even the space for such features, the cheekbones now abutting the forehead. The light that had brought his soul as close to perfection as was possible in the mortal plane had also deformed his body; it was commonly held that this illustrated the superfluity of physical bodies in Heaven. With the limited expressive capacity his face retained, Benny always wore a blissful, rapturous smile.

Neil hoped Benny could say something to help him love God. Benny described Heaven's light as infinitely beautiful, a sight of such compelling majesty that it vanquished all doubts. It constituted incontrovertible proof that God should be loved, an explanation that made it as obvious as 1+1=2. Unfortunately, while Benny could offer many analogies for the effect of Heaven's light, he couldn't duplicate that effect with his own words. Those who were already devout found Benny's descriptions thrilling, but to Neil, they seemed frustratingly vague. So he looked elsewhere for counsel.

Accept the mystery, said the minister of the local church. If you can love God even though your questions go unanswered, you'll be the better for it.

Admit that you need Him, said the popular book of spiritual advice he bought. When you realize that self-sufficiency is an illusion, you'll be ready.

Submit yourself completely and utterly, said the preacher on the television. Receiving torment is how you prove your love. Acceptance may not bring you relief in this life, but resistance will only worsen your punishment.

All of these strategies have proven successful for different individuals; any one of them, once internalized, can bring a person to devotion. But these are not always easy to adopt, and Neil was one who found them impossible.

Neil finally tried talking to Sarah's parents, which was an indication of how desperate he was; his relationship with them had always been tense. While they loved Sarah, they often chided her for not being demonstrative enough in her devotion, and they'd been shocked when she married a man who wasn't devout at all. For her part, Sarah had always considered her parents too judgmental, and their disapproval of Neil only reinforced her opinion. But now Neil felt he had something in common with them—after all, they were all mourning Sarah's loss—and so he visited them in their suburban colonial, hoping they could help him in his grief.

How wrong he was. Instead of sympathy, what Neil got from Sarah's parents was blame for her death. They'd come to this conclusion in the weeks after Sarah's funeral; they reasoned that she'd been taken to send him a message, and that they were forced to endure her loss solely because he hadn't been devout. They were now convinced that, his previous explanations notwithstanding, Neil's deformed leg was in fact God's doing, and if only he'd been properly chastened by it, Sarah might still be alive.

Their reaction shouldn't have come as a surprise: throughout Neil's life, people had attributed moral significance to his leg even though God wasn't responsible for it. Now that he'd suffered a misfortune for which God was unambiguously responsible, it was inevitable that someone would assume he deserved it. It was purely by chance that Neil heard this sentiment when he was at his most vulnerable, and it could have the greatest impact on him.

Neil didn't think his in-laws were right, but he began to wonder if he might not be better off if he did. Perhaps, he thought, it'd be better to live in a story where the righteous were rewarded and the sinners were punished, even if the criteria for righteousness and sinfulness eluded him, than to live in a reality where there was no justice at all. It would mean casting himself in the role of sinner, so it was hardly a comforting lie, but it offered one reward that his own ethics couldn't: believing it would reunite him with Sarah.

Sometimes even bad advice can point a man in the right direction. It was in this manner that his in-laws' accusations ultimately pushed Neil closer to God.

More than once when she was evangelizing, Janice had been asked if she ever wished she had legs, and she had always answered—honestly—no, she didn't. She was content as she was. Sometimes her questioner would point out that she couldn't miss what she'd never known, and she might feel differently if she'd been born with legs and lost them later on. Janice never denied that. But she could truthfully say that she felt no sense of being incomplete, no envy for people with legs; being legless was part of her identity. She'd never bothered with prosthetics, and had a surgical procedure been available to provide her with legs, she'd have turned it down. She had never considered the possibility that God might restore her legs.

One of the unexpected side effects of having legs was the increased attention she received from men. In the past she'd mostly attracted men with amputee fetishes or sainthood complexes; now all sorts of men seemed drawn to her. So when she first noticed Ethan Mead's interest in her, she thought it was romantic in nature; this possibility was particularly distressing since he was obviously married.

༼ Ethan had begun talking to Janice at the support group meetings, and then began attending her public speaking engagements. It was when he suggested they have lunch together that Janice asked him about his intentions, and he explained his theory. He didn't know *how* his fate was intertwined with hers; he knew only that it was. She was skeptical, but she didn't reject his theory outright. Ethan admitted that he didn't have answers for her own questions, but he was eager to do anything he could to help her find them. Janice cautiously agreed to help him in his search for meaning, and Ethan promised that he wouldn't be a burden. They met on a regular basis and talked about the significance of visitations. ༽

༼Meanwhile Ethan's wife, Claire, grew worried. Ethan assured her that he had no romantic feelings toward Janice, but that didn't alleviate her concerns. She knew that extreme circumstances could create a bond between individuals, and she feared that Ethan's relationship with Janice—romantic or not—would threaten their marriage. ༽

Ethan suggested to Janice that he, as a librarian, could help her do some research. Neither of them had ever heard of a previous instance where God had left His mark on a person in one visitation and removed it in another. Ethan looked for previous examples in hopes that they might shed some light on Janice's situation. There were a few instances of individuals receiving multiple miracle cures over their lifetimes, but their illnesses or disabilities had always been of natural origin, not given to them in a visitation. There was one anecdotal report of a man being struck blind for his sins, changing his ways, and later having his sight restored, but it was classified as an urban legend.

Even if that account had a basis in truth, it didn't provide a useful precedent for Janice's situation: her legs had been removed before her birth, and so couldn't have been a punishment for anything she'd done. Was it possible that Janice's condition had been a punishment for something her mother or father had done? Could her restoration mean they had finally earned her cure? She couldn't believe that.

If her deceased relatives were to appear in a vision, Janice would've been reassured about the restoration of her legs. The fact that they didn't made her suspect something was amiss, but she didn't believe that it was a punishment. Perhaps it had been a mistake, and she'd received a miracle meant for someone else; perhaps it was a test, to see how she would respond to being given too much. In either case, there seemed only one course of action: she would, with utmost gratitude and humility, offer to return her gift. To do so, she would go on a pilgrimage.

Pilgrims traveled great distances to visit the holy sites and wait for a visitation, hoping for a miracle cure. Whereas in most of the world one could wait an entire lifetime and never experience a visitation, at a holy site one might only wait months, sometimes weeks. Pilgrims knew that the odds of being cured were still poor; of those who stayed long enough to witness a visitation, the majority did not receive a cure. But they were often happy just to have seen an angel, and they returned home better able to face what awaited them, whether it be imminent death or life with a crippling disability. And of course, just living through a visitation made many people appreciate their situations; invariably, a small number of pilgrims were killed during each visitation.

Janice was willing to accept the outcome whatever it was. If God saw fit to take her, she was ready. If God removed her legs again, she would resume the work she'd always done. If God let her legs remain, she hoped she would receive the epiphany she needed to speak with conviction about her gift.

She hoped, however, that her miracle would be taken back and given to someone who truly needed it. She didn't suggest to anyone that they accompany her in hopes of receiving the miracle she was returning, feeling that that would've been presumptuous, but she privately considered her pilgrimage a request on behalf of those who were in need.

Her friends and family were confused at Janice's decision, seeing it as questioning God. As word spread, she received many letters from followers, variously expressing dismay, bafflement, and admiration for her willingness to make such a sacrifice.

As for Ethan, he was completely supportive of Janice's decision, and excited for himself. He now understood the significance of Rashiel's visitation for him: it indicated that the time had come for him to act. His wife, Claire, strenuously opposed his leaving, pointing out that he had no idea how long he might be away, and that she and their children needed him too.

It grieved him to go without her support, but he had no choice. Ethan would go on a pilgrimage, and at the next visitation, he would learn what God intended for him.

Neil's visit to Sarah's parents caused him to give further thought to his conversation with Benny Vasquez. While he hadn't gotten a lot out of Benny's words, he'd been impressed by the absoluteness of Benny's devotion. No matter what misfortune befell him in the future, Benny's love of God would never waver, and he would ascend to Heaven when he died. That fact offered Neil a very slim opportunity, one that had seemed so unattractive he hadn't considered it before; but now, as he was growing more desperate, it was beginning to look expedient.

Every holy site had its pilgrims who, rather than looking for a miracle cure, deliberately sought out Heaven's light. Those who saw it were always accepted into Heaven when they died, no matter how selfish their motives had been; there were some who wished to have their ambivalence removed so they could be reunited with their loved ones, and others who'd always lived a sinful life and wanted to escape the consequences.

In the past there'd been some doubt as to whether Heaven's light could indeed overcome *all* the spiritual obstacles to becoming saved. The debate ended after the case of Barry Larsen, a serial rapist and murderer who, while disposing of the body of his latest victim, witnessed an angel's visitation and saw Heaven's light. At Larsen's execution, his soul was seen ascending to Heaven, much to the outrage of his victims' families. Priests tried to console them, assuring them—on the basis of no evidence whatsoever—that Heaven's light must have subjected Larsen to many lifetimes' worth of penance in a moment, but their words provided little comfort.

For Neil this offered a loophole, an answer to Phil Soames's objection; it was the one way that he could love Sarah more than he loved God, and still be reunited with her. It was how he could be selfish and still get into Heaven. Others had done it; perhaps he could too. It might not be just, but at least it was predictable.

At an instinctual level, Neil was averse to the idea: it sounded like undergoing brainwashing as a cure for depression. He couldn't help but think that it would change his personality so drastically that he'd cease to be himself. Then he remembered that everyone in Heaven had undergone a similar transformation; the saved were just like the eyeless except that they no longer had bodies. This gave Neil a clearer image of what he was working toward: no matter whether he became devout by seeing Heaven's light or by a lifetime of effort, any ultimate reunion with Sarah couldn't re-create what they'd shared in the mortal plane. In Heaven, they would both be different, and their love for each other would be mixed with the love that all the saved felt for everything.

This realization didn't diminish Neil's longing for a reunion with Sarah. In fact it sharpened his desire, because it meant that the reward would be the same no matter what means he used to achieve it; the shortcut led to precisely the same destination as the conventional path.

On the other hand, seeking Heaven's light was far more difficult than an ordinary pilgrimage, and far more dangerous. Heaven's light leaked through only when an angel entered or left the mortal plane, and since there was no way to predict where an angel would first appear, light-seekers had to converge on the angel after its arrival and follow it until its departure. To maximize their chances of being in the narrow shaft of Heaven's light, they followed the angel as closely as possible during its visitation; depending on the angel involved, this might mean staying alongside the funnel of a tornado, the wavefront of a flash flood, or the expanding tip of a chasm as it split apart the landscape. Far more light-seekers died in the attempt than succeeded.

⌐Statistics about the souls of failed light-seekers were difficult to compile, since there were few witnesses to such expeditions, but the numbers so far were not encouraging. In sharp contrast to ordinary pilgrims who died without receiving their sought-after cure, of which roughly half were admitted into Heaven, every single failed light-seeker had descended to Hell. Perhaps only people who were already lost ever considered seeking Heaven's light, or perhaps death in such circumstances was considered suicide. In any case, it was clear to Neil that he needed to be ready to accept the consequences of embarking on such an attempt.⌐

The entire idea had an all-or-nothing quality to it that Neil found both frightening and attractive. He found the prospect of going on with his life, trying to love God, increasingly maddening. He might try for decades and not succeed. He might not even have that long; as he'd been reminded so often lately, visitations served as a warning to prepare one's soul, because death might come at any time. He could die tomorrow, and there was no chance of his becoming devout in the near future by conventional means.

It's perhaps ironic that, given his history of not following Janice Reilly's example, Neil took notice when she reversed her position. He was eating breakfast when he happened to see an item in the newspaper about her plans for a pilgrimage, and his immediate reaction was anger: how many blessings would it take to satisfy that woman? After considering it more, he decided that if she, having received a blessing, deemed it appropriate to seek God's assistance in coming to terms with it, then there was no reason he, having received such terrible misfortune, shouldn't do the same. And that was enough to tip him over the edge.

Holy sites were invariably in inhospitable places: one was an atoll in the middle of the ocean, while another was in the mountains at an elevation of twenty thousand feet. The one that Neil traveled to was in a desert, an expanse of cracked mud reaching miles in every direction; it was desolate, but it was relatively accessible and thus popular among pilgrims. The appearance of the holy site was an object lesson in what happened when the celestial and terrestrial realms touched: the landscape was variously scarred by lava flows, gaping fissures, and impact craters. Vegetation was scarce and ephemeral, restricted to growing in the interval after soil was deposited by floodwaters or whirlwinds and before it was scoured away again.

Pilgrims took up residence all over the site, forming temporary villages with their tents and camper vans; they all made guesses as to what location would maximize their chances of seeing the angel while minimizing the risk of injury or death. Some protection was offered by curved banks of sandbags, left over from years past and rebuilt as needed. A site-specific paramedic and fire department ensured that paths were kept clear so rescue vehicles could go where they were needed. Pilgrims either brought their own food and water or purchased them from vendors charging exorbitant prices; everyone paid a fee to cover the cost of waste removal.

Light-seekers always had off-road vehicles to better cross rough terrain when it came time to follow the angel. Those who could afford it drove alone; those who couldn't formed groups of two or three or four. Neil didn't want to be a passenger reliant on another person, nor did he want the responsibility of driving anyone else. This might be his final act on earth, and he felt he should do it alone. The cost of Sarah's funeral had depleted their savings, so Neil sold all his possessions in order to purchase a suitable vehicle: a pickup truck equipped with aggressively knurled tires and heavy-duty shock absorbers.

As soon as he arrived, Neil started doing what all the other light-seekers did: criss-crossing the site in his vehicle, trying to familiarize himself with its topography. It was on one of his drives around the site's perimeter that he met Ethan; Ethan flagged him down after his own car had stalled on his return from the nearest grocery store, eighty miles away. Neil helped him get his car started again, and then, at Ethan's insistence, followed him back to his campsite for dinner. Janice wasn't there when they arrived, having gone to visit some pilgrims several tents over; Neil listened politely while Ethan—heating prepackaged meals over a bottle of propane—began describing the events that had brought him to the holy site.

When Ethan mentioned Janice Reilly's name, Neil couldn't mask his surprise. He had no desire to speak with her again, and immediately excused himself to leave. He was explaining to a puzzled Ethan that he'd forgotten a previous engagement when Janice arrived.

She was startled to see Neil there, but asked him to stay. Ethan explained why he'd invited Neil to dinner, and Janice told him where she and Neil had met. Then she asked Neil what had brought him to the holy site. When he told them he was a light-seeker, Ethan and Janice immediately tried to persuade him to reconsider his plans. He might be committing suicide, said Ethan, and there were always better alternatives than suicide. Seeing Heaven's light was not the answer, said Janice; that wasn't what God wanted. Neil stiffly thanked them for their concern, and left.

During the weeks of waiting, Neil spent every day driving around the site; maps were available, and were updated after each visitation, but they were no substitute for driving the terrain yourself. On occasion he would see a light-seeker who was obviously experienced in off-road driving, and ask him—the vast majority of the light-seekers were men—for tips on negotiating a specific type of terrain. Some had been at the site for several visitations, having neither succeeded or failed at their previous attempts. They were glad to share tips on how best to pursue an angel, but never offered any personal information about themselves. Neil found the tone of their conversation peculiar, simultaneously hopeful and hopeless, and wondered if he sounded the same.

Ethan and Janice passed the time by getting to know some of the other pilgrims. Their reactions to Janice's situation were mixed: some thought her ungrateful, while others thought her generous. Most found Ethan's story interesting, since he was one of the very few pilgrims seeking something other than a miracle cure. For the most part, there was a feeling of camaraderie that sustained them during the long wait.

Neil was driving around in his truck when dark clouds began coalescing in the southeast, and the word came over the CB radio that a visitation had begun. He stopped the vehicle to insert earplugs into his ears and don his helmet; by the time he was finished, flashes of lightning were visible, and a light-seeker near the angel reported that it was Barakiel, and it appeared to be moving due north. Neil turned his truck east in anticipation and began driving at full speed.

There was no rain or wind, only dark clouds from which lightning emerged. Over the radio other light-seekers relayed estimates of the angel's direction and speed, and Neil headed northeast to get in front of it. At first he could gauge his distance from the storm by counting how long it took for the thunder to arrive, but soon the lightning bolts were striking so frequently that he couldn't match up the sounds with the individual strikes.

He saw the vehicles of two other light-seekers converging. They began driving in parallel, heading north, over a heavily cratered section of ground, bouncing over small ones and swerving to avoid the larger ones. Bolts of lightning were striking the ground everywhere, but they appeared to be radiating from a point south of Neil's position; the angel was directly behind him, and closing.

Even through his earplugs, the roar was deafening. Neil could feel his hair rising from his skin as the electric charge built up around him. He kept glancing in his rearview mirror, trying to ascertain where the angel was while wondering how close he ought to get.

His vision grew so crowded with afterimages that it became difficult to distinguish actual bolts of lightning among them. Squinting at the dazzle in his mirror, he realized he was looking at a continuous bolt of lightning, undulating but uninterrupted. He tilted the driver's-side mirror upward to get a better look, and saw the source of the lightning bolt, a seething, writhing mass of flames, silver against the dusky clouds: the angel Barakiel.

It was then, while Neil was transfixed and paralyzed by what he saw, that his pickup truck crested a sharp outcropping of rock and became airborne. The truck smashed into a boulder, the entire force of the impact concentrated on the vehicle's left front end, crumpling it like foil. The intrusion into the driver's compartment fractured both of Neil's legs and nicked his left femoral artery. Neil began, slowly but surely, bleeding to death.

He didn't try to move; he wasn't in physical pain at the moment, but he somehow knew that the slightest movement would be excruciating. It was obvious that he was pinned in the truck, and there was no way he could pursue Barakiel even if he weren't. Helplessly, he watched the lightning storm move further and further away.

As he watched it, Neil began crying. He was filled with a mixture of regret and self-contempt, cursing himself for ever thinking that such a scheme could succeed. He would have begged for the opportunity to do it over again, promised to spend the rest of his days learning to love God, if only he could live, but he knew that no bargaining was possible and he had only himself to blame. He apologized to Sarah for losing his chance at being reunited with her, for throwing his life away on a gamble instead of playing it safe. He prayed that she understood that he'd been motivated by his love for her, and that she would forgive him.

Through his tears he saw a woman running toward him, and recognized her as Janice Reilly. He realized his truck had crashed no more than a hundred yards from her and Ethan's campsite. There was nothing she could do, though; he could feel the blood draining out of him, and knew that he wouldn't live long enough for a rescue vehicle to arrive. He thought Janice was calling to him, but his ears were ringing too badly for him to hear anything. He could see Ethan Mead behind her, also starting to run toward him.

Then there was a flash of light and Janice was knocked off her feet as if she'd been struck by a sledgehammer. At first he thought she'd been hit by lightning, but then he realized that the lightning had already ceased. It was when she stood up again that he saw her face, steam rising from newly featureless skin, and he realized that Janice had been struck by Heaven's light.

Neil looked up, but all he saw were clouds; the shaft of light was gone. It seemed as if God were taunting him, not only by showing him the prize he'd lost his life trying to acquire while still holding it out of reach, but also by giving it to someone who didn't need it or even want it. God had already wasted a miracle on Janice, and now He was doing it again.

It was at that moment that another beam of Heaven's light penetrated the cloud cover and struck Neil, trapped in his vehicle.

Like a thousand hypodermic needles the light punctured his flesh and scraped across his bones. The light unmade his eyes, turning him into not a formerly sighted being, but a being never intended to possess vision. And in doing so the light revealed to Neil all the reasons he should love God.

He loved Him with an utterness beyond what humans can experience for one another. To say it was unconditional was inadequate, because even the word "unconditional" required the concept of a condition and such an idea was no longer comprehensible to him: every phenomenon in the universe was nothing less than an explicit reason to love Him. No circumstance could be an obstacle or even an irrelevancy, but only another reason to be grateful, a further inducement to love. Neil thought of the grief that had driven him to suicidal recklessness, and the pain and terror that Sarah had experienced before she died, and still he loved God, not in spite of their suffering, but because of it.

He renounced all his previous anger and ambivalence and desire for answers. He was grateful for all the pain he'd endured, contrite for not previously recognizing it as the gift it was, euphoric that he was now being granted this insight into his true purpose. He understood how life was an undeserved bounty, how even the most virtuous were not worthy of the glories of the mortal plane.

For him the mystery was solved, because he understood that everything in life is love, even pain, especially pain.

So minutes later, when Neil finally bled to death, he was truly worthy of salvation.

And God sent him to Hell anyway.

Ethan saw all of this. He saw Neil and Janice remade by Heaven's light, and he saw the pious love on their eyeless faces. He saw the skies become clear and the sunlight return. He was holding Neil's hand, waiting for the paramedics, when Neil died, and he saw Neil's soul leave his body and rise toward Heaven, only to descend into Hell.

Janice didn't see it, for by then her eyes were already gone. Ethan was the sole witness, and he realized that this was God's purpose for him: to follow Janice Reilly to this point and to see what she could not.

When statistics were compiled for Barakiel's visitation, it turned out that there had been a total of ten casualties, six among light-seekers and four among ordinary pilgrims. Nine pilgrims received miracle cures; the only individuals to see Heaven's light were Janice and Neil. There were no statistics regarding how many pilgrims had felt their lives changed by the visitation, but Ethan counted himself among them.

Upon returning home, Janice resumed her evangelism, but the topic of her speeches has changed. She no longer speaks about how the physically handicapped have the resources to overcome their limitations; instead she, like the other eyeless, speaks about the unbearable beauty of God's creation. Many who used to draw inspiration from her are disappointed, feeling they've lost a spiritual leader. When Janice had spoken of the strength she had as an afflicted person, her message was rare, but now that she's eyeless, her message is commonplace. She doesn't worry about the reduction in her audience, though, because she has complete conviction in what she evangelizes.

Ethan quit his job and became a preacher so that he too could speak about his experiences. His wife, Claire, couldn't accept his new mission and ultimately left him, taking their children with her, but Ethan was willing to continue alone. He's developed a substantial following by telling people what happened to Neil Fisk. He tells people that they can no more expect justice in the afterlife than in the mortal plane, but he doesn't do this to dissuade them from worshiping God; on the contrary, he encourages them to do so. What he insists on is that they not love God under a misapprehension, that if they wish to love God, they be prepared to do so no matter what His intentions. God is not just, God is not kind, God is not merciful, and understanding that is essential to true devotion.

As for Neil, although he is unaware of any of Ethan's sermons, he would understand their message perfectly. His lost soul is the embodiment of Ethan's teachings.

For most of its inhabitants, Hell is not that different from Earth; its principal punishment is the regret of not having loved God enough when alive, and for many that's easily endured. For Neil, however, Hell bears no resemblance whatsoever to the mortal plane. His eternal body has well-formed legs, but he's scarcely aware of them; his eyes have been restored, but he can't bear to open them. Just as seeing Heaven's light gave him an awareness of God's presence in all things in the mortal plane, so it has made him aware of God's absence in all things in Hell. Everything Neil sees, hears, or touches causes him distress, and unlike in the mortal plane this pain is not a form of God's love, but a consequence of His absence. Neil is experiencing more anguish than was possible when he was alive, but his only response is to love God.

Neil still loves Sarah, and misses her as much as he ever did, and the knowledge that he came so close to rejoining her only makes it worse. He knows his being sent to Hell was not a result of anything he did; he knows there was no reason for it, no higher purpose being served. None of this diminishes his love for God. If there were a possibility that he could be admitted to Heaven and his suffering would end, he would not hope for it; such desires no longer occur to him.

Neil even knows that by being beyond God's awareness, he is not loved by God in return. This doesn't affect his feelings either, because unconditional love asks nothing, not even that it be returned.

And though it's been many years that he has been in Hell, beyond the awareness of God, he loves Him still. That is the nature of true devotion.

ↄ Important

Story Notes for Hell is the Absence of God

Ted Chiang

The idea that life is unfair presumes the notion of fairness; where do we get our notions of fairness and justice and moral desert? It's been suggested that, from an evolutionary perspective, our sense of morality arose because the strategy of reciprocal altruism—where individuals reward each other for prosocial actions and punish each other for antisocial ones—provides a selective advantage.[1] This theory jibes with my own thinking, which is that our belief that life should be fair is a kind of anthropomorphic projection onto the universe as a whole: we expect the universe to behave the way people do.

If the universe rewards us when we're good and punishes us when we're bad, our lives make sense. But if we're punished even when we're being good, we need an explanation. Under polytheism, there's an easy one: some deities don't like us or have goals that are opposed to ours, and in the same way that we have to deal with assholes at work, we have to deal with these asshole deities. Under monotheism, however, an explanation is harder to find: why does the same deity that rewards us for being good also punish us when we haven't done anything wrong?

A common answer is to claim that we should think of our relationship with God as being similar to a child's relationship to their parent; note that the Lord's Prayer begins with "Our Father in heaven." This is a tempting analogy, not only because God supposedly created us the way parents create their children, but because when we were very young, we imagined our parents as all powerful. So when God punishes us for no apparent reason, maybe it's because we don't understand how this punishment is ultimately in our best interest, the same way that children can't appreciate that the discipline their parents apply is essential to making them good adults.

Compared to other human relationships, the parent/child relationship is unusually asymmetric, up to and including the fact that the child did not voluntarily enter into it and has no real option of leaving. And while we think it's acceptable to impose such conditions on a child, we wouldn't want them imposed upon us as adults. Which means that if our relationship to God is similar to a child's relationship to a parent, it puts us into a position that we would otherwise consider intolerable: we are forced to live under a system of rules that we're incapable of understanding. Ask why your baby was born with cystic fibrosis, and the only answer you get is that God works in mysterious ways, that his divine plan is beyond our comprehension, i.e. you'll understand when you're older.

There's a legal maxim that says "justice delayed is justice denied," which means that if a court doesn't provide justice within a reasonable amount of time, it's no better than if the court does nothing at all. Now consider the religious assertion that everyone will get their just rewards and punishments in the afterlife. Some people find that comforting, but I think it can also be disquieting. Following such a religion means accepting a cosmic system of morality that runs contrary to everything we think we know; it's saying that our moral intuition is profoundly unreliable. And that's one of the things I wanted to investigate with "Hell is the Absence of God": if you believe that things which feel unjust are actually just, precisely how far are you willing to take that? Neil being sent to Hell feels unjust, but is it really any worse than other things that religions regularly expect us to accept? If cystic fibrosis is actually compatible with divine justice, can we be certain of anything?

Notes

1 Trivers, R. L. (1971). The Evolution of Reciprocal Altruism. *The Quarterly Review of Biology*, 46(1), 35–57; Wright, R. (1994). *The Moral Animal: Evolutionary psychology and everyday life*, New York: Pantheon Books.

Concluding Ventilation

Helen De Cruz, Johan De Smedt, and Eric Schwitzgebel

Helen, Johan, and Eric met again in a conference hotel bar, three years later.

"They are lovely stories," said Johan, running a finger along the edge of the manuscript. "Truly."

"They are, and so many possibilities for the cover," said Helen. "Should I draw a seaside resort with diverse aliens? A weeping scientist creating a baby universe? A woman calligraphing a new maintenance spell on an old filtration machine?"

"But?" nudged Eric, eyeing Johan.

Johan laid his hand atop the stack of stories, meeting first Eric's gaze, then Helen's. "Okay. The first round's on me if you'll both honestly answer this question. What philosophical knowledge do you now have, after having read these stories, which you didn't have before?"

"I'm not sure that's a fair—" began Helen.

"This might require more than one cocktail," said Eric simultaneously. "I must think!" He waved his arm high toward the server across the room.

Johan smiled. "That it's a difficult question is already a bad sign for your view."

The server approached. Eric ordered the frilliest cocktails on the menu for the three of them, a small glass of maraschino cherries on the side ("since," he said, pointing to Johan, "this gentleman is paying"), and extra nuts.[1] "I'll start easy. Being generally ignorant in philosophy of religion, I'd been unaware of the concept of a *sensus divinitatis,* the hypothetical almost sensory knowledge of God. Hudson's story helped me see how that might work."

"A weak answer," said Johan. "You hardly need a whole story for that. A paragraph summation will do. I'm happy to allow that fiction can provide a small amount of philosophical information of that sort."

"But Eric knows it better and differently than he would have known it just by reading a paragraph," interjected Helen. "In fact, he probably *has* encountered a paragraph or a few pages on the *sensus divinitatis* before, in his thirty-plus years of reading philosophy, but it wasn't vivid, it wasn't memorable, it didn't stick."

"And now it has stuck," said Johan. "But Eric will forever think of Hudson's demon when the issue arises, and that will needlessly color his thinking. He'll now pair it in his mind with the less likely *sensus daemoniaci,* creating a small but pointless obstacle to his appreciating the *sensus* in its more common and less demon-ridden understanding."

"I agree it was a weak start," conceded Eric. "Really, I'd rather cut away your question at its root. The presupposition behind your question—that the most important philosophical knowledge is expressible in a summary list of expository statements about what you have learned—that presupposition is exactly what prevents you from properly appreciating the philosophical value of stories, including science fiction stories."

"So, you think you've attained some ineffable, inexpressible knowledge instead?" said Helen. "That's an even weaker reply. Let me try a different angle. What these stories give you isn't theoretical knowledge about philosophical theses but rather imaginative knowledge about what it would be like to live a certain way or to be a certain sort of person. No philosophical exposition could fully express what it's like to reject a high-ranking position under a violent monarch, as in de Bodard's story. How would it feel to be a lawyer trapped in a competitive cycle of cognitive enhancement, as in Liu's story, or an almost accidental creator of a new universe, as in Rose's story? I can't express it in words, but after reading the stories I can imaginatively appreciate these possibilities much better. These narratives have changed me. They've changed me in a way that reading a summary list of positions would not."

"Like a profoundly moving concert?" Johan replied. "Must we relive the conversation we had three years ago? Am I about to disappear in a pink puff of smoke?" He raised his hands, glancing from one to the other as if needing to reassure himself of his continued bodily existence.[2]

Helen shook her head. "No, not like a great concert, or not only like that. Vividly imagining these possibilities through fiction has improved my philosophical acumen in a particular, transformative way.[3] Some possibilities you can fully understand only by living through them, like being a parent, or living in slavery. Experiences like that transform your vision of the world. They change the lens through which you see things, in a way that no philosophical exposition ever could. Fiction probably can't give you a full understanding either, but it can bring you partway there, if you allow yourself to vividly imagine it, becoming fully immersed."

"Okay, Helen, suppose I allow that," said Johan. "I can now better imagine what it would be like to be a dragon's child, or an alien-hating terrorist, or the pilot of a whale-ship. After reading Samatar's story, I can better imagine a world of benevolent nanobots that carry my culture forward and transform me into a godmachine. What's the great use of that? Probably no future human will ever actually experience any of these things. We will live our ordinary, mundane lives here on ordinary, mundane Earth and then go extinct, maybe before too long and by our own doing. If we're going to imagine lives, why not stick with ordinary fiction about ordinary lives instead of these science fictional fantasies? They're lovely fantasies! I'm glad I read them. I'm proud of the fact that we solicited such great stories and brought this collection together, but they are not philosophy. These stories are a wonderful *escape* from philosophy."

Helen laid her hand on Johan's. "And now I'm wondering, what if we lived in a world where technology could help us find or even create our perfect soulmates, as in Baker's story? Would my own perfect soulmate be someone I agreed with or disagreed with on these matters?"

"See the trouble these fictions are causing!" said Johan, in the heat of the moment forgetting his own fictional status. "Our relationship is in the real world. Why compare it with some unrealistic fantasy? That's no better than comparing it with Snow White and Prince Charming. Such fantasies confuse and mislead more than they inform."

The server arrived with three colorful cocktails. Her green sequined dress and bright golden serving tray expressed, Eric would maintain, the hotel's distinctive philosophy of hospitality. "Johan, not only are you wrong about the philosophical merit of these stories," Eric said, "but if we include such a statement in our Concluding Ventilation, we risk upsetting our publisher. The editors at Bloomsbury are hoping that philosophy instructors will assign this book to students in undergraduate courses with course titles like 'Science Fiction and Philosophy.'"

Johan looked skeptically at the flamboyant strawberry daiquiri that the server had set on the table in front of him. Clearing his throat, he announced, "To all students who have been assigned this book, I say: You have been tricked! I hope you enjoyed these stories, but you have probably learned much less philosophy than if you had taken a different course."

"Hold that thought!" said Eric, downing half of his pink Cadillac margarita in a few big gulps.

Helen began arranging a small pyramid of maraschino cherries on a paper napkin. "Johan, if you accept that ordinary fiction can help you better imagine and understand the lives of other people who might be culturally or socially distant from you, then why not grant that science fiction can do the same? Except that science fiction stretches your imagination and understanding because it explores possible worlds that can be very different from our ordinary world. Science fiction deals with the same kinds of possibilities, admittedly sometimes far-fetched, that philosophers also consider in their thought experiments. For example, philosophers have devised thought experiments about empathy, such as whether you should save a drowning child even though it might ruin your new shoes.[4] Howard-Snyder takes this further by presenting an extreme version that distills and displays the implicit commitments of a worldview in which the children of acquaintances are just as important to you as your own children. And note that a real-world philosopher, Mozi[5], has defended such a position. Or consider the philosophical question of whether our psychological point of view is separable from our sensory point of view. Philosophers from different traditions, such as Zhuangzi[6], Maurice Merleau-Ponty[7], and Andy Clark[8], have considered whether our cognition is embodied—in other words, whether our thinking is done by more than just our brains. Schoenberg's story takes that question to the next level by radically separating the psychological and sensory points of view." Helen placed a single peanut neatly atop her pyramid of cherries. "Reading her story helps you think better about what it is to have a point of view. Stories expand our imaginative capacities, and the insights we get from them transform and improve our philosophical thinking. Science fiction is especially good at this. Like expository philosophy, science fiction is constrained only by our concepts and imagination. Both kinds of writing, in their different ways, sharpen our understanding by exploring the boundaries of the possible."

"For entertainment, that's great," said Johan. "Such fantasies are as imaginative and useless and entertaining as your cherry and peanut tower, the possibility of which I confess would never have crossed my mind were it not right here in front of me, in all its glorious eccentricity. Look, a story shows us only one way things might play out, and not always the likeliest way. Stories are subject to the demands of fiction. We want fun characters and an entertaining plot, not the most plausible characters and the most likely outcomes. We want a pyramid of cherries, not a bowl of oatmeal. In Silcox's story, for instance, we experience the point of view of a fascist who is disgusted by everyone different from him. It's an exciting read, and we enjoy seeing him get his comeuppance. But is that representative of the nature of bigotry? People already tend too much to think of bigots as basically hateful fascists like Silcox's protagonist. That's an attractive way to think, emotionally, since we know that *we* aren't like that. But if we're really interested in understanding bigotry, we'd be better served by thinking more broadly about bigotry, including subtler types that are more common and which we might, after reading a good expository treatment, be better prepared to discover in ourselves."

"Johan, will you drink that daiquiri? I hope that was part of the deal we made." Eric pointed at Johan's untouched glass while finishing the last swig of his own.

"If inebriation can help me sustain this conversation, I will." Johan dutifully drank.

"Science fiction, alcohol, and philosophy have something in common," said Eric. "They change the structure of your thinking. What's great about philosophy? Some people love philosophy because they think it reveals truths about the fundamental structure of the universe, which they wouldn't otherwise have known. Others love the combat of philosophical argument or the beauty of grand systems. But what I love most about philosophy is its capacity to produce doubt and wonder, its tendency to upset my mundane ways of thinking and show me that things could be different from how I've always assumed they would be. Might the world be a dream[9] or a computer simulation[10]? Probably not, but can I 100% rule this out?[11] Might many of the ethical views I ordinarily take for granted simply be my contingent cultural inheritance, which reasonable people from very different backgrounds might entirely reject? The society I imagine, the god or the atheism I prefer, my understanding what it is to be a person—all of these can be thrown into doubt, and will be thrown into doubt, by good philosophy. Philosophy at its best fills us with uncertainty, awe, and wonder. Our parochial assumptions crack. Spend a day engaged with the thoughts of a great philosopher whose worldview and foundational assumptions differ from your own, and you will emerge thinking differently, more expansively and more reflectively, than you had been thinking before. Even mundane facts—like that you have hands and will not disappear in a pink puff of smoke—become sources of fascination and inquiry."

Helen plucked the topmost peanut and cherry from her pyramid and popped them in her mouth. "What if God is the author of evil? Philosophers of religion, such as John Hick[12] have proposed this. But it can be difficult to wrap your head around this if you've grown up in a tradition where God is seen as an all-good being. A story like Chiang's helps you start to imagine different forms of God who might thoughtlessly or intentionally or incomprehensibly cause our suffering." She lifted another cherry, gazed briefly at it, and bit it in half. "Dry exposition couldn't do that half as well."

"Wait a minute, Eric," said Johan. "Why, on your view, do you still need science fiction? If you're struck with wonder reading Descartes' *Meditations* and then start doubting the existence of an external world, why would you still need science fiction such as *The Matrix* trilogy to achieve the same effect? We already have Hannah Arendt to help us understand how people can be lured into supporting awful regimes.[13] Do we need Nikel's story to help us see how they can then betray those regimes? What's distinct about science fiction?"

"It's not distinct!" Eric replied. "That's my point. Science fiction and expository philosophy can deliver exactly the same doubt and wonder, exactly the same expansion of the mind. Science fiction works in a way that is entirely continuous with the imaginative exercises of great philosophers of the past who were not constrained, as most of our colleagues at this APA are, to writing philosophy in the form of expository arguments. Take Ibn Tufayl[14], who tells the story of Hayy, a boy who grows up on an island, raised by gazelles. He learns about the world around him through observation and reason, and basically restates Aristotelian physics and metaphysical principles. Or take Rousseau's *Julie, or the New Heloise*[15], which is at first sight an epistolary novel, but it is also a discussion about authenticity, especially moral authenticity. Eighteenth-century readers believed the characters in this novel were real, but we now read this as a great work of philosophy."

"I can see why you wanted to impair my judgment with alcohol before delivering these tawdry arguments, Eric! Your feeling of wonder and Helen's feeling of having been transformed, which I suspect you've both overstated, might be a *side effect* of philosophical thinking, which philosophy sometimes shares with science fiction. But doubts of this sort—especially doubts about whether you're dreaming or living inside a computer simulation—they are signs of philosophy's failure, not its success."

The three of them argued late into the night, never reaching agreement, an ending that Eric found wonderful, Johan disappointing, and Helen tantalizing.

Notes

1   Oh sheesh, not this issue again! See endnote 10 of the *Introductory Dispute*.
2   G.E. Moore famously argued that he could prove the existence of an external world by holding up his hands and saying "here is one hand" and "here is another": Moore, G.E. (1939). Proof of an external world. *Proceedings of the British Academy, 25*, 273–300. However, it remains unclear how well the proof works when the hands belong to a fictional character.
3   See L.A. Paul (2014). *Transformative experience.* Oxford: Oxford University Press.
4   Singer, P. (1972). Famine, affluence, and morality. *Philosophy and Public Affairs*, 1(3), 229–243.
5   Mozi (5th/4th c. BCE/2009). *The Mozi* (Ian Johnston, trans.). Hong Kong: Chinese University of Hong Kong Press.
6   Zhuangzi (3rd c. BCE/2020). *Zhuangzi: The complete writings* (B. Ziporyn, trans.). Indianapolis: Hackett.
7   Merleau-Ponty, M. (1962). *Phenomenology of perception* (C. Smith, trans). London: Routledge and Kegan Paul.
8   Clark, A. (1997). *Being there. Putting brain, body, and world together again.* Cambridge, MA: MIT Press.
9   Descartes, R. (1641/1984). Meditations on first philosophy. In: *The philosophical writings of Descartes*, Vol II (J. Cottingham, R. Stoothoff & D. Murdoch, trans). 1–62, Cambridge: Cambridge University Press.

10 Bostrom, N. (2003). Are we living in a computer simulation? *Philosophical Quarterly, 53*(211), 243–255.

11 Non-fictional Eric argues that it's reasonable to regard it as about 99% likely that the world is approximately how you think it is, and 1% likely that you're dreaming, or living in a computer simulation, or in some other radically skeptical scenario. See Schwitzgebel, E. (2017). 1% Skepticism. *Noûs, 51*(2), 271–290.

12 Hick, J. (1966). *Evil and the god of love.* London: Macmillan.

13 Arendt, H. (1963). *Eichmann in Jerusalem. A report on the banality of evil.* New York: Viking Press.

14 Ibn Tufayl (12th c./2009). *Hayy Ibn Yaqzan, a philosophical tale* (L.E. Goodman, ed. and trans.). Chicago: University of Chicago Press.

15 Rousseau, J.-J. (1761/1997). *Julie, or the new Heloise. Letters of two lovers who live in a small town at the foot of the Alps.* (Philip Stewart and Jean Vache, trans.). Hanover and London: University Press of New England.

List of Contributors

David John Baker is a philosophy professor at the University of Michigan, where he studies the conceptual foundations of modern physics. He has defended the view that space and time are as real as material objects, and that there is no fundamental difference between your left hand and your right hand. He has held fellowships from the National Science Foundation, and in 2010 he was awarded the James Cushing Prize in the History and Philosophy of Physics. His recent stories have appeared in *A E: The Canadian Review of Science Fiction, Escape Pod, Crowded Magazine,* and the PS Publishing anthology *Catastrophia*; his earlier fiction was the recipient of the Writers of the Future and Phobos awards. Visit him online at www-personal.umich. edu/~djbaker.

Ted Chiang's fiction has won four Hugo, four Nebula, and four Locus Awards, and has been reprinted in *Best American Short Stories*. His first collection *Stories of Your Life and Others* has been translated into twenty-one languages, and the title story was the basis for the Oscar-nominated film *Arrival* starring Amy Adams. His second collection *Exhalation* was chosen by *The New York Times* as one of the 10 Best Books of 2019.

Aliette de Bodard writes speculative fiction: she has won three Nebula Awards, a Locus Award and four British Science Fiction Association Awards, and was a double Hugo finalist for 2019 (Best Series and Best Novella). She is the author of the Dominion of the Fallen series, set in a turn-of-the-century Paris devastated by a magical war, which comprises *The House of Shattered Wings, The House of Binding Thorns,* and *The House of Sundering Flames* (July 2019, Gollancz/JABberwocky Literary Agency). Her short story collection *Of Wars, and Memories, and Starlight* is out from Subterranean Press. She lives in Paris.

Helen De Cruz holds the Danforth Chair in the Humanities at Saint Louis University. Her current research is on meta-ethics, on the question of what archaeological evidence can bring to the study of the evolution of morality. Another current research interest is how fiction and other media can contribute to the study of philosophy. Her most recent books include *Religious Disagreement* (Cambridge) and *The Challenge of Evolution to Religion* (Cambridge, co-authored with Johan De Smedt); her book *Philosophy illustrated: 42 Thought Experiments to Broaden your Mind* is forthcoming with Oxford University Press.

Johan De Smedt is Postdoctoral Fellow at Saint Louis University. He currently works on evolutionary ethics and religious pluralism. His most recent book is *The Challenge of Evolution to Religion* (Cambridge, co-authored with Helen De Cruz).

Frances Howard-Snyder is a philosophy professor at Western Washington University. Her research interests focus on ethics, philosophy of religion, and philosophy of fiction. She has published short fiction at *Halfway Down the Stairs, The Magnolia Review, Oxford Studies in Philosophy of Religion*, and other places.

Hud Hudson is a professor of philosophy at Western Washington University, where he works primarily in the areas of metaphysics, philosophy of religion, and the history of philosophy. An award-winning teacher and scholar, he is the author of *A Grotesque in the Garden* (Eerdmans), *The Fall and Hypertime* (Oxford), *The Metaphysics of Hyperspace* (Oxford), *A Materialist Metaphysics of the Human Person* (Cornell), and *Kant's Compatibilism* (Cornell).

Ken Liu (http://kenliu.name) is an American author of speculative fiction. A winner of the Nebula, Hugo, and World Fantasy awards, he wrote *The Dandelion Dynasty*, a silkpunk epic fantasy series (starting with *The Grace of Kings*), as well as *The Paper Menagerie and Other Stories* and *The Hidden Girl and Other Stories*. Prior to becoming a full-time writer, Liu worked as a software engineer, corporate lawyer, and litigation consultant. Liu frequently speaks at conferences and universities on a variety of topics, including futurism, cryptocurrency, history of technology, bookmaking, the mathematics of origami, and other subjects of his expertise.

Wendy Nikel is a speculative fiction author with a degree in elementary education, a fondness for road trips, and a terrible habit of forgetting where she's left her cup of tea. Her short fiction has been published by *Analog, Nature, Podcastle,* and elsewhere. Her time travel novella series, beginning with *The Continuum,* is available from World Weaver Press. For more info, visit https://wendynikel.com/.

Christopher Mark Rose is senior professional staff at Johns Hopkins University Applied Physics Laboratory and an electrical engineer for NASA missions. His avionics firmware has flown on the Van Allen Probes, Parker Solar Probe, and soon with DART, the Double Asteroid Redirection Test. He is a winner of the Baltimore Science Fiction Society's Amateur Writing Contest, and a founder of Charm City Spec, Baltimore's premiere reading series in speculative fiction. His fiction has appeared in *Escape Pod, Interzone,* and *DreamForge*. He hopes his stories are affecting, humane, and concerned with large questions.

Sofia Samatar is the author of the novels *A Stranger in Olondria* and *The Winged Histories*, the short story collection, *Tender*, and *Monster Portraits*, a collaboration with her brother, the artist Del Samatar. Her work has received several honors, including the Astounding Award, the British Fantasy Award, and the World Fantasy Award. She teaches Arabic literature, African literature, and speculative fiction at James Madison University.

Lisa Schoenberg is Associate Professor of Philosophy at Slippery Rock University of Pennsylvania. Her research interests include philosophy of art, ethics of technology, and philosophy of education. She has published on the aesthetics of the art museum and the pedagogy of critical thinking.

Eric Schwitzgebel is Professor of Philosophy at University of California at Riverside and cooperating member of UCR's program in Speculative Fiction and Cultures of Science. His most recent book, *A Theory of Jerks and Other Philosophical Misadventures*, blends philosophy, psychology, cosmology, science fiction, and personal narrative. He has published philosophical short fiction in *Clarkesworld* and *F&SF*, nonfiction philosophy in *Philosophical Review* and *Noûs*, empirical psychology in *Cognition* and *Mind & Language*, and op-eds in the *Los Angeles Times* and *Salon*. He blogs at The Splintered Mind.

Mark Silcox is professor and chair of Humanities and Philosophy at the University of Central Oklahoma. His most recent research focuses on literary aesthetics and theories of distributive justice. His science fiction novel *The Face on the Mountain* was published in 2015, and *A Defense of Simulated Experience*, a philosophical monograph, came out in 2019.

Index

Acclimation Center 134, 136, 140
Adams, Richard 98
action 153
addiction 184
"Adjoiners" (Schoenberg) 12, 35–48
   story notes 49–51
aliens 133–4, 135, 136, 138, 140, 145,
   146
ambiguous utopia 71
Ancient China 120
angels 210, 213, 219, 224, 225, 227,
   228
Animal Intra-Mental Manipulation
   Study 36–9, 40–2, 46–7
animals 167–8. *See also* dogs; eagles;
   horses
Arendt, Hannah 239
Aristotle 95
artificial brains 83, 85
atheism 163
Atwood, Margaret 7
authenticity 51

Barakiel 227, 228, 230
Battlestar Galactica (Moore) 155
beliefs 163–4
Bentham, Jeremy 150, 192
Bhagavad Gītā 153
Big Bang 195, 199, 293
Big Bang In A Little Room, A (Zeeya)
   205, 206
Bioshock (Irrational Games) 98
birds. *See* eagles
Blazing World (Cavendish) 96
bodies 80, 81–2, 88, 178
Boehm, Christopher 95
Borges, Jorge Luis 156
Bostrom, Nick 15, 241
brain boosters 18–20, 21, 22–30
brains, artificial 83, 85

breathing 84
Brinker's World 134, 135
Brothers Karamazov (Dostoyevsky)
   153
Bublitz, J.C. 50
Buddhism 154
Burke, Edmund 12

cancer 79, 213, 217
Categorical Imperative 191
Cavendish, Margaret 96
children
   "eye of the needle, The" (Howard-
      Snyder) 176
   "God on a bad night" (Rose) 195,
      196, 197, 202, 205, 206
   "Out of a dragon's womb"
      (Bodard) 101, 103, 104,
      106, 107, 115, 117, 119, 120
   "Whale fall" (Nikel) 124
China 120
choice 120–1
cognition 238
cognitive enhancement devices
   (boosters) 18–20, 21, 22–30
collective unconscious 79
community 120
compassion 87
compatibilism 71–2
congenital abnormalities 209, 212
consciousness 79, 83, 91
consent 50, 51
conservatism 12
constellations 53, 65, 70
continuity 79, 91
copyright 28
cosmogenesis 203, 206
cosmology 205, 206
cramming 42–3, 44–5, 51
creation 199, 203–4, 205–6, 230

crime 43, 49, 51
cruelty 103–4, 112, 115, 117, 120, 209
cultural continuity 91
culture 79
  of carbon 79

Daoists 120
data 28, 29, 86, 87
demons
  "I, player in a demon tale"
    (Hudson) 154, 159–71
    story notes 172–3
  "New Book of the Dead, The"
    (Samatar) 77, 78
Descartes, René 239, 240
determinism 71
devotion 218–21, 224, 231
Diaspora (Egan) 14
Dick, Philip K. 97
Digestible Oceanic Vessel
    Experiment (DOVE) pods
    125, 126–7
direct manipulation 50
disability 212–13, 214
disappointment 160, 178
Dispossessed, The (Le Guin) 97
dissatisfaction 160
dogs 159, 160
dragons 101, 105, 111, 117, 119
dreaming 38–9, 176
drugs 59, 76
dying 79, 80, 123–4, 127, 229–30
dystopias 96, 130–1

eagles 36–9, 40–2, 44, 46–8
Egan, Greg 8, 14
Egyptian Book of the Dead, The 91, 92
embodied cognition 238
emotions 153–4. *See also* feelings
empathy 177–8, 186, 191, 237–8
  medical treatments for lack of
    179–80
empires 102, 104, 114, 115
enrichment opportunist phase 125
eternal life 81

ethics 205
  of love 191
eudaimonism 13
evangelism 213–14, 230
evil 154
"Excerpt from *Theuth*" (Liu) 12,
    17–30
  story notes 31–3
"eye of the needle, The" (Howard-
    Snyder) 155, 175–90
  story notes 191–2

fairness 232
family 101, 111–12, 155. *See also*
    children
Feed (Anderson) 14
feelings 63, 78. *See also* emotions;
    empathy
fiction 1–2, 5, 6, 7, 178, 235, 236,
    237
  and philosophy of religion
    153–4
  speculative 96, 154
Flowers for Algernon (Keyes) 14
fragmentation 77
free will 71, 120–1

gardening 62, 64, 69–70
Gattaca (Niccol) 14
God 154–5
  "Hell is the absence of God"
    (Chiang) 154–5, 209–31
    story notes 232–3
  "I, player in a demon tale"
    (Hudson) 163, 164, 166,
    167, 168–9
  "God on a bad night" (Rose) 154, 155,
    193–204
    story notes 205–7
godmachines 75, 76, 77, 78, 79, 81, 86,
    88–9
good 12–13
grapholects 32
grief 209, 217
guilt 46, 49

hallucination 39, 170
Handmaid's tale, The (Atwood) 7
happiness 64
Hayy Ibn Yaqzan (Ibn Tufayl) 240
heart 82–3
   of carnelian 87
Heaven 210, 212, 217, 224
Heaven's light 220, 225, 229
hedonism 13
Heinlein, Robert 98
"Hell is the absence of God" (Chiang)
   154–5, 209–31
   story notes 232–3
Hick, John 241
holy sites 215, 223, 224, 226
horses 193–4, 195, 205
human enhancement 11–12.
      See also cognitive
      enhancement devices
      (boosters)
humanist movement 219
Hunger Games, The (Collins) 130

"I, player in a demon tale" (Hudson)
   154, 159–71
   story notes 172–3
Icarus eagles 36–9, 40–2, 44, 46–8
image world 79
images 79
immortality 91
indirect manipulation 50
"Intended, The" (Baker) 13, 52–70
   story notes 71–3
inter-species co-operation 136
iron 75
Isis 76, 79, 82, 89

Jonah 2:3 123
Julie, or the new Heloise (Rousseau)
   240
justice 232, 233
Justice as Fairness (Rawls) 99

Kant, Immanuel 191
knowledge 28, 33, 235, 236

Left Hand of Darkness, The
   (Le Guin) 96, 99
Legalists 120
Le Guin, Ursula K. 71, 97
Levy, Neil 50, 51
liberal political philosophy
   148–9
literary fiction 178
Locke, John 72
Lorax, The (Seuss) 130
Lord of Light (Zelazny) 154
love
   ethics of 191
   "Hell is the absence of God"
      (Chiang) 211, 215,
      218–21, 224, 228, 229, 230,
      231
   "Intended, The" (Baker) 62, 68, 69,
      72
   "New Book of the Dead, The"
      (Samatar) 87
   "Out of a dragon's womb"
      (Bodard) 113, 115, 120

Machiavelli, Niccolò 120
magical circles 105–6, 107–8, 115
Man in the High Castle (Dick) 97
manual labor 64
Melchert-Dinkel, William 49
memory 22, 75–6, 77, 78–9, 80, 91
mental manipulation 49–51
   Animal Intra-Mental
      Manipulation Study 36–9,
      40–2, 46–7
Merkel, R. 50
metaphysics 199
Mill, John Stuart 71
minds 178
miracles 210
monotheism 232
"Monsters and soldiers" (Silcox) 97,
   133–47
   story notes 148–50
Moon is a Harsh Mistress, The
   (Heinlein) 98

morality 191, 232, 233
multiplicity 91
mummification 81

Nathanael 210
nature/nurture question 57, 72
Nautical Alliance 125–6, 128, 129
neural enhancement devices
        (boosters) 18–20, 21,
        22–30
"New Book of the Dead, The"
        (Samatar) 13, 75–90
    story notes 91–2
Nineteen eighty-four (Orwell) 8
Nussbaum, Martha 15

Ong, Walter 32
Open Society and Its Enemies, The
        (Popper) 148
oral culture 32
orcas 126
Orwell, George 8
Osiris 76, 77, 80, 82, 89, 91
"Out of the dragon's womb" (Bodard)
        97, 101–19
    story notes 120–1

pain 159, 166, 167, 168, 171, 198, 202,
        229
paintings 2–3
Panopticon 149, 150n
paradox of tolerance 148, 149
paramilitary organizations 136
"passive billables" 23–6
Paul, L.A. 192
Phaedrus (Plato) 31
philosophical knowledge 235, 236
philosophy 2–4, 6, 239–40
    political 95, 148–9
    of religion 153–5, 235, 239
physics 195, 205, 206
pilgrimages 223–4, 225–7
plagiarism 28
Plato 6, 31–4
pleasure 13

political imagination 96
political philosophy 95, 148–9
political values 97
Politics (Aristotle) 95
poly relationships 54
polytheism 232
Popper, Karl 148, 149
prayer 139, 170, 178, 180, 181–4, 232
Prince, The (Machiavelli) 121

Qin dynasty 120

Rashiel 213, 216
Rawls, John 95
reciprocal altruism 232
reduplication 78
Reflections on the Revolution in
        France (Burke) 12
relationships 54, 55, 222
    with God 232–3
religion, philosophy of 153–5, 235,
        239
Remembrance of Earth's Past (Liu)
        98
righteousness 221
Rousseau, Jean-Jacques 98, 240

science 172
science fiction stories 5, 237, 238,
        239–40
self 91–2
self-creation 51
sensus daemoniaci 165, 167, 171, 173
sensus divinitatis 164, 173
sex 55, 59, 61, 68
sex change 182
sinfulness 221
Sirius (Stapleton) 14
Small Gods (Pratchett) 156
Socrates 31
Sparrow, The (Russell) 156
speculative fiction 96, 154
spells 108, 115
sperm whales 125–6
star sculpting 53, 62, 67, 70

stories 96. *See also* science fiction stories
structured imagination 96
suffering 153
suicide 43, 49, 127, 217–18, 227
supernatural agents 172. *See also* demons
surveillance 149
sympathy 178

Terra Federation 125–6, 127, 128
Theuth 31. *See also* "Excerpt from *Theuth*" (Liu)
Thoreau, Henry David 72
Three Versions of Judas (Borges) 156
tolerance, paradox of 148, 149
transcendentalism 72–3
transformations 89–90, 224
transformative experience 191–2
trolley problem 4–5, 5–6
Tufayl, Ibn 240

universe 199, 204, 205, 206
utilitarianism 191
utopias 96–7
    ambiguous 71

Van Norden, Bryan 8
Virgin Mary 79
visions 212, 220
visitations 210, 213, 216–17, 224, 230
    support groups 210–11, 213, 214–15, 216, 217–18, 219

Walden; or, life in the woods (Thoreau) 72
Ward, Thomas 96
water filtration tank 105–7, 113–14, 115–16
Watership Down (Adams) 98
"Whale fall" (Nikel) 97, 123–9
    story notes 130–1
what-if thinking 154
Witness, The (Thekla) 155
working short-term memory 22
writing 31, 32–3

Zeeya, Merali 194, 196, 199, 201, 205, 206
Zelazny, Roger 154